Robert Davenport

Alpha
Teach Yourself

American
History

in 24 hours

A member of
Penguin Group (USA) Inc.

Alpha Teach Yourself American History in 24 Hours

Copyright © 2002 by Robert Davenport

International Standard Book Number: 0-02-864407-7
Library of Congress Catalog Card Number: 2002108502

Printed in the United States of America

First printing: 2002

06   05   6   5   4

Note: This publication contains the opinions and ideas of its author. It is intended to provide helpful and informative material on the subject matter covered. It is sold with the understanding that the author and publisher are not engaged in rendering professional services in the book. If the reader requires personal assistance or advice, a competent professional should be consulted.

TRADEMARKS

ACQUISITIONS EDITOR
Eric Heagy

DEVELOPMENT EDITOR
Nancy D. Lewis

SENIOR PRODUCTION EDITOR
Christy Wagner

COPY EDITOR
Drew Patty

INDEXER
Brad Herriman

PRODUCTION
Stacey Richwine-DeRome
Mary Hunt

COVER DESIGNER
Alan Clements

BOOK DESIGNER
Gary Adair

MANAGING EDITOR
Jennifer Chisholm

PRODUCT MANAGER
Phil Kitchel

PUBLISHER
Marie Butler-Knight

Robert Davenport dedicates this book to my parents, Harry Augustus Davenport III and Jean Yeager Davenport, who first instilled in me a passion for history.

Overview

Contents

Appendixes

Introduction

Ever feel that you should have learned the history of the United States in high school, but somehow missed it? Imagine. You're sipping a cocktail among friends, and they start talking about the Bull Moose Party. If only you had remembered it was an American *political* party, not a theme for a *frat* party, fewer people might have fallen off their chairs, laughing at you! Oh, well, we can't all be scholars of American history ... or can we?

Here is a chance for you to learn the entire history of the United States in just 24 easy lessons of 1 hour each. When you've finished this book, you will be armed with enough information about American history to hold your own in any conversation.

And just to make things a little more interesting, we've included a variety of sidebar boxes that present nifty insights and little-known trivia about America's past.

STRICTLY DEFINED

These sidebars offer insight into how other languages have helped transform the King's English into American English.

QUOTABLE QUOTES

These sidebars offer interesting statements from interesting people throughout history.

JUST A MINUTE

These sidebars offer statistics from the history of the United States.

These sidebars offer biographies of notable people throughout history; byways of history that we guarantee are true, even though you might not believe it; and some descriptions of very strange occurrences from yesteryear.

About the Author

ROBERT DAVENPORT is a Los Angeles–based writer. He is a member of the Writer's Guild of America (screenwriters), the Academy of Television Arts and Sciences, and the Hollywood Radio and Television Society; he is also listed in *Who's Who in America*.

After attending high school in England, where he was an Eagle Scout, Robert majored in history at Middlebury College in Vermont. He then enlisted in the United States Navy and entered Officer Candidate School in Pensacola, Florida. After commissioning as an Ensign, he was selected for flight training and after receiving his wings, became commander of Combat Aircrew Crew Eight, making two overseas deployments during his tour with Patrol Squadron Forty-Four.

In addition to *Alpha Teach Yourself American History in 24 Hours* (Alpha Books), Robert is the author of such books as *Roots of the Rich and Famous*, about celebrities and their famous ancestors, and is "Genealogist to the Stars." His other published books include *The Rich and Famous Baby Name Book* (St. Martin's Press), *The Celebrity Almanac* (Random House), *Pet Names of the Rich and Famous* (General Publishing through Warner), *The Celebrity Birthday Book* (General Publishing through Warner), and *The Encyclopedia of War Films* (Facts On File). He has also been the editor on eight editions of the *Hereditary Society Blue Book* and is the author of the *History and Genealogy of the Davenport Family, 1086–1982*.

Robert was the winner of the prestigious UCLA Screenwriting Showcase for his script *The Six Court Martials of Uriah Levy*, the story of the most court-martialed officer in American military history.

He finished this book while serving in the war against terrorism in Kabul, Afghanistan.

Acknowledgments

The author, Robert Davenport, would like to acknowledge the help and assistance of the following persons in the compilation of this book, and the management of his career. I would like to thank my agent, Jake Elwell, from the agency of Wieser and Wieser, who not only helped me with this book, but also my books *Roots of the Rich and Famous*, and the *Encyclopedia of War Films*. Special thanks goes to Eric Heagy of Alpha Books, editor extraordinaire, who helped me immeasurably with the preparation of this book. Finally, I would like to acknowledge the help and assistance that Lenny Bekerman, my personal manager, has provided me in guiding my career.

PART I

The Foundations of America

HOUR 1

Coming to America

Thousands of years before the arrival of the first Europeans, the continent of North America was populated with Asians who had emigrated from Siberia. Their culture flourished and spread throughout the entire continent, and they were there to welcome the first Europeans when they "discovered" the continent in their voyages of exploration across the Atlantic. At first, only interested in export and trade with this new land, these first adventurers were soon replaced with ships laden with settlers determined to carve a life for themselves in this new land.

THE EMIGRATION BEGINS

During the Ice Age, a large percentage of the world's water was frozen in vast continental ice sheets. As a result, the Bering Sea was hundreds of feet below its current sea level, and a land bridge, known as Beringia, existed between Asia and North America. A vast tundra, it was covered with grasses and other plant life, which attracted the large animals that early humans hunted for their survival. As the game wandered in their search for forage, the humans followed, across the land bridge to North America. The first people to reach North America probably did so without knowing they had crossed into a new continent.

CHAPTER SUMMARY

LESSON PLAN:

In this hour, you will learn about the first people to arrive in America, the Indians, about the first European adventurers to explore America, and about the early European settlements.

You will also learn ...

- What the Indians were really up to before they were discovered.
- What Christopher Columbus really thought he was doing in 1492, when he sailed the ocean blue.
- How everyone in America has gotten into the act of mangling the King's English.
- Who is really to blame for smoking sections in restaurants.

FYI Some scientists, disgusted with what they perceived to be the Euro-centric approach to history, have advanced the theory that man originated in the Americas, and then subsequently migrated through Asia to Europe. Unfortunately, these scientists have not been able to produce any fossils to support their theory. They're still digging.

From Alaska, it took these first North Americans thousands of years to work their way south through the gaps in the great ice glaciers to what is now the United States. The earliest evidence of life in North America dates back to around 12000 B.C.E., and man had migrated to most of South America by around 10000 B.C.E.

The mastodon, or mammoth, was a principle source of food for the early Indians as they migrated to America.

As the mammoth began to die out, the buffalo took its place as a principal source of food and hides for these early North Americans. Over time, as more and more species of large game vanished, whether from overhunting or by a change in the global climate, plants, berries, and seeds became an increasingly important part of the early American's diet. Gradually, foraging was replaced by the first attempts at agriculture. Indians in what is now central Mexico were the first to cultivate corn, squash, and beans, perhaps as early as 8000 B.C.E. Slowly, this knowledge spread northward. By 3000 B.C.E., a primitive type of corn was being grown in the river valleys of New Mexico and Arizona. By 300 B.C.E., the peoples of America were living in villages.

By the first century C.E., Native Americans known as the Hohokum were living in settlements near what is now Phoenix, Arizona, where they built ball courts and pyramidlike mounds, as well as canals and irrigation systems.

BUILDING MOUNDS

The first Native American group to build mounds in what is now the United States were called the Adenans. They began constructing earthen burial sites and fortifications around 600 B.C.E. Some mounds from that era are in the shape of birds or serpents, and might have also served religious purposes.

The Adenans appear to have been absorbed or displaced by mound builders known as the Hopewellians. One of the most important centers of their culture was in southern Ohio, where the remains of several thousand of their mounds still remain. Believed to be great traders, the Hopewellians exchanged goods across a region hundreds of miles wide.

By around 500 C.E., the Hopewellians, too, had disappeared, gradually giving way to a new tribe of mound builders, the Mississippians. One of their cities, Cahokia, located just east of what is now St. Louis, Missouri, is thought at its peak in the early twelfth century to have had a population of more than 20,000. At the center of the city stood a huge earthen mound, flat on top, which was 30 meters high and 37 hectares at its base. Eighty other mounds have been found in the vicinity.

JUST A MINUTE

In the 1150s, Cahokia, a Native American city with a population of 20,000 people, was larger than London. It was not until the 1800s that another city in the United States would reach that population.

Early native cities such as Cahokia depended on a combination of hunting, foraging, trading, and agriculture. Influenced by the thriving societies to the south, such as the Aztec and Mayan, they evolved into complex hierarchical societies that practiced slavery and offered human sacrifices to the gods.

POTLATCH

Perhaps the most affluent of the early American Indians lived in the Pacific Northwest, where the lush forests and the abundance of fish made food supplies plentiful and permanent villages possible as early as 1000 B.C.E. The opulence of their *potlatch* gatherings remains a standard for extravagance and festivity unmatched in early American history.

STRICTLY DEFINED

Potlatch, common among Native Americans of the Northwest, entailed the lavish distribution of gifts such as slaves and goat-hair blankets, as well as feasting and ritual boasting, often lasting for several days. The potlatch came to serve as a means by which aspiring nobles validated their tenuous claims to high rank, increasingly through the ostentatious destruction of property. This led both the U.S. and Canadian governments to outlaw the practice in 1884. Potlatching, nevertheless, continued covertly, until the ban was lifted in 1951.

NATIVE AMERICAN CULTURES

Indian customs and culture across America were extraordinarily diverse as a result of the great many different environments to which they had to adapt. However, all Native American tribal groups had some characteristics in common. Tribes combined aspects of hunting and gathering with the cultivation of maize and other crops to supplement their food supplies. Generally, the women were responsible for farming and raising the children; the men hunted and provided warriors for the constant inter-tribal warfare.

JUST A MINUTE

When the Europeans arrived, there were as many Native Americans in the Western Hemisphere, about 40 million, as there were inhabitants in Western Europe.

Indian society in North America was closely tied to the land. Identification with nature and the elements was integral to their religious beliefs. Native American life was essentially clan-oriented and communal, and children were allowed more freedom and tolerance than was the European custom of the day.

JUST A MINUTE

Life in America required the British settlers to start adopting their own version of English. New words had to evolve to describe the new plants, fish, clothing, foods, and customs that they discovered. One simple way was to borrow from the Native American languages. Examples include words like *hickory, pecan, chipmunk, tomahawk, teepee,* and *raccoon.*

Although some North American tribes developed a type of hieroglyphic to represent certain events, the preservation of Indian tradition was primarily oral, with a high value placed on the recounting of tales and dreams.

There was a good deal of trade among various tribes and clans, and strong evidence exists that tribes maintained extensive and formal relations over long distances.

WHO WERE THE ANASAZI?

In the southwest United States, the *Anasazi* began building stone and adobe pueblos around 900 C.E. These unique and amazing apartment-like structures were often built along cliff faces; the most famous, the "cliff palace" of Mesa Verde, Colorado, had more than 200 rooms. Another site, the Pueblo Bonito ruins along New Mexico's Chaco River, once contained more than 800 rooms.

STRICTLY DEFINED

The Navajo believe they are descended from these ancient peoples; **Anasazi** means "ancient ones" in the Navajo language.

By 500 C.E. the Anasazi had established villages where they grew crops such as corn, squash, and beans. The Anasazi developed sophisticated dams and irrigation systems; created a distinctive pottery; and carved intricate, multi-room dwellings into the sheer sides of cliffs that remain among the most striking archaeological sites in the United States today.

However, by the year 1300, the Anasazi culture had disappeared into history. The area where they had lived remained empty of inhabitants for more than a century, until new tribes, such as the Navajo and the Ute, settled the area.

The story of the Anasazi is tied inextricably to the beautiful but harsh environment in which they chose to live. Early settlements, consisting of simple pit houses scooped out of the ground, evolved into sunken structures that served as meeting and religious sites. Later generations developed the masonry techniques for building square, stone pueblos. But the most dramatic change in Anasazi living (for reasons that are still unclear) was the move to the cliff sides below the flat-topped mesas, where the Anasazi carved their amazing, multilevel dwellings.

The Anasazi lived in a communal society that evolved very slowly over the centuries. They traded with other peoples in the region, but signs of warfare are few and isolated. And although the Anasazi certainly had religious and civil leaders, as well as skilled artisans, social or class distinctions were virtually nonexistent.

Religious and social motives might have played a part in the building of the cliff communities and their final abandonment. But the struggle to raise food in an increasingly difficult environment was probably the paramount factor. As populations grew, farmers planted larger areas on the mesas, causing some communities to farm marginal lands, while others left the mesa tops for the cliffs. But the Anasazi couldn't halt the steady loss of the land's fertility from constant use, nor withstand the region's cyclical droughts. Analysis of tree rings shows that a drought lasting 23 years, from 1276 to 1299, is probably what finally forced the last groups of Anasazi to abandon their lands and search for a home elsewhere.

THE FIRST EUROPEANS

With so many native peoples, the America that greeted the first Europeans was far from an empty wilderness. However, the arrival of the settlers had an immediate and devastating effect on the native populations. The Europeans were carriers of diseases for which they had some natural immunity, but the Native Americans did not. Smallpox, in particular, ravaged whole communities. While the wars with the new settlers caused some reduction in the population, it was really the infectious diseases that caused the precipitous decline in Indian population in the 1600s.

JUST A MINUTE

Twenty million Indians lived in North America when Columbus landed, but diseases brought by the Europeans reduced the Indian population to about two million by the time the Declaration of Independence was signed. Some of this was inadvertent. After a slave ship brought Africans with smallpox to South Carolina in 1737, half the Cherokee population was dead within the year. However, some infection was outright bioterrorism. In 1763, Lord Jeffrey Amherst, knowing the local Indians penchant for thievery, made sure that the Indians he was fighting stole smallpox-infected blankets.

The first Europeans who arrived in North America (for which there is solid evidence) were the Norsemen, who traveled west from Greenland, where Erik the Red had founded a settlement around the year 985. In 1001, his son Leif is thought to have explored the northeast coast of what is now Canada and to have spent at least one winter there.

While Norse sagas suggest that Viking sailors explored the Atlantic coast of North America as far down as the Bahamas, such claims remain unproven. In 1963, however, the ruins of some Norse houses dating from that era were discovered at L'Anse-aux-Meadows in northern Newfoundland, thus, supporting at least some of the claims made by the Norse sagas.

FYI Columbus set out to prove the earth was round. At the end of the fifteenth century, only idiots thought the world was flat. What was in question was the circumference of the sphere. It was because Columbus underestimated the size of the earth by one-fourth that he thought he was in India. Columbus thought he had arrived in India, even though it was quite obvious to every one else in his crew that nobody meeting the boat was wearing a turban. Even so, he announced to the inhabitants "you are Indians," and in time they came to believe it themselves.

In 1497, just five years after Christopher Columbus landed in the Caribbean looking for a western route to Asia, a Venetian sailor named John Cabot arrived in Newfoundland on a mission for the British king. Although quickly forgotten, Cabot's journey was later to provide the basis for British claims to North America. It also opened the way to the rich fishing grounds off George's Banks, to which European fishermen, particularly the Portuguese, were soon making regular visits.

Columbus, of course, never saw the United States, but the first explorations of the mainland were launched from the Spanish possessions that he helped establish. The first of these took place in 1513 when a group of men under Juan Ponce de León landed on the Florida coast near the present city of St. Augustine.

With their conquest of Mexico in 1522, the Spanish further solidified their position in the Western Hemisphere. The ensuing discoveries added to Europe's knowledge of what was now called America, after the Italian Amerigo Vespucci.

FYI Amerigo Vespucci came to the world's attention through the publication in 1503 and 1504 of two letters. Obviously the work of an educated man, the letters combined a sober discussion of navigational issues with the news that the natives of the New World would have sex with anyone, including their relatives. The letters caused a sensation that far exceeded that of Columbus 10 years earlier, were reprinted in every European language, and soon came to the attention of a group who were publishing "Introduction to Cosmography," the first attempt to update maps in centuries. Vespucci called the first letter *Novus Mundus,* the New World. They were quite taken with Amerigo's idea that it was a new land, rejected calling it Vespucciland, and thus it came to be christened America on the maps of the day.

By 1529, reliable maps of the Atlantic coastline from Labrador to Tierra del Fuego had been drawn up, although it would take more than another century before hope of discovering a "Northwest Passage" to Asia would be completely abandoned.

Among the most significant early Spanish explorations was that of Hernando de Soto, a veteran conquistador who had accompanied Francisco

Pizzaro during the conquest of Peru. Leaving Havana in 1539, de Soto's expedition landed in Florida and traveled through the southeastern United States as far as the Mississippi River in search of cities of gold.

JUST A MINUTE

American English also borrowed from the Spanish settlers. Words incorporated from the Spanish include *poncho, bronco, sombrero, canyon, enchilada, taco,* and *tequila.*

Another Spaniard, Francisco Coronado, set out from Mexico in 1540 in search of the mythical Seven Cities of Cibola. Coronado's travels took him to the Grand Canyon and to Kansas, but he also failed to find gold or treasure. Coronado's expedition left the region a remarkable, if unintended gift: Enough horses escaped from his party to change life on the Great Plains forever. The horse is not native to America. It wasn't long before the Plains Indians, rather than running around their enemies (which must have been very exhausting), were able to ride around them in style on their new horses.

While some Spanish explorers were traversing the south in search of mythical cities of gold, in the north of the present-day United States a Florentine who sailed for the French, Giovanni da Verrazano, made landfall in North Carolina in 1524, then sailed north along the Atlantic coast into what is now the harbor of New York City.

FYI The Verrazano Bridge in New York Harbor, named for the explorer, is the longest suspension bridge in North America. The towers are so high and far apart that in designing the bridge it was necessary to take into account the curvature of the earth's surface.

A decade later, the Frenchman Jacques Cartier set sail with the hope of finding the fabled Northwest Passage to Asia and India. Cartier's expeditions along the St. Lawrence River laid the foundations for the French claims to North America, which were to last until the British conquered the province in 1763.

JUST A MINUTE

American English was also influenced by the French settlers. Words borrowed from the French include *chowder, praline, prairie, bureau, cent,* and *dime.* However, we have rejected the kilometer, and stick stubbornly to our old-fashioned and antiquated English measuring system.

Following the collapse of their first Quebec colony in the 1540s, French Huguenots attempted to settle the northern coast of Florida. The Spanish, viewing the French as a threat to their trade route along the Gulf Stream, destroyed the colony in 1565. Ironically, the leader of the Spanish forces, Pedro Menendez, would soon establish his own settlement nearby in St. Augustine. It was to become the first permanent European settlement in what would later become the United States.

The great wealth which poured into Spain from the colonies in Mexico, the Caribbean Islands, and Peru provoked great interest on the part of the other European powers. Soon emerging maritime nations such as England, drawn in part by Francis Drake's successful raids on Spanish treasure ships, began to take a more serious interest in the New World.

EARLY SETTLEMENTS

The early 1600s saw the beginning of a great tide of emigration from Europe to North America. Spanning more than three centuries, this movement grew from a trickle of a few hundred English colonists to a flood of millions of newcomers.

The first English immigrants to what is now the United States crossed the Atlantic long after Spanish colonies had been established in Mexico, the West Indies, and South America. Like all early travelers to the New World, they came in small, overcrowded ships. During their 6- to 12-week voyages (in which passage cost 7 years of wages) they were half starved on meager rations, and many died from disease. Ships often encountered impossible storms that sent these fragile crafts quickly to the bottom.

The reasons that drove emigrants to leave Europe were as diverse as the peoples. They left their homelands to escape political oppression, for religious freedom, to escape poverty, or simply for adventure. Between 1620 and 1635, economic devastation swept England. People could not find work, even skilled artisans could earn little more than a meager living. Poor crop yields added to the distress. In addition, the Industrial Revolution created a burgeoning textile industry, which demanded an ever-increasing supply of wool to keep the looms running. Landlords enclosed farmlands and evicted the peasants in order to graze sheep. Colonial emigration became a natural outlet for this disenfranchised peasant population.

The colonists' first glimpse of the new land was that of a dark, dense, cold, and impenetrable forest. The settlers might not have survived had it not been for the help of friendly Indians, who taught them how to grow native plants such as pumpkin, squash, beans, and corn. The vast, virgin forests of the Eastern seaboard ultimately proved a rich source of game and firewood. They also provided abundant raw materials to build houses, furniture, ships, and profitable cargoes for export.

Although the new continent could supply some of the needs of the colonists, trade with Europe was vital for the many articles the settlers could not produce. The coast, with its many inlets and harbors, made coastal and transatlantic trade relatively easy. Only two colonies, North Carolina and southern New Jersey, lacked harbors that could support ocean-going vessels.

Great rivers, like the Kennebec, Hudson, Delaware, Susquehanna, and Potomac, made travel from the coast to the inland settlements possible. Only one river, however, the St. Lawrence, controlled by the French in Canada, offered a deep water passage to the Great Lakes and into the middle of the continent. Dense forests, the resistance of some Indian tribes, and the formidable barrier of the Appalachian Mountains discouraged settlement beyond the coastal plain. For the first hundred years, only trappers and traders ventured that far into the wilderness; the rest of the colonists were content to build their settlements close to the coast.

As mentioned previously, political and religious considerations drove many people to emigrate to America. In the 1630s, tyrannical rule by England's Charles I, and his persecution of the Puritans, gave impetus to the religious migration to New England. The subsequent revolt and triumph of the Puritans under Oliver Cromwell over the monarch in the 1640s led many cavaliers, who were supporters of the king, to in turn flee from England and cast their lot in Virginia, far from the Puritans in New England. This English civil war between the Puritans and the Cavaliers was to repeat itself in America in the 1860s, with the southern gentleman of the Confederacy continuing to style themselves as "cavaliers."

In the German-speaking regions of Europe, the oppressive policies of various petty princes—particularly with regard to religion and the devastation caused by a long series of wars—helped drive even more emigrants to America in the late seventeenth and eighteenth centuries. The main concentration of German emigration was in the Pennsylvania colony.

Going to America in the seventeenth century entailed careful planning and management, as well as considerable expense and risk. Settlers had to not only cross three thousand miles of sea, but they had to bring with them all of their utensils, clothing, seed, tools, building materials, livestock, arms, and ammunition. In contrast to the colonization policies of other countries, such as Spain, the emigration from England was not directly sponsored by the government, but by private groups of individuals whose chief motive was profit.

QUOTABLE QUOTES

William Mullins, one of the passengers on the Mayflower, realizing that there was no stores to be found in the wilderness, brought with him from England 126 pairs of shoes and 13 pairs of boots, enough to last him the rest of his life. He stated, "When settling a new continent, you don't want to run out of shoes."

JAMESTOWN

In 1578 Humphrey Gilbert, who had written a book on the search for the elusive Northwest Passage to India, received a patent from Queen Elizabeth to colonize those "heathen and barbarous lands" in the New World which other European nations had not yet claimed. When he was lost at sea, his half-brother, Sir Walter Raleigh, took up the mission. In 1585 Raleigh established the first British colony in North America, on Roanoke Island off the coast of North Carolina. It was later abandoned, and a second effort two years later also proved a failure.

 FYI Sir Walter Raleigh dropped out of college to become a pirate. He is best known for the occasion on which he spread his coat over a puddle, so that Queen Elizabeth (the first one, the virgin), would not get her new shoes dirty (even then women were fanatical about their shoes). Although best known for introducing tobacco to England, he also was the first one to take a potato (also native to America) to Ireland.

In 1607, the first of the British colonies to take hold in North America was Jamestown, named after King James I, who had granted to the Virginia Company a charter to settle in the Chesapeake Bay region. Seeking to avoid conflict with the Spanish, they chose a site up the James River (which they also named after him).

The colonists were mainly adventurers looking to find gold, and being city people, wouldn't have known how to farm even if they had the inclination. The group was unequipped by temperament or ability to embark upon a completely new life in the wilderness. Captain John Smith soon emerged as the dominant figure. Despite constant quarrels, frequent periods of starvation, and repeated Indian attacks, his ability to enforce discipline held the little colony together through its first year.

FYI "Pocahontas" was her childhood nickname, which when translated from the native Indian language means "little wanton," so named because her father could not control her. She was only about 10 years old when she asked her father, the chief, to spare John Smith's life so that he could make toys for her. If the Disney romance were true, given the differences in their ages, in modern days that would have made John Smith subject to arrest in most states.

In 1609 Smith returned to England, and in his absence, the colony descended into complete anarchy. During the winter, those colonists that did not starve to death succumbed to disease. By the following spring, only 60 of the original 300 settlers were still alive.

It was not long, however, before a new leader, John Rolfe, revolutionized Virginia's economy, and put the struggling colony in the black. In 1612, he began cross-breeding imported tobacco seed from the West Indies with native plants used by the Indians, and produced a new "smoke" that was pleasing to European tastes. He then married Pocahontas, who as an Indian princess brought to the marriage as her dowry vast lands to add to his plantation. The first shipment of this new tobacco reached London in 1614. Within a decade it had become Virginia's chief source of revenue.

Prosperity did not come quickly, however, and the death rate from disease and Indian attacks remained extraordinarily high. Between 1607 and 1624, approximately 14,000 people migrated to the colony, yet only 1,132 were living there in 1624. As is usual with such disastrous situations, the government stepped in, appointed a royal commission to investigate, and on their recommendation the king revoked the company's charter, and made Virginia a royal colony.

HOUR'S UP!

1. How did the Native Americans originally journey from Asia to America?

   A. By boat

   B. By canoe

   C. Across a land bridge where the Bering Sea is now located

   D. On horseback

2. Words incorporated into English by the Spanish include all of the following except:

   A. Tequila

   B. Sombrero

   C. Canyon

   D. Immigration

3. All of the following discovered America, except:

   A. Christopher Columbus

   B. Vikings

   C. Indians

   D. Amerigo Vespucci

4. Tobacco was brought back from America by:

   A. Phillip Morris

   B. Sir Walter Raleigh

   C. Duke of Marlborough

   D. Earl of Chesterfield

5. All of the following were friends of Pocahontas, except:

   A. Captain John Smith

   B. Queen of England

   C. John Rolfe

   D. King James I

HOUR 2

The Europeans Keep Coming

The 13 original colonies that made up early America were not all founded at the same time. In addition, there was great variety in the countries of origin of those who settled them, the industries in which they were engaged, and the religions to which they subscribed. Yet by the end of the first century of settlement, as they all came firmly under the control of the same sovereignty of England, they were already taking on the attributes of a single group of "American colonies."

PLYMOUTH AND THE MASSACHUSETTS BAY COLONY

England in the early 1600s was wracked by religious dissent that threatened to tear apart the country, and eventually was to result in civil war. This religious controversy was created by Puritans who sought to reform the Established Church of England. They demanded that the rituals and structures associated with the Roman Catholics be replaced by plainer Protestant methods of worship. Their ideas of reform were thought to undermine the absolute authority of the state church, divide the people, and to dilute the absolute authority of the king.

FYI MYTH: The *Mayflower* passengers always wore black and white clothes, and had big buckles. FACT: *Mayflower* wills show what clothing they left to their family. John Howland had two red waistcoats. William Bradford had a green gown, a violet cloak, and a red waistcoat. William Brewster had green drawers, a red cap, and a violet coat. The Pilgrims did not have buckles on their clothing, shoes, or hats. Buckles did not come into fashion until the late 1600s, more trendy and stylish for the Salem Witchcraft trials than for the Pilgrims.

CHAPTER SUMMARY

LESSON PLAN:

In this hour, you will learn about the settlement of the original 13 colonies, the differences between the colonies, and how the early colonists carved a life from the wilderness.

You will also learn ...

- Why the Pilgrims served turkey, and not spaghetti, at the first Thanksgiving.
- Why New York City has places like Bedford-Stuyvesant, Amsterdam Avenue, and the Van Wyck Expressway.
- Why freedom of religion was a popular contender for the Bill of Rights.
- Why Africans, and not Indians, made the best slaves.

One radical sect of English Puritans was known as the Separatists. They did not believe that the Established Church could ever be reformed from within, and therefore established their own, separate church. In 1607, they departed for Leyden, Holland, where the Dutch granted them complete freedom of religion. However, the Dutch did restrict them to low-paid menial jobs as laborers. Members of the congregation became increasingly dissatisfied with this discrimination, and decided to transplant their colony to the New World.

In 1620, a group of Separatists from Leyden secured a land patent from the Virginia Company, and a group of 101 men, women, and children set out for the New World on board the *Mayflower*. They were going to settle on the Hudson River, in present-day New York, but a storm blew them off course and they landed on Cape Cod in New England. Believing themselves outside the jurisdiction of the Virginia Company, and therefore the English king, they drew up a formal agreement to abide by "just and equal laws" of their own choosing, known as the Mayflower Compact. This was the first declaration of independence from the English king in the New World.

Because the *Mayflower* reached Plymouth harbor in December, the Pilgrims had to build their settlement in the middle of the winter, and nearly half the colonists died of exposure and disease before spring. Then, friendly neighboring Wampanoag Indians provided them with help on planting and growing maize, a type of native corn. By the next fall, the Pilgrims had a plentiful crop of corn and were able to celebrate a bountiful Thanksgiving.

Although idealized, this painting encapsulates the feeling that most Americans have about the first Thanksgiving.

FYI MYTH: The original Thanksgiving feast took place on the fourth Thursday of November. FACT: The original feast in 1621 occurred sometime between September 21 and November 11. The event was based on English harvest festivals, which traditionally occurred around the twenty-ninth of September. President Franklin D. Roosevelt set the date for Thanksgiving to the fourth Thursday of November in 1939 (approved by Congress in 1941). Abraham Lincoln had previously designated it as the last Thursday in November.

Inspired by the success of the Plymouth colony, a wave of Puritan immigrants arrived on the shores of Massachusetts Bay in 1630, under the authority of a grant from King Charles I of England. The king thought that by encouraging them to emigrate, he would remove them as a source of dissension, and as a threat to his monarchy. He was wrong on both accounts. There were still enough Puritans left in England to remove him from his throne and cut off his head during the English Civil War, and subsequently, the descendants of these troublesome immigrants would successfully rebel against a future king, and form the United States of America.

The leader of this new expedition, John Winthrop, set out to create a place where Puritans could live in strict accordance with their religious beliefs. The Massachusetts Bay Colony was to play a significant role in the development of the entire New England region.

Winthrop and his Puritans brought their charter with them, and in their opinion, the authority for the colony's government resided in Massachusetts, not in England. Under the charter's provisions, power rested with the General Court, which was made up of "freemen" who were required to be members of the Puritan Church. This guaranteed that the Puritans would be the dominant political force in the colony. It was the General Court that elected the governor, and for an entire generation, this governor would be John Winthrop.

RHODE ISLAND

The rigid dictatorship of the Puritan's was not to everyone's liking. One of the first to openly challenge the General Court was a young minister named Roger Williams, who objected to the colony's seizure of Indian lands. Banished from the Massachusetts Bay Colony for his heresy, in 1636 he purchased land from the Narragansett Indians in what is now Providence, Rhode Island. Determined not to create another settlement dominated by a single religion, he set up the first American colony where complete separation of church and state, as well as freedom of religion, was the rule. The freedom of religion clause in the U.S. Constitution is credited with originating in the Rhode Island colony.

NEW HAVEN COLONY

Settlers were flooding into New England faster than the Massachusetts Bay Colony could absorb them. In addition, those arriving did not always want to submit to the absolute dictatorship of John Winthrop and the Massachusetts Bay Colony.

One such group was the Davenport-Eaton party, who arrived in 1637 under the leadership of the minister John Davenport and businessman Theophilus Eaton. Disgusted with the conditions under which they would be forced to live in Boston, they created their own settlement in New Haven, equidistant from Winthrop in the north, and the Dutch settlement in New York.

QUOTABLE QUOTES

The Rev. John Davenport was a Puritan leader on the King's special "hit list" of rebellious leaders that the king wanted to imprison. A special enemy of Archbishop Laud, the head of the church of England, Davenport was forced to flee to Holland. When he learned that the King's men were going to abduct him there, he decided that New England would make a better hideout. When Laud learned that Davenport had made it to America, he vowed "my hand shall reach him, even there." However, luckily for the author, who is his direct descendant, it never did.

Other settlements began cropping up along the New Hampshire and Maine coasts, and in the Connecticut River Valley, as more and more immigrants were enticed to come to America by the free land of the New World.

 The grandson of Theophilus Eaton was Elihu Yale, who went to India and made an incredible fortune. The grandson of the Rev. John Davenport, also known as the Rev. John Davenport, needed money to start a college, so he promised they would name it after him, if Yale would write the check. He did, and they did.

NEW NETHERLAND

Henry Hudson, in 1609, explored the area around New York City on behalf of the Dutch East India Company, venturing up the river, which now bears his name as far north as Albany, New York, and laying claim to the entire region for the Dutch.

In 1624, the island of Manhattan was purchased from local Indians for the reported price of $24, and the colony was christened New Netherland, with it's capital at New Amsterdam. Like the French in Canada, the Dutch were interested in the fur trade. They cultivated close relations with the Five Nations of the Iroquois, who controlled the fur-rich inland areas, and in 1617 Dutch settlers built a fort at the junction of the Hudson and the Mohawk rivers, present-day Albany.

JUST A MINUTE

The Indians actually got a very good deal for the island of Manhattan. The $24 was actually 60 guilders in Dutch money. According to Wall Street maven Peter Lynch, if the Indians had invested the 60 guilders at 8 percent interest, today they would have built up a net worth of more than $20 trillion, which is many times Manhattan Island's present value.

In order to attract investors to the Hudson River region, the Dutch encouraged a type of feudal aristocracy, known as the *patroon* system. The first of these huge estates was established in 1630 along the Hudson River. Under the patroon system, any stockholder, or patroon, who could convince 50 settlers to move onto his estate over a 4-year period was given a riverfront plot, exclusive fishing and hunting privileges, and civil and criminal jurisdiction over his lands. In turn, he provided livestock, tools, and buildings to the settlers. These settlers paid the patroon rent and gave him first option on their surplus crops.

JUST A MINUTE

The borrowings from Dutch into American English include such words as *coleslaw, cookie, waffle, sleigh, boss, Yankee,* and *Santa Claus.*

Further to the south, a Swedish trading company tried to found a settlement called New Sweden along the Delaware River. Without the resources to consolidate its position, New Sweden was gradually absorbed into New Netherland, and later became part of Pennsylvania and Delaware.

MARYLAND

In 1632, Lord Baltimore obtained a charter from King Charles I for land north of the Potomac River, in what became known as the colony of Maryland. Because he was Catholic (who were as persecuted in England as the Puritans) he cleverly drew up a charter that did not expressly prohibit the establishment of non-Protestant churches, and he then encouraged fellow Catholics to settle in the colony. Maryland's first town, St. Mary's, was established in 1634 near the junction of the Potomac River and the Chesapeake Bay.

FYI Maryland was actually Lord Baltimore's second attempt at founding a colony. His first venture was Avalon, a harbor located on the southeastern coast of Newfoundland. In 1622, he obtained a charter from the King, equipped a group of colonists, and sent them off. In spite of Lord Baltimore investing a large portion of his fortune in the venture, the harsh winters were too much for the colonists. He visited the colony in 1628, realized it was a lost cause, and abandoned it in favor of a warmer climate.

The royal charter granted to Lord Baltimore had a mixture of feudal and modern elements. On the one hand he had the power to create manorial estates, similar to those of the Dutch patroons in New York. However, the charter constricted him to only making laws with the consent of freemen (property holders). He found that in order to attract settlers, which he needed to make a profit from his holdings, he had to offer people farms, not just tenancy on the manorial estates. As a result, the number of independent farms multiplied, and their owners demanded their fair vote and control over the affairs of the colony. By 1635, Maryland had it's own legislature.

RELATIONS WITH THE INDIANS

Sometimes friendly, sometimes hostile, by the 1640s the Indian tribes of the east coast were no longer strangers to the European settlers. On the positive side, the Native Americans benefited from access to new technology and trade with the settlers; on the negative side, the settlers brought disease and an unquenchable thirst for land, both of which posed a serious challenge to the Indian's long-established way of life.

Trade with the European settlers brought many advantages, primarily metal implements for which the Indians did not have the technology, such as knives, axes, weapons, cooking utensils, and fish hooks. In addition, those Indians who traded with the settlers obtained a significant advantage in war over their enemies who did not. To obtain goods for trade with the settlers, tribes such as the Iroquois began to devote more attention to fur trapping during the 1600s. Furs and pelts provided these tribes the means by which to obtain European goods up until the late eighteenth century.

FYI Luis Gomez (1660–1740) was representative of the early Jewish fur traders on the frontier. The possibility that the Indians were descended from the Ten Lost Tribes of Israel was seriously discussed and considered in the Jewish community of New York, and rabbis insisted that Indians be dealt with as fellow Jews. The belief that the Indians were the lost tribes of Israel persisted into the nineteenth century.

Relations between settlers and Native Americans were an uneasy mix of cooperation and conflict. On the one hand, in the Pennsylvania Colony there were the near-perfect relations during the first half-century. On the other hand, in other colonies there were numerous conflicts that almost always led to an Indian defeat and to further loss of their tribal lands.

The Pequot War of 1637 resulted from the Pequots rather brutal raids on local settlers in the Connecticut River valley. Even other local Indian tribes hated the Pequots, and a combined force of the Connecticut militia and their Indian allies virtually annihilated the Pequots.

King Phillip's War occurred in 1675 when Phillip, the son of the chief who had made the original peace with the Pilgrims in 1621 at Plymouth, attempted to unite the tribes of southern New England against further European settlement. However, 50 years had passed, and the colonial militias were now a powerful force. In the struggle, Phillip was killed, and many of the captured Indians were sold into slavery.

In the west, the Pueblo Indians rose up against the Spanish missionaries in 1680 in the area near Taos, New Mexico. For the next dozen years, the Pueblo Indians controlled their land, only to lose it again when the Spanish crushed their revolt. Sixty years later, another Indian revolt threw out the Spanish, this time in Arizona, when the Pima Indians rose up.

The steady influx of settlers into the interior regions of the eastern colonies signaled the end of the Indians' way of life. As the game was killed off, tribes who subsisted as hunter-gatherers were faced with difficult decisions: They could slowly starve, they could go to war and try to push back the almost endless stream of European settlers, or they could move west and be pushed into conflict with the western tribes. Each of the alternatives was a sure road to destruction.

The Iroquois, who lived in northern New York and Pennsylvania, were more successful than most tribes in resisting European immigration, as a result of their unique form of government. In 1570, the five tribes of the Iroquois had joined to form the most democratic nation of its time, the "Ho-De-No-Sau-Nee," or League of the Iroquois. The League was run by a council made up of 50 representatives from each of the 5 member tribes. The council dealt with matters common to all the tribes, but it had no say in how the free and equal tribes ran their internal day-to-day affairs. No tribe was allowed to make war by itself—it was always a united effort. This league was later used as the basis for the federal system of government in the United States.

QUOTABLE QUOTES

 Benjamin Franklin used the structure of the League of the Iroquois as the model for the U.S. Constitution. He had this to say about the Indians:

> He that would speak, rises. The rest observe a profound silence. When he has finished and sits down, they leave him five or six minutes to recollect, so that if he has omitted anything he intended to say or has anything to add, he may rise again and deliver it. To interrupt another, even in common conversation, is reckoned highly indecent. How different it is from the conduct of the British House of Commons, where scarce a day passes without some confusion that makes the Speaker hoarse in calling to order; and how different from the mode of conversation in Europe, where if you do not deliver your sentence with great rapidity, you are cut off in the middle of it by the impatient loquacity of those you converse with and never allowed to finish it.

The League was a formidable power in the 1600s and 1700s. It sided with the British against the French in the war for control of the American continent between 1754 and 1763. The British might not have won that war without the support of the League of the Iroquois. The League stayed strong until the American Revolution. Then, for the first time, the council could not reach a unanimous decision on whom to support. In defiance of their constitution, member tribes made their own decision. Some fought with the British, some with the Revolution, some remained neutral. As a result, everyone at one time or the other launched a campaign against the Iroquois. The tribes suffered greatly during the war, and the League was permanently destroyed. The Iroquois were never able to regain their former power.

SECOND GENERATION OF BRITISH COLONIES

The English Civil War in the mid-seventeenth century limited immigration, as well as the attention the mother country paid to the fledgling American colonies. This allowed the colonies to exert a great deal of independence, more than might otherwise have been allowed.

In order to provide for the defense that mother England was neglecting, in 1643 the colonies of Massachusetts Bay, Plymouth, Connecticut, and New

Haven formed the New England Confederation. It was the American colonies first attempt at uniting.

The House of Burgesses, the first legislative assembly in the American colonies, held its first meeting in the choir of Jamestown Church in the summer of 1619. Its first order of business was setting a minimum price for the sale of tobacco in the colony. This small body established a tradition of colonial self rule, and with the subsequent formation of each new English colony, the citizens demanded their own legislature.

The first significant revolt against royal authority was Bacon's Rebellion. The small farmers of Virginia, embittered by low tobacco prices, hard living conditions, and Indian raids, rallied around Nathaniel Bacon. The governor refused to grant Bacon a commission to conduct Indian raids, but he did agree to call new elections to the House of Burgesses, which had remained unchanged since 1661. Defying the governor's orders, Bacon led an attack against the friendly Ocaneechee tribe, nearly wiping them out. Then he turned his mob on Jamestown in September 1676. He burned the town, and forced the governor to flee. Most of the state was now under Bacon's control. His victory was short lived, however; he died of a fever the following month. Without Bacon, and with the arrival of British regulars, the rebellion soon lost its momentum. The governor reestablished his authority, and hung 23 of Bacon's followers.

Nathaniel Bacon promised freedom to black and white indentured servants who joined the rebellion. This was the greatest fear of the ruling class, that the poor would unite against them. This fear hastened the transition to race-based slavery. In 1705, the Virginia General Assembly decided that only blacks would be slaves, with the passage of the Virginia Slave Codes. Henceforth, only servants imported and brought into the state, who were not Christians in their native country, were to be slaves. Because the whites were Christians, and the blacks Muslims, or in any event not Christians, their fate was sealed.

With the restoration of King Charles II in 1660, the English Civil War was over, and the British could once again turn their full attention to North America.

NEW AMSTERDAM

As a general rule, Dutch settlements had been ruled by autocratic governors appointed in Europe, and New Amsterdam was no exception. As a result, the local population had no loyalty to their governor. When British colonists began settling in increasing numbers on Dutch lands on Long

Island and Manhattan, the unpopular royal governor was unable to rally the population in opposition. The English colonists were soon calling for the King to take over the colony of New Netherland, and in 1664 a fleet was sent to take control. Once again, the Dutch governor received no support from his own people, who cut their own deal with the Duke of York: The Dutch settlers were able to retain their property and worship as they pleased, in return for which they gave up without a fight.

THE CAROLINAS

As early as the 1650s, the Ablemarle Sound region off the coast of what is now northern North Carolina was inhabited by settlers trickling down from Virginia. The first royal governor was appointed in 1664. However, the first town in the area was not established until the arrival of a group of French Huguenots in 1704.

 FYI John Locke, the British educator, statesman, and philosopher of liberty, wrote the first constitution for the colony of Carolina. He had studied medicine, and then served for many years as private physician and secretary to Anthony Ashley Cooper, the first Earl of Shaftesbury, and one of the Lord Proprietors of the Carolina Colonies.

In 1670 the first settlers, coming both from New England and the Caribbean island of Barbados, arrived in what is now Charleston, South Carolina. One of the most curious features of this new settlement was an abortive attempt to create a hereditary nobility. They also tried to create a trade in Indian slaves, but it was soon learned what the Spanish had discovered over a century earlier: The Indians made extremely poor slaves. They either found a way to run away, back to their tribe, or they simply died when applied to any sort of hard work. In either event, they were useless as slaves. Soon, however, timber, rice, and indigo gave the colony an economic base.

PENNSYLVANIA

In 1681, William Penn, a wealthy Quaker and personal friend of King Charles II, received a charter and a large tract of land west of the Delaware River, which he modestly named after himself. To boost immigration, Penn actively recruited those Europeans most willing to emigrate—religious dissenters such as Quakers, Mennonites, Amish, Moravians, and Baptists—by guaranteeing them religious freedom similar to that already in place in Rhode Island.

When Penn arrived in his new colony, there were already Dutch, Swedish, and English settlers living along the Delaware River. That was where he founded Philadelphia, the "City of Brotherly Love."

In keeping with his Quaker religion, William Penn was motivated by a sense of equality not found in other American colonies at the time. For example, women in Pennsylvania had rights long before they did anywhere else in America. Penn and his deputies also tried to be fair to the Delaware Indians, ensuring that they were paid for any land settled on by Europeans.

GEORGIA

Georgia was finally settled in 1732, the last of the 13 colonies. Because it was close to, if not actually part of, Spanish Florida, the colony was viewed as a buffer against Spanish incursion. And it had another unique quality: The man charged with Georgia's fortifications, General James Oglethorpe, was a reformer who deliberately set out to create a refuge where the poor and former prisoners would be given new opportunities.

 FYI James Oglethorpe was the only founder of an American colony to see it become a state. Before his death the general enthusiastically greeted John Adams, ambassador to England from the newly formed United States, and he ultimately lived until 1785.

SETTLERS, SLAVES, AND SERVANTS

Few emigrants could afford the cost of passage for themselves and their families to make a start in the new land. Judges and prison authorities offered convicts a chance to migrate to colonies like Georgia instead of serving prison sentences. Ships' captains received large rewards from the sale of service contracts for poor migrants, and the migrants in turn became indentured servants to the person paying for their passage. Captains used every method from extravagant promises to actual kidnapping to take on as many passengers as their vessels could hold.

In some cases, the expenses of transportation and maintenance were paid by colonizing agencies like the Virginia or Massachusetts Bay companies. In return, indentured servants agreed to work for the agencies as contract laborers, usually for four to seven years. When freed at the end of this term, they would be given "freedom dues," which usually included a small tract of land in the colony on which they could settle.

Half the settlers living in the southern colonies came to America under the indentured servant system. Some of them faithfully fulfilled their obligations, others ran away from their employers and settled in another colony. Probably because it was so prevalent, no social stigma was attached to a family that had come to America under this type of slavery. Every colony had its share of civic and military leaders who were former indentured servants.

The important exception to this rule was African slaves. The first black Africans were brought to Virginia in 1619. At first, they were regarded as indentured servants who could earn their freedom in the same manner as white immigrants. By the 1660s, however, as the demand for plantation labor in the Southern colonies grew, the institution of black slavery began to solidify. Ultimately, the law became different for black and white slaves, where whites could earn their freedom but Africans could not.

JUST A MINUTE

Another big group of immigrants who influenced American English were African slaves. Such words as *tote, gumbo, jazz, voodoo, okra,* and *chigger* are from Africa. In addition, many black American expressions like "be with it," "do your thing," and "bad mouth" are word-for-word translations of phrases widely used in West Africa.

NEW ENGLAND

The need for black slaves did not exist in the north. New England has thin, stony soil, relatively little level land, and long winters, making it difficult to eke out an existence from farming. The sturdy Yankees soon turned their attention to other ways of making a living. New Englanders harnessed the water power of their many streams and rivers and established mills and factories.

Good stands of timber encouraged shipbuilding. Oak timber for ships' hulls, tall pines for spars and masts, and pitch for the seams of ships came from the New England forests. Building their own vessels and sailing them to ports all over the world, the shipmasters of Massachusetts Bay laid the foundation for a trade that was to grow steadily in importance. By the end of the colonial period, one third of all vessels under the British flag were built in New England.

New England shippers soon discovered that rum and slaves were profitable commodities. One of the most enterprising, and unsavory, of the trading practices of the colonial period was the "triangular trade." In the first side of the triangle, merchants and shippers would purchase slaves off the coast of Africa for New England rum. In the second side of the triangle, they would sell the slaves in the West Indies, and in the third leg, they would buy molasses to bring home for sale to the local rum producers. Each leg of the triangle was profitable, and massive fortunes were made in the North by supplying slaves to the South.

FYI MYTH: The Civil War ended the slave trade in 1865. FACT: In the U.S. Constitution, there was a provision that the slave trade would end 20 years after its ratification. However, even though this provision ended the slave trade in 1807, it would take the Civil War to end all slavery in America. By the time of the Civil War, only a few very old slaves remained who had actually been born in Africa; the vast majority had been born in America.

Hour's Up!

1. The Pilgrims celebrated the first Thanksgiving:
    - **A.** The last Thursday in November
    - **B.** The fourth Thursday in November
    - **C.** The Thursday before the first Wednesday in December
    - **D.** Nobody knows

2. New York City was sold to the Dutch by:
    - **A.** The Duke of York
    - **B.** The Duke of Earl
    - **C.** The Manhattan Indians
    - **D.** The Cleveland Indians

3. The founder of Maryland was:
    - **A.** Lord Baltimore
    - **B.** Lord Oriole
    - **C.** Queen Mary
    - **D.** Mary, Queen of Scots

QUIZ

QUIZ

4. The League of the Iroquois became the model for the:
   A. National League
   B. American League
   C. U.S. Constitution
   D. Urban League

5. African words that American slaves contributed to English include all of the following except:
   A. *gumbo*
   B. *jazz*
   C. *voodoo*
   D. *hood*

HOUR 3

The Colonies Grow

CHAPTER SUMMARY

LESSON PLAN:

In this hour, you will learn about the emergence of the early American colonies, their culture, their schools, and their early government.

You will also learn ...

- Why they found so many witches in Salem, Massachusetts.
- Why the center of finance in America is called Wall Street and not Tin Pan Alley.
- Why the Johnny who couldn't read probably lived in the south.
- Why the American colonies always thought they were independent, even before the Revolution.

The colonies, which had begun as a few isolated villages hugging the Atlantic seaboard, quickly began to prosper and grow as their burgeoning populations began to push inland. With their increased population, the need arose for representative government, since the entire business of the colony could no longer be conducted in the intimate atmosphere of a town meeting. Domestic industry began to develop, producing goods that spurred foreign trade. The isolated outposts were quickly transformed into urbane settlements.

THE MIDDLE COLONIES

Society in the middle colonies was much more tolerant of nonconformity than in New England. Under William Penn's guidance, Pennsylvania grew rapidly. By 1685, its population was almost 9,000. The heart of the colony was Philadelphia, a city known for its broad, tree-shaded streets, substantial brick and stone houses, and busy docks. By the end of the colonial period, its population had reached 30,000, a cosmopolitan mix of languages, creeds, and trades. Philadelphia's bent for successful business enterprise made the city one of the thriving centers of colonial America.

Though the Quakers dominated Philadelphia, the Germans, mainly from the Rhine region of Germany, transplanted their farming skills to Pennsylvania, and were the majority in the countryside. They also brought with them important cottage industries such as weaving, shoemaking, and cabinetmaking.

Pennsylvania was also the principal gateway into the New World for the Scots-Irish, who emigrated in larger numbers into the colony in the early eighteenth century. They hated the English, whom they had been fighting for centuries, and were generally suspicious of all government. The Scots-Irish tended to settle in the back country, away from British colonial rule, where they lived by hunting and subsistence farming. They were a group of immigrants whom it would not be hard for the revolutionaries to convince to throw off the yoke of British rule.

Even in the colonial period, New York outdid Pennsylvania in its ethnic and polyglot nature. By 1646, the population of the former Dutch colony on the Hudson River included French, Danes, Norwegians, Swedes, English, Scots, Irish, Germans, Poles, Bohemians, Portuguese, and Italians, an ethnic migration that was to continue for centuries.

FYI The old Dutch city of New Amsterdam had built a protective wall to defend against those Indians on Manhattan who still refused to understand the concept of land transfer. When the wall was later torn down, it was replaced with a street, aptly named Wall Street, which became the center for trading in the city.

The Dutch continued to exercise an important social and economic influence on New York long after the fall of New Netherland and their integration into the British colonial system. Their sharp-stepped, gable roofs were a permanent part of the city's architecture until replaced in the nineteenth century by new methods of building, and their merchants gave lower Manhattan its original bustling, commercial atmosphere.

THE SOUTHERN COLONIES

The southern colonies, even in the colonial period, were very different from their northern neighbors. Virginia, Maryland, North and South Carolina, and Georgia were predominantly agrarian, rural areas, which relied on farming for their subsistence.

By the end of the first century, Virginia and Maryland had established an economic and social structure based on two distinct groups, great planters and yeoman farmers. The planters of the tidewater region, whose wealth was derived from their slave labor, held most of the political power. They built great houses, adopted an aristocratic way of life, and affected pretensions to the culture of Europe. At the other end of the social scale were the yeoman farmers, who worked small tracts of land, were often elected to the assemblies, and who constantly challenged the political elite. Their outspoken independence was a constant warning to the planter oligarchy not to encroach too far upon the rights of free men. These yeoman farmers were another potential hotbed of dissent, and it would not take much to stir them to revolution.

Further south, Charleston, South Carolina, became the leading port and trading center for the southern colonies. Settlers in this area balanced their plantation economy with commerce, and therefore were not bound to a single crop as was Virginia. North and South Carolina also produced and exported indigo, a blue dye obtained from native plants, which was used in coloring fabric. By 1750, the population in the Carolinas had topped 100,000.

JUST A MINUTE

No sooner had South Carolina sent its first export shipment of indigo to England, than Parliament in 1747 passed a trade act placing a large bounty on each pound on indigo imported from the American colonies. The seeds of revolution continue ....

In the southern colonies, like in the North, German immigrants and the Scots-Irish, unwilling to live in the tidewater settlements where English influence was strong, pushed inland. By the 1730s they were pouring into the Shenandoah Valley of Virginia, and moving into the mountains of Appalachia.

JUST A MINUTE

If you want to find areas where they still speak the English of Shakespeare, you need to venture in the hollers of Appalachia. Cut off from mainstream civilization for centuries, you can still find people that speak like Granny Clampet and Queen Elizabeth. For both of them, *vittles* was a perfectly proper word for "food."

Living on the leading edge of the colony, such families were encroaching on the Indian lands, and were constant victims of attack. On the frontier, families built cabins, cleared tracts in the wilderness and cultivated maize and wheat. The men made leather from the skin of deer, called "buck" skin, the women wore garments of cloth they spun at home, known as "homespun." They ate venison, wild turkey, and fish.

 FYI You couldn't get cable on the frontier, so they had to make their own fun. Barbecues, dances, housewarmings, barn raisings, shooting matches, and quilt contests helped to break the tedium of survival in the wilderness.

THE WITCHES OF SALEM

Witchcraft was widely believed to exist in the 1600s, and in mother England, witchcraft trials were a common occurrence, with hundreds of witches burned at the stake annually. The New World had managed to avoid these troubles, until 1692 when a group of adolescent girls in Salem Village, Massachusetts, accused women of being witches.

Town officials immediately convened a court to hear the charges of witchcraft, and swiftly convicted and hung six women. The hysteria continued because the court permitted witnesses to testify that they had seen the accused as spirits or in visions. Such "spectral evidence" could neither be verified nor subject to objective examination. By the fall of 1692, more than 20 victims, including several men, had been executed, and more than 100 others were in jail, among them some of the town's most prominent citizens. But as the hysteria threatened to spread beyond Salem, ministers throughout the colony called for an end to the trials. The governor of the colony agreed and dismissed the court ... the *witch hunts* were over.

STRICTLY DEFINED

The Salem witch trials have come to represent the deadly consequences of making sensational, but false, charges. Today, making false accusations against a number of people is still called a **witch hunt.**

What was the real motivation behind the witch trails? It was actually a manifestation of the social change that was occurring throughout New England. Salem Village, like much of colonial New England at that time, was undergoing an economic and political transition from a largely agrarian, Puritan-dominated community to a more commercial, secular society. The accusers were tied to the traditional way of life of farming and the church, whereas the accused witches were members of the rising commercial class of small shopkeepers and tradesmen. The old-line Puritans really were seeing the devil—it was the end of the society they had come to America to preserve.

NEW PEOPLES

Although the majority of the settlers who came to America in the early years were English, there were also Dutch, Swedes, Germans, French Huguenots, slaves from Africa, Spaniards, Italians, and Portuguese. Amazingly, although the English dominated immigration from 1620 to 1680, ever since that time they have been swamped by other immigrant groups.

JUST A MINUTE

By 1690, the American population had risen to 250,000. From then on, it doubled every 25 years until, in 1775, at the beginning of the American Revolution, it numbered more than 2.5 million.

Although a family could move from Massachusetts to Virginia or from South Carolina to Pennsylvania without major readjustment, distinctions between individual colonies continued to exist. There were even more differences between the three regional groupings of colonies. New England, the southern colonies, and the middle colonies each had their own distinctive regional flavor, with the differences being the most marked between New England and the south, differences which were to play an important part in future American history.

AN AMERICAN CULTURE EMERGES

From its very beginnings, America had a strong democratic form of government, even in the south where the aristocratic planter class attempted to create a hereditary nobility of sorts. A significant factor deterring the rise of a powerful aristocratic or gentry class in the colonies was the fact that if they subjugated the common people too much, they could simply move west. Time after time, dominant tidewater figures were obliged, by the threat of a mass exodus to the frontier, to liberalize political policies, land-grant requirements, and religious practices.

COLONIAL EDUCATION

American education also had a significant impact on the democratic facet of colonial life. From the very beginning, institutions of higher learning were established by the colonists. Harvard College was the first, founded in 1636 in Cambridge, Massachusetts. The Rev. John Davenport founded the Hopkins Grammar School in New Haven, Connecticut, within a year of the colony's founding. Near the end of the century, the College of William and Mary was established in Virginia.

FYI Colonial children learned to read on a "hornbook." It was usually a small, wooden paddle with just one sheet of paper glued to it. Because paper was so expensive, parents and teachers wanted to protect it. So they covered the paper with a very thin piece of cow's horn. The piece of cow's horn was so thin, you could see through it. The paper usually had the alphabet, some pairs of letters, and a religious verse, often the Lord's Prayer.

On the town level, a free education was available to all. The Puritan emphasis on reading directly from the Scriptures underscored the importance of literacy. In 1647, the Massachusetts Bay Colony enacted the "ye olde deluder Satan" Act, requiring every town having more than 50 families to establish a grammar school to prepare students for college. Shortly thereafter, other New England colonies followed its example.

The first immigrants to New England brought their own books, and as the colonies grew they continued to import books directly from London. Booksellers in the colonies were doing a thriving business in works of classical literature, history, politics, philosophy, science, theology, and belles-lettres. In 1639, the first printing press in the English colonies was installed at Harvard College.

The first school in Pennsylvania, which began in 1683, taught reading, writing, and accounting. Every Quaker community provided for the teaching of its children. Advanced training in classical languages, history, and literature was available at the Friends Public School, founded in 1689, where tuition was free to the poor. The Friends Public School still operates in Philadelphia as the William Penn Charter School.

Women were not entirely overlooked, but their educational opportunities were limited to training in home economics. Private teachers were often hired to instruct the wealthy daughters of Philadelphia in French, music, dancing, painting, singing, and grammar.

Benjamin Franklin was a prime mover and shaker in the intellectual development of Philadelphia. He formed a debating club that became the American Philosophical Society. His endeavors led to the founding of the University of Pennsylvania. He was also a key figure in the establishment of a subscription library, which he modestly dubbed "the mother of all North American subscription libraries."

FYI Ben Franklin played several musical instruments, including the guitar. His great interest in music lead him to invent the armonica. This simple musical instrument is played by touching the edge of the spinning glass with dampened fingers. The armonica's beautiful tones appealed to many composers, including Mozart and Beethoven.

In the southern colonies, wealthy planters and merchants imported private tutors from Ireland or Scotland to teach their children, or sent their children to school in England. Because of these opportunities, the upper classes in the south were not interested in supporting public education. In addition, they did not have closely packed villages like in the north, and the scattered farms and plantations of the south made community schools difficult.

New England was the cradle of literary effort in the colonies, at first confined primarily to the works of famous ministers. One such Puritan minister, the Reverend Cotton Mather, wrote some 400 works. His masterpiece, *Magnalia Christi Americana*, detailed New England's history.

FYI Michael Wigglesworth had the biggest single colonial best-seller, titled *The Day of Doom*. It described in lurid detail the many agonies and tortures that would befall those who fell into hell at the last judgment, a sort of colonial *Nightmare on Elm Street*.

FREE PRESS

Another bastion of America's democracy has always been its free press. In 1704, the first successful newspaper was launched at Cambridge, Massachusetts, and by 1745 there were 22 newspapers being published throughout the colonies. In New York, an important step in establishing the principle of freedom of the press took place with the trial of Johann Peter Zenger, whose *New York Weekly Journal*, begun in 1733, represented the opposition to the government. The colonial governor, who could not tolerate Zenger's satirical barbs, had him thrown into prison on a charge of seditious libel. Zenger continued to publish his paper from jail during his nine-month trial, which provided excellent copy, and which sold throughout the colonies. Zenger argued that the charges he printed were true and hence not libelous. The jury returned a verdict of not guilty, and Zenger went free. Since then, truth has always been an absolute defense to the charge of libel.

THE GREAT AWAKENING

The growing wealth of the merchant class prompted fears among the populace that the devil was at work, luring society into the evil pursuit of worldly gain. This fear produced a religious reaction in the 1730s that came to be known as the Great Awakening. Leaders arose to fan the fears of the populace, in a frenzy reminiscent of the witch trials.

The Rev. Whitefield, an initial instigator of this mania, began his religious revival in Philadelphia and then moved on to New England. He could command audiences of 20,000 people at a time, and engaged them with histrionic displays, gestures, and emotional oratory. Religious turmoil swept throughout New England and the middle colonies as ministers left established churches to follow his word and to preach the revival.

Whitefield's converts were sometimes even more outspoken. The Reverend James Davenport, the son of the Rev. John Davenport, the founder of Yale, and the great-grandson of the Rev. John Davenport who was the founder of New Haven, was thought by many to be completely insane. He could easily command audiences in the thousands, and regularly exhorted his followers to abandon their regular minister, whom he would accuse of not being sufficiently devout. The legislature of Connecticut could finally take no more of him, and passed a law against "exhorters." In one of his greatest public appearances, he built a great bonfire, and exhorted his followers to throw all of their worldly possessions into the flames.

FYI Another of the preachers who followed Whitefield with great zeal was Eleazar Wheelock, Davenport's brother-in-law, who became so carried away with the Great Awakening that his parish refused to pay him his salary. He later founded Dartmouth College as a school for converting the Indians.

Yet another influenced by Whitefield was the Rev. Jonathan Edwards, Davenport's cousin, and the Great Awakening reached its zenith in 1741 with his sermon "Sinners in the Hands of an Angry God." His magnum opus, *Of Freedom of Will* (1754), attempted to reconcile Calvinism with the Enlightenment.

The Great Awakening gave rise to numerous evangelical denominations and to the spirit of revivalism, which continues to play a significant role in American religious and cultural life today. It further weakened the status of the established clergy, and provoked believers to rely on their own conscience in matters of religion. Perhaps most important, it led to the proliferation of so many different sects and denominations that it was impossible to maintain any sort of state religion, even in New England, where the Puritan Church (now called Congregational), had held sway over the people for several generations. With so many different religions, religious toleration and freedom were inevitable.

THE EMERGENCE OF COLONIAL GOVERNMENT

All the colonies, except Georgia, had emerged as companies of shareholders, or as feudal proprietorships, authorized by charters granted by the Crown. The fact that the king had transferred his immediate sovereignty over the New World settlements to stock companies and proprietors did not, of course, mean that the colonists in America were free of his control. The crown expected that inhabitants of Virginia, for example, would have no more voice in their government than if the king himself had retained absolute rule.

In direct contrast, the colonies had never thought of themselves as subservient. Rather, they considered themselves chiefly as commonwealths or states, much like England itself, having only a loose association with the authorities in London. The colonists, inheritors of the traditions of the Englishman's long struggle for political liberty, had incorporated concepts of freedom into Virginia's first charter. In 1618, the Virginia Company issued instructions to its appointed governor providing that free inhabitants of the plantations should elect representatives to join with the governor and an appointive council in passing ordinances for the welfare of the colony.

These measures proved to be some of the most far-reaching in the entire colonial period. From then on, it was generally accepted that the colonists had a right to participate in their own government. The king provided in the charters of other colonies that the free men of the colony should have a voice in legislation affecting them. Thus, charters awarded to the Calverts in Maryland, William Penn in Pennsylvania, the proprietors in North and South Carolina, and the proprietors in New Jersey specified that legislation should be enacted with "the consent of the freemen."

In New England, for many years, there was even more complete self-government than in the other colonies. Aboard the *Mayflower*, the Pilgrims adopted the "Mayflower Compact." Although there was no legal basis for the Pilgrims to establish a system of self-government, their action was not contested and, under the compact, the Plymouth settlers conducted their own affairs without outside interference.

The Massachusetts Bay Company had also been given the right to govern itself, with full authority vested in the hands of persons residing in the colony. At first, the dozen or so original members of the company who had come to America attempted to rule autocratically. But the other colonists soon made it clear that they would have none of that, and demanded a voice in public affairs. Faced with mass migration, the leaders had no choice but to give in, and control of the government passed to elected representatives.

Subsequently, other New England colonies, such as Connecticut and Rhode Island, also succeeded in becoming self-governing simply by announcing that they were beyond any governmental authority, and then setting up their own political system modeled after that of the Pilgrims at Plymouth.

In only two colonies was the self-government provision omitted in the original charter. These were New York, which was granted to Charles II's brother, the Duke of York, who was himself later to become King James II, and Georgia, in whose charter power was granted to a group of "trustees." In both instances these provisions for control were short-lived, for the colonists demanded legislative representation, and faced with the choice of a mass exodus, or a determined mob, the authorities were forced to surrender power to a local legislature.

Even though the colonies were self-governing, they were technically still subject to the absolute authority of the king. However, in the critical early years of the seventeenth century, the king was distracted by the Civil War (1642–1649), and then the Revolution cut off his head. After the death of the king, Oliver Cromwell's Puritan Commonwealth and Protectorate were too busy with their own establishment of a new government, and with maintaining their own power against Cavalier plots, to concern themselves with reigning in their wayward colonial possessions, who were in any event governed by their fellow Puritan revolutionaries. After the restoration of Charles II to the throne, England could have looked to tighten their hold on the colonies, but inexplicably, the colonies were left largely to their own devices.

Why did England have such a difficult time controlling their American colonies? The remoteness afforded by a vast ocean, in the days of very primitive travel, made any sort of direct control very difficult. By the time that a ship could come from America, the king could decide an issue, and another ship return with an answer, the colonists had long since come to their own conclusion. Another factor was the rugged individualism of the colonists. They had conquered a wilderness, and they were loath to listen to anyone who had never even set foot in their country. And as the generations passed, the colonists no longer considered themselves Englishmen, except when it came to demanding their inalienable rights. Their allegiance was to the colony where they were born. Lastly, America was a vast country, and the reach of any foreign government, if it had any impact, went only as far as the coastal cities; it did not extend to the settlers who had lived for generations in the interior regions.

However, the colonies assertion of total self-government did not go entirely unchallenged. In the 1670s, for example, the Lords of Trade and Plantations, a royal committee established to enforce the mercantile system on the colonies, tried to annul the Massachusetts Bay charter, because the colony was refusing to comply with the government's economic policy.

FYI Sometimes it is best to do nothing at all. James II was having his troubles, but at least no one was throwing him off the throne. However, he did two stupid things. First, he became a Catholic, in a country that had a law that said the king had to be Protestant. That they put up with, but when his wife had a son, ensuring that he would be followed by another Catholic king, the Protestant opposition invited William of Orange, who was James's nephew, and who was married to Mary, James's daughter, to come to England and take charge. The bloodless coup was dubbed the Glorious Revolution.

In 1685, James II tried to create a consortium of colonies he dubbed the Dominion of New England, putting New England, New York, and New Jersey under a single jurisdiction, in an attempt to tighten Crown control over the region. He appointed a royal governor, Sir Edmund Andros, who levied taxes by executive order, implemented harsh measures, and jailed those who resisted. However, the colonies were in luck. The Glorious Revolution in England (1688–1689) deposed James II, at which point the colonies took advantage of the situation, rebelled, and imprisoned Andros. The colonies that were supposed to be part of the Dominion of New England reinstalled their previous governments, and went back to ignoring the king.

The Glorious Revolution had other positive effects on the colonies. The Bill of Rights and Toleration Act of 1689 affirmed that freedom of worship was the right of all those subject to the king, and enforced limits on the Crown. Equally important, John Locke's book *Second Treatise on Government* (1690) set forth a new theory of government, one that was not based on divine right of kings, but on the fact that people are endowed with the natural rights of life, liberty, and property, and that they had the right to rebel when governments violated these natural rights.

When Thomas Jefferson was writing the Declaration of Independence, he made an important tweak to the classic Lockean formulation on inalienable human rights: "Life, liberty, and property." Jefferson changed it to "Life, liberty, and the pursuit of happiness."

The colonial legislatures, mindful of the rights that Parliament had gained over the king through the civil war and the Glorious Revolution, proceeded to make the same demands on their colonial governors. The colonial assemblies constantly asserted their "rights" and "liberties." By the early eighteenth century, the colonial legislatures held two significant powers similar to those of the English Parliament: the right to vote on taxes and expenditures and the right to initiate their own legislation. The legislatures used these rights to check the power of royal governors and to pass additional measures to expand their power and influence. In many cases, the royal authorities did not understand the importance of the bills the colonial assemblies were passing, and simply ignored them. However, they should have been paying attention, because these acts established precedents and principles that the colonies would later assert during the revolution.

Hour's Up!

QUIZ

1. A *hornbook* was:

   A. A place for a frontiersman to keep his powder dry

   B. A book on the care and treatment of horns

   C. A learning aid for children

   D. A music book primer

2. Benjamin Franklin invented all of the following, except:

   A. Public library

   B. University of Pennsylvania

   C. Armonica

   D. Electric guitar

3. The Great Awakening was:

   A. A solar eclipse

   B. A religious revival

   C. Judgment Day

   D. A scientific breakthrough

4. All of the following would think that victuals (pronounced *vittles*) is a perfectly good word for food, except:

    A. William Shakespeare

    B. Queen Elizabeth I

    C. Inhabitants of Appalachia

    D. Emily Post

5. The Pilgrims who came over on the *Mayflower* and settled at Plymouth drew up a document under which they would all live, which was called the:

    A. Constitution

    B. Declaration of Independence

    C. Mayflower Compact

    D. Plymouth Compact

QUIZ

HOUR 4

A Country Forms

LESSON PLAN:

In this hour, you will learn about how the expense of the French and Indian War led the English Crown to try a number of different ways to squeeze money out of the American colonies. Each idea was worse than the last, and only served to further fan the flames of revolution.

You will also learn ...

- That it wasn't the French fighting the Indians in the French and Indian War.
- Why nobody was ever served any tea to drink at the Boston Tea Party.
- Why the Stamp Act didn't have anything to do with the Post Office.
- Why the Boston Massacre wasn't a really bad game for the Boston Celtics.

Great Britain was slowly discovering the costs of being a superpower and ruling a worldwide empire. A tiny island kingdom, it was becoming increasingly important to them for their far-flung colonies to not only be self-supporting, but to contribute to the costs of administering this vast domain. After Great Britain finally won their war with France for control of the North American continent, the French and Indian War, the royal exchequer decided that it was finally time for the colonies to contribute and help repay the costs of this war. As they tried different ways of extracting money from the American colonies, each successive method resulted in increasingly deteriorating relations between the mother country and her colonies.

THE FRENCH AND INDIAN WAR

France and England fought a succession of wars in Europe and the Caribbean during the eighteenth century. Though Britain made some gains, primarily in the sugar islands of the Caribbean, France remained a powerful force in North America.

France had alliances with Indian tribes in Canada and along the Great Lakes, possession of the Mississippi River, and a line of forts and trading posts stretching from Quebec to New Orleans. This effectively limited the American colonies to the eastern seaboard, with no possibility of expanding west of the Appalachian Mountains as long as the French controlled the Mississippi Valley.

With two superpowers on the same continent, conflict was inevitable, and it occurred on the fault line between the two empires. An armed clash took place in 1754 at Fort Duquesne, the site where Pittsburgh, Pennsylvania, is now located, between a band of French regulars and Virginia militiamen under the command of George Washington, then just 22 years old. This was the beginning of the North American theater of the worldwide conflict between France and England known as the Seven Years' War, which in America was also called the French and Indian War.

FYI Washington was eager to be a regular British officer, and was bitterly disappointed when he failed to obtain a commission in the British Army. As a result, he threw all of his energies into serving in the Virginia militia, and he was serving in that capacity with the British army during the French and Indian War.

In response to the French threat, a congress was called, with representatives from New York, Pennsylvania, Maryland, and the New England colonies. The Albany Congress, as it came to be known, met with the Iroquois at Albany, New York, in order to bring them into the alliance against the French. What they had done so far was in accord with their instructions from London, but then they went further. The delegates decided that a union of the American colonies was "absolutely necessary," and adopted the Albany Plan of Union. Drafted by Benjamin Franklin, the plan provided that a president act with a grand council of delegates chosen by the assemblies, with each colony to be represented in proportion to its financial contributions to the general treasury. This organization would have charge of defense, Indian relations, trade, and settlement of the West, as well as having the power to levy taxes. This would have been the perfect instrument with which to later lay the groundwork for future independence, but none of the colonies would accept Franklin's plan. They did not want to give up their power of taxation and their control over the development of the western lands to a central government.

England defeated the French in the Seven Years' War. In the Peace of Paris, signed in 1763, France gave up her claim to all of Canada, the Great Lakes, and the upper Mississippi Valley. Any possibility of a French empire in North America was over.

JUST A MINUTE

At the end of the French and Indian War in 1760, the colonies had a combined population of 1,500,000, a sixfold increase since 1700.

Having finally defeated France, Britain now had to face a problem that it had sorely neglected, governing its vast empire. With not only its old colonies, but also its new French lands to govern, London had to reorganize its possessions to provide for the common defense, reconcile the divergent interests of different areas and peoples, and raise taxes to pay for the cost of imperial administration.

In North America alone, British territories had more than doubled. In addition to the 13 colonies on the eastern seaboard, added to the British empire was Canada and all of the territory west from the Allegheny Mountains to the Mississippi River. A population that was predominantly Protestant and English now included French-speaking Catholics in Quebec, and large numbers of Native Americans, some of whom were Christians. Defense and administration of these territories would require huge sums of money and many new administrators. The old colonial system would have to be completely overhauled.

A NEW COLONIAL SYSTEM

Britain needed a new imperial plan for the colonies, but the situation in America was not favorable to such a sudden and drastic change. The colonies had had their virtual independence for too long, and they were ready to demand more freedom, particularly now that the French were no longer a threat. If England was going to try to implement a new imperial system, Parliament would have to contend with colonists accustomed to self-government, who had their own battle-tested colonial militia.

One of the first moves made by the British after the war was to attempt to organize their newly conquered lands. Canada and the Ohio Valley required policies that would not alienate their non-British subjects, the French and the Indians. Unfortunately for the British Foreign Office, any attempts to treat the newly conquered peoples fairly put them into direct conflict with their own original colonies. With their populations increasing, the colonies were looking to the newly conquered lands as living space. Almost immediately, the coastal colonies took a straight edge, and extended their borders directly west to the Mississippi River.

FYI Evidence of this land grab by the original colonies can be seen even today. One look at a map of the United States will reveal that Kentucky is the natural extension of the borders of Virginia, and Tennessee is an extension of North Carolina all the way to the Mississippi.

London, fearful that settlers migrating into the new lands would provoke new, and expensive, Indian wars, decided that the lands should only be opened to settlement on a gradual basis. Restricting movement was also a way of ensuring royal control over existing settlements before allowing the formation of new ones. The Royal Proclamation of 1763 reserved all the western territory between the Alleghenies, Florida, the Mississippi River, and Quebec for use by Native Americans. This measure, in the eyes of the American colonists, constituted a high-handed disregard by the king of their manifest destiny, and of their inalienable right to move west, dispossess the Indians, and settle new lands.

FYI Manifest Destiny was a phrase used by leaders and politicians to explain the continental expansion by the United States outward from the original thirteen colonies. The people of the United States felt it was their national destiny to extend the "boundaries of freedom" to others by imparting their idealism and belief in democratic institutions across the entire continent, from "sea to shining sea." The idealism behind this desire to expand the American dream was fueled by a high birth rate on the east coast, and massive immigration from Europe, both of which combined to provide an unending supply of settlers eager to push west where they could make a new and better life for themselves.

Another repressive course of action of the British government was their new financial policy, brought about because of their pressing need to raise money to administrate and defend their expanded empire. The logic advanced by Parliament was that the money that was being raised in the colonies, would actually be returned to the colonies in the form of administration and defense, so that the new taxes would be to the mutual benefit of both England and her colonies. What Parliament did not seem to recognize was that they were usurping the colonies long-standing prerogative of taxation, which they had successfully employed for years to pay their own militia and to run their own affairs. The colonies bitterly resented what they considered royal usurpation of their traditional rights.

The first move by Parliament in implementing their new system was the passage of the Sugar Act of 1764. This act forbade the importation of foreign rum, and put a duty on molasses, wine, silk, coffee, and a number of other luxury items. To enforce the Sugar Act, more customs officials were hired. British warships in American waters were instructed to seize smugglers, and "writs of assistance," or warrants, authorized the king's officers to search suspected premises. Both the duty imposed by the Sugar Act and the measures created to enforce it enraged New England merchants. They contended that payment of the duty would be ruinous to their businesses. Merchants, legislatures, and town meetings protested the law.

FYI In response to the Sugar Act of 1764, Samuel Adams charged Britain with levying a tax on its colonial citizens without proper colonial representation in Parliament, thus giving birth to the battle cry "no taxation without representation." Adams spent the next ten years writing essays and making speeches to encourage the patriot cause, as well as organizing the Sons of Liberty, a group of men devoted to harassing British troops stationed in Massachusetts.

The Sugar Act was only the beginning of what the colonists considered to be new and repressive laws enacted by Parliament for the subjugation of the colonies. Their next law was the Currency Act, passed "to prevent paper bills of credit hereafter issued in any of His Majesty's colonies from being made legal tender." Because the colonies were a deficit trade area and constantly short of hard currency, this measure added a serious burden to the colonial economy. This was followed by an even more objectionable law, the Quartering Act. Passed in 1765, it required colonies to provide royal troops with provisions and barracks, often in the homes of private individuals. Providing room and board for thousands of British Regulars was not only a serious financial drain on the resources of each colony, which had to be made up with additional taxes, but the quartering in private homes was considered a serious infringement on the inalienable rights to which every Englishman considered himself entitled.

FYI The Quartering Act wasn't forgotten by the colonists, and when the Bill of Rights to the Constitution was drafted, they quickly added the 3rd Amendment, which states: "No Soldier shall, in time of peace be quartered in any house, without the consent of the Owner, nor in time of war, but in a manner to be prescribed by law." This made it quite clear that they didn't like quartering, and they weren't going to stand for it any more.

STAMP ACT

However, it wasn't until the Stamp Act that the people were aroused to action, perhaps because this affected each and every citizen in the colonies. The Stamp Act bore equally on people who did any kind of business. Thus it aroused the hostility of the most powerful and vocal groups of Americans: journalists, lawyers, clergymen, merchants, and businessmen.

JUST A MINUTE

The Stamp Act was not about mailing a letter—these "stamps" were revenue stamps, which have survived to present day in the form of the revenue stamps found on packages of cigarettes. However, these revenue stamps had to be affixed to all newspapers, broadsides, pamphlets, licenses, leases, and legal documents. The revenue was to be used for "defending, protecting and securing" the colonies.

Leading merchants organized for resistance and formed nonimportation associations. Trade with England fell off precipitously in the summer of 1765, as prominent men organized themselves into the *Sons of Liberty*, a secret organization formed to protest the Stamp Act. From Massachusetts to Georgia, mobs forced customs agents to resign, and destroyed the hated revenue stamps.

STRICTLY DEFINED

Ironically, the **Sons of Liberty** took their name from a debate on the Stamp Act in Parliament in 1765. Charles Townshend, speaking in support of the act, spoke contemptuously of the American colonists as being "children." Isaac Barre jumped to his feet in outrage, and said that these Americans were not children, they were "Sons of Liberty."

Patrick Henry introduced a resolution in the Virginia House of Burgesses denouncing taxation without representation as a threat to the liberties of all Virginians. In his opinion, they had the same rights as all natural-born Englishmen, and hence could be taxed only by their own representatives. Then, the Massachusetts Assembly convened a "Stamp Act Congress" in New York, inviting each colony to send delegates. Twenty-seven representatives from nine colonies answered the summons. After much debate, the congress adopted a resolution asserting that "no taxes ever have been or can be constitutionally imposed on them, but by their respective legislatures," and further, that the Stamp Act had a "manifest tendency to subvert the rights and liberties of the colonists."

TAXATION WITHOUT REPRESENTATION

The colonies had a number of reasons why they did not feel that English Parliament had any power to levy taxes on the colonies in America. First of all, from the point of view of the colonies, it was impossible to consider themselves represented in Parliament unless they actually had their own citizens elected to be members to the House of Commons. The English, on the other hand, advanced the principle of "virtual representation," believing that each member of Parliament represented the interests of the whole empire, despite the fact that he was elected by the property owners from his own district.

Second, the American leaders argued that no "imperial" Parliament existed; the only legal relations that existed between the colonies and England were with the Crown. It was the king who had established the colonies, and the king who had authorized them to have their own governments. While they admitted that the king was both the king of England, and the king of the colonies, they held to the belief that the English Parliament had no more right to pass laws for the colonies than the colonial legislatures had the right to pass laws for England.

The British Parliament was unwilling to accept the colonial position. However, British merchants were not so intransigent. They were being hit hard by the American boycott, and they threw all of their power and influence behind a repeal movement. In 1766, Parliament bowed to the political pressure, repealed the Stamp Act, and then modified the Sugar Act. However, not wishing to be perceived as giving in completely, and to mollify the supporters of central control over the colonies, Parliament then passed the Declaratory Act. This law asserted that Parliament had the authority to make laws regarding the colonies "in all cases whatsoever." Such a bold declaration of their power might have been a "feel good" provision in England, but it only served to further enrage the hotspurs in the colonies.

TOWNSHEND ACTS

The next act by the British government to incite the American colonists was initiated by Charles Townshend, the British Chancellor of the Exchequer (the British equivalent of the Secretary of the Treasury). He drafted a new fiscal program, which was intended to reduce British deficits by imposing new taxes on the American colonies. Townshend reasoned that while internal taxes, such as the Stamp Act, arguably might be considered illegal, no one could question that the British government had a perfect right to tax any goods coming into the colonies from abroad, so he imposed duties on imported paper, glass, lead, and tea.

FYI Charles Townshend was unable to foresee the ramifications of his policies in national and colonial affairs, and his abrasive, ham-handed political style often aroused opposition as much as it worked to his benefit. Despite an engaging wit and occasional charm, Townshend's mercurial disposition and unprincipled behavior guaranteed him enemies in every administration. The Townshend Acts galvanized antiimperial sentiment in North America, and were ultimately far more costly to England than any gain in revenue. Ironically, Townshend never lived to see the American reaction to his policies: the nonimportation agreements, the riots, and finally the Revolution. He died suddenly on September 4, 1767, "of a neglected fever."

The British government did need to raise revenue: They were spending large sums to support colonial governors, judges, and customs officers, as well as garrisoning a large British army in America to protect the settlers from the Indians, and to ensure that the French did not reacquire their lost North American empire. However, by this point any attempt at taxation levied on the colonists from England was going to be the subject of controversy.

The response was not long in coming. Philadelphia lawyer John Dickinson, in his *Letters of a Pennsylvania Farmer*, argued that Parliament, while it might have the right to control imperial commerce in the rest of their empire, did not have any right to tax the American colonies, whether the duties were external or internal.

Following enactment of the Townshend duties, colonial merchants once again resorted to nonimportation agreements, and the people refused to buy imported goods. Especially in the northeast, colonists made do with local products. It became the mark of a true patriot, for example, to dress in homespun clothing, and to drink anything but tea. They used homemade paper, and they refused to paint their houses with imported paint. In Boston, when officials tried to enforce the new regulations, the people turned to violence. Customs officials were set upon by the populace. Alarmed at the way in which his soldiers were being treated, the king dispatched two regiments of British regulars to the city.

Sending the troops to Boston was not one of the best ideas ever generated by the British government in Whitehall. The presence of the British regulars was an open invitation to the firebrands to stir up trouble. On March 5, 1770, some local patriots began throwing snowballs at soldiers on guard duty. The incident quickly escalated, as the sergeant of the guard called for more men, and then the mob grew larger and larger. Someone gave the order to fire. When the smoke cleared, three citizens of Boston lay dead in the snow. It was immediately dubbed the "Boston Massacre" by the patriots, and the incident was dramatically pictured in the press as conclusive proof of British tyranny.

The Boston Massacre was painted by a revolutionary Paul Revere. An early form of propaganda, it encouraged many who were undecided to join the patriot cause.

FYI Crispus Attucks, half black and half Indian, became the first casualty of the American Revolution when he was killed in the Boston Massacre. The soldiers were put on trial, and the crown did everything to vilify Attucks. He was described as the leader of "a motley rabble of saucy boys, Negroes and mulattos, Irish teagues and outlandish jack tars." The soldiers were acquitted, which further inflamed the citizens. Despite laws regulating the burial of blacks, Attucks was buried in the Park Street cemetery along with the other honored dead. The citizens of Boston observed the anniversary of the Boston Massacre every year leading up to the war. In ceremonies designed to stir revolutionary fervor, they summoned up the "discontented ghosts" of the victims." Attucks was immortalized as "the first to defy, the first to die."

Faced with mounting opposition from their American colonies, Parliament in 1770 decided that a policy of mollification might be a better idea, and repealed all the Townshend duties except that on tea, which was considered a luxury item. This action by Parliament was heralded in the colonies as a great victory, and greatly diffused the building sentiment for revolution. The colonial embargo on "English tea" continued, but in light of the decreasing tensions, was not too scrupulously observed.

Samuel Adams

During the following three-year period, a small number of radicals strove energetically to keep the controversy alive. They were determined to escalate tensions, and to bring about a complete severance of the American colonies from England. They continued to repeat the argument that payment of any tax, even a luxury tax, constituted an outright acceptance of the principle that Parliament had the right to rule the colonies. They raised the specter that at any time Parliament might once again decide to trample on the liberties of the colonials.

Samuel Adams was the acknowledged leader of the radicals, and he worked incessantly for independence. A graduate of Harvard College, which even in those days was a hotbed of radicalism, Adams was shrewd and able in politics, and deft at using the New England town meeting to mobilize public opinion. Adams published articles in newspapers, made speeches in town meetings, and initiated resolutions that appealed to the democratic fervor of the citizenry.

In 1772, he persuaded the Boston town meeting to elect a "Committee of Correspondence," whose mission was to record the grievances of the colonists, and to transmit them to other towns and colonies. The first action of the committee was to oppose a British decision to pay the salaries of judges from customs revenues. The committee realized that the judges would no longer be dependent on the legislature for their incomes, and would thereafter refuse to be held accountable to the people. In the opinion of Adams and the committee, this was the first step toward "a despotic form of government." The committee of correspondence, true to their name, sent letters to the other towns about this problem, and requested that each town draft their own reply. As a result, committees were set up in practically every colony. Adams had achieved his first goal: He had created an organization that could be used as the basis for the upcoming revolution he envisioned.

Sam Adams Hosts a "Tea Party"

Adams knew that he needed an incident to incite the populace, to rally the people to armed insurrection. Not realizing that they were playing right into the hands of the revolutionaries, in 1773, Britain furnished Adams and his firebrands with an incendiary issue.

The East India Company, a powerful government-within-a-government because of the immense riches they had made in colonial trade, found itself in critical financial trouble. To bail them out, it went straight to the British government, and asked for a monopoly on all tea exported to the colonies. The government also gave them the authority to supply retailers directly, bypassing colonial wholesalers who had previously handled the transactions. By selling its tea through its own agents at a price well below that of the Yankee tea smugglers, the East India Company made smuggling unprofitable and threatened to eliminate the independent colonial merchants at the same time. Aroused not only by the loss of the tea trade, but also by the monopoly which the crown had conferred on a non-American company, colonial merchants joined the radicals agitating for independence. All along the Atlantic coast, agents of the East India Company were forced to resign, and as shipments of tea arrived, they were returned to England.

JUST A MINUTE

The colonists' boycott of English tea was quite effective. Consumption in the colonies fell from 900,000 pounds in 1769 to 237,000 pounds just 3 years later. The Boston Tea Party was not just a couple of tea bags—the "Indians" plunked 9,659 pounds sterling (a small fortune) worth of tea into Boston Bay. This was in a day when 100 pounds was a very good *yearly* salary.

In Boston, however, the agents of the East India Company defied the colonists. With the support of the royal governor, they announced that they would land incoming cargoes of tea regardless of opposition.

On the night of December 16, 1773, a band of men disguised as Mohawk Indians, and led by Samuel Adams and Paul Revere, boarded three British ships lying at anchor and dumped the cargo of tea into the Boston harbor. They realized that if the tea were landed, colonists would comply with the tax and purchase the tea. Adams and his band of radical revolutionists were not going to rely on their fellow countrymen's commitment to principle, they were going to ensure that they did the right thing.

The tea was shipped by Davison, Newman & Company, the oldest tea merchants and exporters in London. They are still in business, and today sell a fine blend of Ceylon and Indian teas they have ironically named "Boston Harbor."

Britain was now confronted by a problem. The East India Company had been authorized the tea monopoly by act of parliament. Therefore, the Boston Tea Party was not just an act against the company, it was against the

British government as well. If the dumping of the tea was allowed to go unpunished, Parliament would in effect be admitting to the world that it had lost control of its American colonies. Opinion in Britain almost unanimously condemned the Boston Tea Party as an act of vandalism, and supported measures to bring the insurgent colonists into line.

THE INTOLERABLE ACTS

Parliament responded to the Boston Tea Party with new laws that the colonists named the "Coercive or Intolerable Acts." The first, the Boston Port Bill, closed the port of Boston until the tea was paid for. Of course, no thought was given to who would pay for the tea. It was certain the revolutionaries wouldn't pay a single farthing—the last thing in the world they wanted was a reconciliation between England and the colonies. This act played right into the hands of the revolutionaries. Closing the port was an action that threatened the very life of the city, because preventing Boston access to the sea meant economic disaster and ruin. Every day that the port was closed, more and more citizens became resentful and dissatisfied with English rule.

Parliament also restricted local authority, and required that towns seek the governor's consent before they held a town meeting. A new Quartering Act required local authorities to find suitable quarters for British troops, and this usually meant in private homes.

The Quebec Act extended the boundaries of the province of *Quebec* and guaranteed the right of the French inhabitants to remain Catholic. This act, by one stroke of the pen, nullified all of the claims to western lands contained in the charters of the colonies. In addition, the colonies, as a predominantly Protestant state that spoke English, did not want to be hemmed in by a Catholic country that spoke French. Though the Quebec Act had not been passed by Parliament as a punitive measure against the colonies, but as an enlightened approach to governing Canada, it was nevertheless classified by the Americans with the other Coercive Acts, and together they became known as the "Intolerable Acts."

STRICTLY DEFINED

The Indians used the name kebek for the region around the city of **Quebec.** It is a reference to the Algonquin word for "narrow passage" or "strait" to indicate the narrowing of the river at Cape Diamond.

These Intolerable Acts became the call to action for the colonies. Representatives met in Philadelphia on September 5, 1774, "to consult upon the present unhappy state of the Colonies," at what they called the First Continental Congress. Every colony except Georgia sent at least 1 delegate, and the group of 55 representatives was large enough for diversity of opinion and to spark debate, but small enough for genuine discussion and effective action.

The division of opinion in the colonies posed a genuine dilemma for the delegates. They would have to give an appearance of total unanimity to induce the British government to recognize their authority and to make concessions. At the same time, they would have to mask the opinions of the radicals, who were insisting on independence, because that would alarm the majority of Americans, who believed that a peaceful solution, one which retained ties to England, could work.

Congress passed a resolution which stated that the colonies would refuse to obey the Coercive Acts, and that should have been enough for their first session. However, having taken the leap, they couldn't stop there. They declared the right of the colonists to "life, liberty and property," and the right of the colonial legislatures to rule on "all cases of taxation and internal polity."

The most important action taken by the Congress, however, was the formation of a "Continental Association." This organization was given the power to renew the trade boycott, to create a system of committees to inspect customs entries, to publish the names of merchants who violated the agreements, and to confiscate the imports of violators.

FYI The Continental Association, in their message to the king, referred to themselves as the "free Protestant colonies." While they may have stood for freedom of religion, they were definitely only thinking about the freedom to be Protestant.

The association immediately assumed leadership of the colonies, spurring new local organizations to terminate what remained of royal authority. Led by the pro-independence leaders, they drew their support not only from the less well-to-do, but from many members of the professional class, especially lawyers, most of the planters of the Southern colonies, and of course many merchants. They intimidated the hesitant into joining the popular movement and punished those who defied their authority. They began to amass military supplies, and to mobilize the militia. In one bold stroke, the colonies had virtually set themselves up as an independent country.

The revolutionaries might have taken control, but many Americans, even though they opposed British encroachment on American rights, nonetheless favored compromise. The king at this point might well have appealed to these large numbers of moderates and, with swift and timely concessions, so strengthened their position that the revolutionaries would have found it difficult to proceed. But the temperament of George III did not lend itself to compromise. In September 1774, scorning a petition by Philadelphia Quakers who were trying to effect a reconciliation, he wrote, "The die is now cast, the Colonies must either submit or triumph."

QUIZ

HOUR'S UP!

1. The group most influential in fanning the flames of revolt in the colonies was:

   A. Sons of the American Revolution

   B. Daughters of the American Revolution

   C. Daughters of Liberty

   D. Sons of Liberty

2. Which of the following were not mailed an engraved invitation to the Boston Tea Party?

   A. Daughters of the American Revolution

   B. Sam Adams

   C. Sons of Liberty

   D. Citizens disguised as Mohawk Indians

3. Who was the most opposed to the Stamp Act?

   A. Post Office

   B. Federal Express

   C. United Parcel Service

   D. Committee of Correspondence

4. According to John Adams, future president of the United States, who of the following were not present at the Boston Massacre?

   A. Irish Teagues

   B. Paul Revere

   C. Saucy Boys

   D. Outlandish Jack Tars

5. American colonists hated the Quartering Act because:

    A. It increased the number of crimes for which a colonist could be drawn and quartered.

    B. Nickels, dimes, and pennies were enough.

    C. British regulars made lousy house guests.

    D. Colonists wanted their own elected legislatures to decide how many quarters there should be before halftime.

QUIZ

HOUR 5

The Road to Independence

LESSON PLAN:

In this hour, you will learn how the American colonies declared their independence, allied with France, fought the British, and finally won their independence, becoming the United States of America.

You will also learn ...

- How General Washington was able to win the war in spite of losing virtually every battle.

- Why the revolution needed a Declaration of Independence, when they were already fighting the British.

- Why Lord Cornwallis, with one of the greatest armies ever assembled in North America, was forced to surrender.

- Where the Loyalists who supported the king ran to after the end of the Revolution.

The American colonies, chaffing under the increasingly oppressive rule of Great Britain, finally decide that they can no longer tolerate foreign rule, and declare their independence. However, the king is not going to let his colonies go without a fight. It is a long, hard war, seven years of deprivation as the fledgling nation struggles to defeat the most powerful superpower in the world.

THE REVOLUTION BEGINS

General Thomas Gage, who commanded the British garrison at Boston, learned that the Massachusetts colonists were collecting powder and military stores at the town of Concord, a town near Boston. Realizing that seizing the powder would cripple the fledgling revolt, and also discourage many who were uncertain about the revolution, Gage sent an expedition to confiscate the munitions.

FYI Paul Revere had been a leader of the Sons of Liberty, and his famous midnight ride was to warn the militia at Concord that the redcoats were coming. Unfortunately, he was captured, and it was actually a man named Dawes who finished the ride. However, "Listen my children, and you shall hear, of the midnight ride of William Dawes" doesn't rhyme, so he was shortchanged by history.

After a long night of marching, the British troops reached the village of Lexington on April 19, 1775, and saw a determined band of *Minutemen* waiting for them in the early morning mist. Major John Pitcairn, the leader of the British troops, yelled, "Disperse, you damned rebels! Run, you dogs, run!" The leader of the Minutemen, Captain John Parker, warned his men not to fire. Suddenly, someone (no one will ever know if it was British or colonial), fired a shot, and the British opened fire. The British then charged with bayonets, leaving eight dead and ten Minutemen wounded. Ralph Waldo Emerson dubbed it "the shot heard 'round the world." The war had begun, and there was no stopping it.

STRICTLY DEFINED

The Massachusetts militia were called **Minutemen** because they could be mobilized to fight within a minute.

Having routed the rebels at Lexington, the British pushed on to Concord, only to discover that the Americans had removed most of the munitions. However, by this point, the countryside had been awakened, and the colonial militias for miles around had been mobilized. As the British made their long march back to Boston, the colonial militia dogged their trail. Behind stone walls, hillocks and houses, militiamen from "every Middlesex village and farm" made targets of the bright red coats of the British soldiers. By the time the weary soldiers finally stumbled into Boston, they had suffered 250 killed and wounded. The Americans, for their part, only had 93 casualties.

Shortly thereafter, the Second Continental Congress convened in Phila-delphia on May 10, 1775. Encouraged by the success at Lexington and Concord, it took them only five days to decide to declare war on England. In the colonial equivalent of mobilizing the National Guard, they called up the colonial militias into continental (regular army) service, promoted Colonel George Washington of the Virginia Militia to Major General, and appointed him commander-in-chief of the American forces. Hoping to bring Canada into the revolution as the fourteenth colony, Congress ordered American expeditions to march northward into Canada.

QUOTABLE QUOTES

During the Battle of Bunker Hill, near Boston, an officer sternly admonished the militiamen, "Do not fire until you see the whites of their eyes!" This order was given because the patriots did not have enough bullets or powder for their rifles, and they wanted every shot to find its mark.

Despite their declaration of war, many members of the Continental Congress were not ready to vote for complete independence. In July 1775, John

Dickinson drafted a resolution, known as the Olive Branch Petition, begging the king not to launch a military punitive expedition against the colonies, to give the diplomats a chance to work out a peaceful solution. The petition fell on deaf ears, however, and King George III issued a proclamation on August 23, 1775, declaring the colonies to be in a state of rebellion.

JUST A MINUTE

The musket of the militiaman has given us a number of words and phrases, such as "lock, stock, and barrel." A "flash in the pan" was a misfire, and still means something that is ineffective. "Going off half-cocked" was not very effective, because half-cock was the safety position on a flintlock.

Britain had thought that the Southern colonies, because of their reliance on slavery, would remain loyal. If the southern colonies were in rebellion, it was thought, then slaves would take that opportunity to rise up, and try to gain their freedom. To take advantage of that possibility, in November 1775, Lord Dunmore, the royal governor of Virginia, offered freedom to any slave who would fight for the British. However, Dunmore's proclamation backfired, not only did he obtain very few slave recruits, but he drove over to the rebel cause many Virginians who would otherwise have remained Loyalists.

QUOTABLE QUOTES

In arguing for all of the colonies to stand united, Benjamin Franklin quipped, "We had best all hang together, or we'll be hanging separately."

In the Carolinas, Josiah Martin urged North Carolinians to remain loyal to the Crown. When 1,500 men rallied to Martin, they were overrun by the revolutionary army before British troops could reach them. The British warships continued down the coast to Charleston, South Carolina, and opened fire on the city in early June 1776. But South Carolinians had had time to mobilize, and were able to drive the British off. The English would not return to the South for more than two years.

COMMON SENSE AND INDEPENDENCE

Thomas Paine, a political theorist and writer, published a 50-page pamphlet, *Common Sense*, which sold more than 100,000 copies. In his treatise, Paine attacked the concept of hereditary monarchy, declaring that one common citizen, who did an honest days work, was worth more to society than "all the crowned ruffians that have ever lived." He stressed that the colonists had only two alternatives: either to continue to submit to a tyrannical king and his archaic system of government, or to pursue liberty and happiness as a self-sufficient, free, and independent republic. *Common Sense* helped to mobilize the people toward complete separation, silencing those who wanted to maintain ties with England.

On May 10, 1776, the Second Continental Congress adopted a resolution calling for separation. On June 7, Richard Henry Lee of Virginia declared "That these United Colonies are, and of right ought to be, free and independent states …." Now, only a formal declaration was needed. A committee of five, headed by Thomas Jefferson of Virginia, was appointed to prepare the actual document.

QUOTABLE QUOTES

When you sign your name, that's known as "giving your John Hancock." On August 2, 1776, Hancock was the first member of the Continental Congress to sign the Declaration of Independence, in a very large and bold script. He said, "The King won't need his glasses to read this."

The Declaration of Independence was adopted on the fourth of July. It not only announced the birth of the new nation, but it also set forth a philosophy of human freedom that would ultimately rock the entire world. Drawn from the works of the French and English Enlightenment, one influence overshadows the rest: John Locke's *Second Treatise on Government*. Locke transformed the historical rights of Englishmen into natural rights for everyone. The Declaration's opening passage echoes his theory of government, based on a social contract between the people and their government:

> We hold these truths to be self-evident, that all men are created equal, that they are endowed by their Creator with certain unalienable Rights, that among these are Life, Liberty and the pursuit of Happiness. That to secure these rights, Governments are instituted among Men, deriving their just powers from the consent of the governed, that whenever any Form of Government becomes destructive of these ends, it is the Right of the People to alter or to abolish it, and to institute a new Government, laying its foundation on such principles, and organizing its powers in such form, as to them shall seem most likely to effect their Safety and Happiness.

Jefferson linked Locke's principles directly to the revolution. To fight for American independence was to depose a king who had "combined with others to subject us to a jurisdiction foreign to our constitution, and unacknowledged by our laws ...." Only a government created by the people could secure natural rights to life, liberty and the pursuit of happiness. Thus, to fight for the revolution was to assert one's own natural rights. Put in such terms, it was hard for any patriot to resist the call to arms.

DEFEATS AND VICTORIES

The rebels suffered severe setbacks for months after independence was declared. In August 1776, after the disastrous Battle of Long Island, Washington was able to evacuate his army in small boats from the shores of Brooklyn to Manhattan, due in large part to the hesitation of British General William Howe. By November, however, Howe had also forced the patriots out of Manhattan, and New York City would remain under British control until the end of the war.

By December, Washington's army was near total collapse. Congress was having trouble raising money, and supplies for the army failed to materialize. But Howe once again missed his chance to crush the Americans. Not wanting to mount a winter campaign, he decided to wait until spring to resume the offensive.

While criticized by many for its lack of historical accuracy (for example, the flag depicted in the painting had not been adopted at the time of the crossing), this painting has come to encapsulate the determination of Washington and his soldiers to forge the freedom of the new nation.

Washington, on the other hand, decided that a winter campaign might be just what the waning fortunes of the republic needed. On the day after Christmas, he crossed the Delaware River. In the early morning hours, his troops surprised the garrison at Trenton, New Jersey, taking more than 900 prisoners, primarily Hessian mercenaries. A week later, Washington attacked the British at Princeton, and won again. While the victories did not have that much military value, they did revive the declining spirits of the patriots.

JUST A MINUTE

The King of England, short of British regulars, hired 30,000 German soldiers. Since the majority were from Hess, they were all known as Hessians. Many were taken prisoner, and sent by the colonials to work on frontier farms to support the war effort. By the end of the war, most had married the farmer's daughter and never returned to Europe.

Washington's victory was short lived. Later, in 1777, Howe defeated the American army at Brandywine, Pennsylvania, and occupied Philadelphia, the rebel capitol, forcing the continental congress to flee for their lives. The British now had the two major cities, New York and Philadelphia, under their control. The war was not going well for the rebels.

Washington withdrew what was left of his army into the Pennsylvania countryside, to a remote location called Valley Forge. The winter was harsh, and his men lacked adequate food, clothing, and supplies. To make things even worse, the local farmers and merchants preferred to sell their produce to the British for gold and silver instead of using *continentals*, because the paper money issued by the Continental Congress and the individual colonies was becoming increasingly worthless. Valley Forge was the absolute low point in the fortunes of the struggling young country and its army.

STRICTLY DEFINED

The expression "not worth a continental" derives from the currency of the continental congress, which were called **continentals.** By the end of the war, they had about as much value as Confederate money did at the end of the Civil War.

In late 1776, British General John Burgoyne decided to invade New York and New England via Lake Champlain and the Hudson River. Poor reconnaissance and planning resulted in the army trying to move too much heavy equipment through the forests and marshes along their line of march. At Oriskany, New York, a band of Loyalists and Indians under Burgoyne's command were harassed by a mobile and seasoned American force.

Then at Bennington, Vermont, more of Burgoyne's forces, while foraging for supplies, encountered additional American troops. The resulting battle delayed Burgoyne's army again, and by this time reinforcements were on their way from Washington's main army. By the time Burgoyne could resume his advance, the Americans had mustered a large army. Led by Benedict Arnold, then a Major General in the American army, the Americans twice repulsed the British. Burgoyne was forced to fall back to Saratoga, New York, where another American army under General Horatio Gates was waiting for them. The British troops were cut off, then surrounded, and Burgoyne was forced to surrender his entire army. The British lost 6 generals, 300 officers, and 5,500 enlisted men.

 FYI Benedict Arnold, famous as the greatest traitor in American history, was also one of its best generals. And that was the problem. While Washington as a rule lost battles, Arnold won them. Resentful that Congress kept Washington in the top spot, he finally quit and went over to the enemy. This was extremely lucky for the United States; otherwise we would have been saddled with a capital called Arnold, D.C.

FRANCE ENTERS THE WAR

In France, the common people were enthusiastic about the American cause, and the French intellectual world wrote heavily against the concepts of feudalism and privilege. However, the king had more practical reasons for wanting to support the rebels. France was eager for revenge ever since their defeat at the hands of England during the French and Indian wars. Realizing that France was a potential ally, Benjamin Franklin was sent to Paris in 1776. A self-made millionaire and Renaissance man, his wit, guile, and intellect soon garnered him influence at the French court, where he lobbied for the French king to declare war on England.

France began by providing aid to the colonies. In May 1776, they sent fourteen ships with war supplies to America. Soon, they were the major supplier of gunpowder to the beleaguered American forces. However, it was Britain's defeat at the hand of the colonials at Saratoga that convinced France that they should do more than simply send musket balls. On February 6, 1778, America and France signed a Treaty of Amity and Commerce, in which France formally recognized America as a free and independent country. They also signed a Treaty of Alliance, which provided that if France entered the war, they would not sign a peace treaty with Great Britain that did not include complete independence for the United States.

JUST A MINUTE

 The treaty between the United States and France was the first bilateral defense treaty to be signed by the United States, and the United States would not sign another one until 1949.

The Franco-American alliance meant that what had been an internal revolution had the potential to expand into a worldwide conflict. In June 1778, British ships fired on French vessels, and the two superpowers were officially at war. In 1779, Spain, hoping to reacquire the territories taken by Britain from them during the Seven Years' War, entered the conflict on the side of France. In 1780, Britain declared war on the Dutch, who had continued to trade with the colonies. The combination of these three European powers, France, Holland, and Spain, fighting the British was a great boost to the rebels' cause. They were no longer fighting alone against the world's greatest superpower.

THE BRITISH MOVE SOUTH

With the French in the war, the British decided to move their main effort into the southern colonies, since those in the north were for the most part solidly patriots, but the South had large numbers of Loyalists. In 1778, they captured Savannah, Georgia, followed by Charleston, South Carolina, the largest and most important Southern port. Making good use of joint operations, the British used their naval and amphibious forces to support their ground troops, and bottled up the Americans on the Charleston peninsula. On May 12, General Benjamin Lincoln was forced to surrender the city and its 5,000 troops, the greatest American defeat of the war.

However, the setback only served to enrage the rebel forces. The British found it was easier to take an American colony than to hold it. The rebels, under such guerilla fighters as Francis Marion, were soon attacking British supply lines. Lord Cornwallis, the British general, tried several times to engage the rebels, but they weren't ready for a fight, so the militia would constantly run when they encountered British regulars. Finally, Cornwallis was able to get into a major battle at Cowpens, South Carolina, in early 1781, only to be soundly defeated by the Americans. Discouraged, Cornwallis now set his sights on Virginia.

VICTORY AND INDEPENDENCE

In July 1780, a French expeditionary force of 6,000 men, along with a major French fleet, arrived in America under the command of the Comte Jean de Rochambeau. While the French fleet harassed British shipping and prevented reinforcement and resupply of British forces, Washington set about massing the entire American army. Men from the northern states all marched south, regular and militia alike, to close for the final battle with the British.

Cornwallis, not realizing the extent of the American army, and always confident that he could be evacuated by the British navy, was surprised to find himself trapped on the Yorktown peninsula. The French fleet held the British fleet at bay, and Cornwallis found himself not only cut off, but hopelessly outnumbered by the infernal rebels. He was forced to surrender his entire army on October 19, 1781.

FYI You would think that losing a major army and the American colonies in a single defeat would be a career-ender, but Cornwallis was then appointed governor-general and commander in chief of India, which was then in turmoil. He restored the military situation and laid the administrative foundation of British rule in India.

A new British government, dedicated to ending the American war, decided to pursue peace negotiations in Paris in early 1782. American delegates included Benjamin Franklin, John Adams, and John Jay. On April 15, 1783, Congress approved the final treaty, known as the Treaty of Paris. The peace settlement acknowledged the independence, freedom, and sovereignty of the 13 colonies. Great Britain acknowledged that the new country ran west all the way to the Mississippi River, north to Canada, and south to Florida. The fledgling colonies were finally "free and independent states."

LOYALISTS DURING THE AMERICAN REVOLUTION

The War for Independence was a revolution, but it was also a civil war. American Loyalists, also known as "Tories" or "Royalists," fought with the king against the rebels. The Loyalists, like the rebels, hated British actions like the Stamp Act and the Coercive Acts. But Loyalists believed in the status quo, fearing that the revolution would give rise to mob rule, a fear that was actually to come true some years later in the French Revolution. They also believed that independence would mean the loss of the economic benefits that they derived from being part of the British empire.

JUST A MINUTE

Estimates of the number of Loyalists range as high as 500,000, or 20 percent of the white population of the colonies at the time of the Revolution.

Loyalists came from all strata of American society, and included small farmers, artisans, and shopkeepers. Wealthy merchants tended to remain loyal, as did Anglican ministers, Crown officials and bureaucrats, slaves who wanted to be free, Indian tribes who had been allied with the British in previous wars, and indentured servants.

The percentage of Loyalists varied from colony to colony. For example, New York, which was occupied during the entire war, had a high percentage of loyalists, because any other course of action was very risky. In the Carolinas, back-country farmers tended to be Loyalist, whereas the Tidewater planters, with their large investment in slavery and the plantation system, tended to support the Revolution.

During the Revolution, because they were allied with the government, most Loyalists suffered little for their views. However, even though the Paris Peace Treaty required Congress to restore property confiscated from the Loyalists, the patriots were ready to take their revenge. In the Carolinas, where enmity between rebels and Loyalists was especially strong, few regained their property. In many states, confiscations from Loyalists resulted in a social revolution as the large estates of rich Loyalists were divided up among their former tenants.

FYI When the Loyalists started arriving in large numbers in Canada, a country that was primarily French, it began to cause problems. Accordingly, in 1791, the British Parliament enacted the Constitutional Act, whereby Quebec was split into two provinces, Upper and Lower Canada. The United Empire Loyalists, descendants of those Loyalists who fled America at the end of the Revolution, are still a large and powerful group in Canada today.

Many Loyalists fled the country, including William Franklin, the son of Benjamin Franklin, and John Singleton Copley, the greatest American painter of the period. Most of them settled in Canada. In the decades after the Revolution, Americans preferred to forget about the Loyalists, and they were quickly forgotten as people moved on with building the new country.

State Constitutions

As early as May 10, 1776, Congress had passed a resolution authorizing the colonies to form new governments "such as shall best conduce to the happiness and safety of their constituents." Within a year after the signing of the Declaration of Independence, all but three colonies had drawn up their own individual state constitutions.

The new state constitutions presented a perfect opportunity to incorporate all of the new democratic ideas championed by the patriots. Each was animated by the spirit of republicanism, an ideal that had long been praised by Enlightenment philosophers.

The first objective of the framers of the state constitutions was to secure those "unalienable rights" whose violation had caused the former colonies to repudiate their connection with Britain. Virginia's state constitution served as a model for all the others. It's provisions included popular sovereignty, rotation in office, freedom of elections, and a listing of basic and fundamental liberties common to all citizens: moderate bail and humane punishment, speedy trial by jury, freedom of the press, freedom of religion, and the inalienable right of the majority to govern.

Other states enlarged the list of liberties, and included freedom of speech, freedom of assembly, freedom of petition, the right to bear arms, the right to a writ of *habeas corpus,* and the right to equal protection under the law. In addition, each state constitution divided the government into three branches, executive, legislative, and judiciary, each branch to serve as a check and balance on the other.

STRICTLY DEFINED

A **habeas corpus** petition is filed with a court by a person who objects to his own or another's imprisonment. Once the petition is filed, the court is required to make a review of the legal and factual basis for the imprisonment. If they cannot justify the prisoner being held, then he must be released. The primary purpose of habeas corpus is to prevent the illegal imprisonment of citizens.

The state constitutions did have some problems, by modern standards. The colonies south of Pennsylvania did not grant these inalienable rights to slaves or to women. No state granted universal male suffrage, although Delaware, North Carolina, Georgia, and Pennsylvania permitted all taxpayers to vote.

However, despite their limitations, the state constitutions were radical documents, in a time when the whole of Europe was still ruled by kings and princes, and when serfs were still tied to the land on which they were born. A bold new country had sprung forth on a world that little realized or appreciated the changes that its birth had brought forth.

QUIZ

Hour's Up!

1. "Minutemen" were called that:

   A. By disgruntled colonial wives

   B. Because they could dance the *minuet*; the word is an English corruption of the French minuet-man

   C. Because they could get ready to fight in a minute

   D. By the English regulars, because they would only fight for a minute, before they would run

2. All of the following countries fought with the United States against England during America's war for Independence, except:

   A. France

   B. Spain

   C. South Vietnam

   D. Holland

3. Those Americans who sided with the British during the Revolution were called all of the following, except:

   A. Royalists

   B. Loyalists

   C. Tories

   D. Federalists

4. The first battle of the American Revolution was:

   A. Bunker Hill

   B. Lexington

   C. Concord

   D. Yorktown

5. All of the following American phrases derive from the colonial musket, except:

   A. Lock, stock, and barrel

   B. Flash in the pan

   C. Going off half-cocked

   D. At loggerheads

HOUR 6

The Constitution

LESSON PLAN:

In this hour, you will learn why the Articles of Confederation didn't work, and why the delegates to the convention assigned to fix it decided to throw the whole thing out, start over, and create a whole new Constitution.

You will also learn ...

- Why every state gets two Senators, but some only get one Congressman.

- Why some states thought it would be a good idea to treat the territories in the West like colonies, just like they had been treated by England.

- Why most of the men who framed the Constitution were young, with the notable exception of Benjamin Franklin.

- Why they left the Bill of Rights out of the original Constitution, and how they finally got it in there.

The United States had won their freedom from England, and it was now incumbent on the revolutionaries to forge a new country from 13 separate and often-times competing interests. The first document that the newly independent colonies adopted, the Articles of Confederation, was a dismal failure. The founding fathers started over, and forged a new document, the Constitution, which has endured ever since.

ARTICLES OF CONFEDERATION

John Dickinson had written the "Articles of Confederation and Perpetual Union" in 1776, the Continental Congress had adopted them in November 1777, and they had gone into effect in 1781, after having been ratified by all the states. The Articles established a government with many critical weaknesses. The national government lacked the authority to set tariffs, to regulate commerce, or to levy taxes. It also lacked control of international relations, and some of the states were actually engaged in their own negotiations with foreign countries. Nine states had organized their own armies, and several had their own navies. In addition, there was also a curious hodge-podge of coins and a bewildering variety of state and national paper bills in circulation, all fast depreciating in value. In short, under the Articles of Confederation, there were 13 separate countries, each doing their own thing, and the central government had virtually no authority to take control of any of the traditional powers of a central government.

The end of the war had a severe effect on merchants, who had done well supplying the armies of both sides. That revenue was now gone, and in addition, they had also lost the advantages derived from being in the British empire. The states gave preference to American goods in their tariff policies, but these tariffs were inconsistent across state lines, leading to the demand for a stronger central government to implement a uniform policy of import duties.

Farmers also suffered severely from the economic difficulties following the Revolution. With the war over, the supply of farm produce exceeded demand, and farmer-debtors wanted strong remedies to avoid foreclosure on their property and imprisonment for debt. The courts were clogged with these suits for debt. All through the summer of 1786, the people demanded reform.

Growing Pains

The problem of farmer debt came to a head in the autumn of 1786, when mobs of farmers, lead by a former army captain, Daniel Shays, began to intimidate, by force, the county courts from passing judgments for debt. In January of 1787 a ragtag army of 12,000 farmers advanced on the federal arsenal at Springfield, Massachusetts. The local state militia was mobilized, and they were able to stop the rebels, who were only armed with staves and pitchforks. Then, General Benjamin Lincoln arrived with reinforcements from Boston and routed the remaining rebels. The government captured fourteen and sentenced them to death, but in the end some were pardoned and the rest were let off with short prison terms. After the defeat of Shays's Rebellion, the newly elected legislature, who sympathized with the rebels, passed laws to provide debt relief.

 FYI One of the leaders in Shays's Rebellion, a farmer named Stone, had led a group of 400 farmers during the actions of 1786 and 1787. He left a rebellious legacy, his great-granddaughter Lucy Stone. She was the first American woman to retain her maiden name when she married. She learned Greek and Hebrew so that she could translate the Bible herself and challenge its sexist interpretations. When Lucy married Henry Blackwell, Lucy omitted the word *obey* from her vows. In 1847, her husband's sister Elizabeth received the first doctorate of medicine conferred on a woman in the United States. In her time, the expression "Lucy-Stoner" was commonly used to describe women who were independent thinkers.

Thirteen State Limit

The fledgling republic had another problem to face, the old chestnut of the western lands. No sooner had the new country ceased to be a colony, then it was itself in the colony business. Lured by rich, free land, pioneers poured through the Appalachian Mountains and into the lush lands beyond. The new country was faced with the problem of expansion, with the resulting complication of warfare instigated by the Indians who were losing their land. By the conclusion of the Revolution, there were far-flung outposts scattered along the inland waterways with tens of thousands of settlers. Separated by tall mountain ranges and hundreds of miles from any eastern political authority, the inhabitants, like their colonial ancestors before them, simply established their own governments.

JUST A MINUTE

By 1790, the population of the lands west of the Appalachians numbered well over 120,000.

Before the war, many of the colonies had made extensive claims, and in some cases contradictory and overlapping claims, to land beyond the Appalachians. Some colonies, such as Maryland, had no western claims, and she led the way toward a solution by introducing a resolution that the western lands be considered property common to the entire new country, to be apportioned and parceled out by Congress as free and independent colonies, who would ultimately become states in their own right.

This idea did not receive a very warm welcome from those states with western claims. Then, in an unexpected move of generosity, in 1780 New York ceded all of its claims to western lands to the United States. They were followed in 1784 by Virginia, which had previously made the most outlandish claims, and they signed over all of their land north of the Ohio River. The ice having been broken, it wasn't long before all of the other states followed suit, and Congress was in possession of all of the lands north of the Ohio River and west of the Allegheny Mountains. This mass donation of illusionary claims, but very real territory, was a great statement of national unity, and gave the central government a solid claim to national sovereignty.

However, having acquired these vast territories, they posed a great problem for the struggling new country. How would they be administered? Were they going to be colonies, and then states, in the same manner as the original 13 colonies?

The Articles of Confederation offered an answer. The Articles had created a system, further delineated in the Northwest Ordinance of 1787, which provided for the organization of the Northwest Territory as a single governmental unit, ruled by a governor. When this territory had 5,000 free male inhabitants of voting age, it was to be entitled to a legislature of two chambers, and the right to send a nonvoting delegate to Congress. As the population increased, the territory would be allowed to divide, however they could not form more than five nor less than three states. When one of these new states reached a population of 60,000 free inhabitants, it was to be admitted to the Union "on an equal footing with the original states in all respects."

QUOTABLE QUOTES

The Northwest Ordinance stated that "there shall be neither slavery nor involuntary servitude in the said territory." If only the founding fathers had made that a requirement for every new state beyond the original 13, we might never have had a Civil War.

This policy for the Northwest Territory was in keeping with the spirit of the Revolution. It repudiated the concept that colonies existed for the benefit of the mother country and were politically subordinate and socially inferior. There was no way that the new country was going to make the same mistake that had resulted in revolution. The new policy boldly embraced the concepts upon which the entire revolution was based, that colonies are but an extension of the nation and are entitled, not as a privilege but as a right, to all the benefits of equality. Although originally designed to apply to the Northwest Territory, these became the principles upon which every new acquisition of land would be treated, right up until the admission of Alaska and Hawaii after the end of World War II.

CONSTITUTIONAL CONVENTION

The Articles of Confederation was by and large a weak document on which to found a national government. When disputes between Maryland and Virginia over navigation on the Potomac River could not be worked out amicably, a conference of representatives from five states met at Annapolis, Maryland, in 1786. One of the delegates, Alexander Hamilton, convinced his colleagues that the situation was too serious to be dealt with by a council that did not represent all of the states.

QUOTABLE QUOTES

George Washington described the period in American history between the Treaty of Paris and the adoption of the Constitution. He stated that the states were only held together by a "rope of sand."

Hamilton advocated asking all the states to appoint representatives for a meeting to be held the following spring in Philadelphia. The Continental Congress was indignant, feeling that this trampled directly on their prerogatives. The whole idea might have died stillborn had not Virginia immediately elected George Washington as their delegate. Such was the power and prestige of Washington, that all objections immediately faded away.

The Federal Convention assembled at the Philadelphia State House in May 1787. The state legislatures sent leaders with experience in colonial and state governments, in Congress, on the bench, and in the army. George Washington, regarded as a virtual demigod because of his integrity and his military leadership during the Revolution, was unanimously and immediately chosen as presiding officer.

From Virginia came James Madison, a young statesman, a thorough student of politics and history and, according to a colleague, "from a spirit of industry and application … the best-informed man on any point in debate."

FYI James Madison, who was later to become president, is today recognized as the "Father of the Constitution." However, of 71 specific proposals that Madison supported, he was on the losing side 40 times.

Noticeably absent from the Convention was Thomas Jefferson, who was serving in France as minister, and John Adams, ambassador to Great Britain. Youth predominated among the 55 delegates; the average age was 42.

The Convention had been authorized merely to fix the Articles of Confederation, by drafting new amendments, but, as Madison later wrote, the delegates, "with a manly confidence in their country," simply tossed out the Articles and started composing a whole new document.

The delegates recognized that they needed to reconcile the power of the state governments, who could solve local problems, with a national and central government who could provide for the common defense, and handle international affairs. They adopted the principle that the functions and powers of the national government had to be carefully defined and stated, and if the central government did not expressly have a power, it was reserved to the states. However, realizing that the central government had to have real authority, or they would be right back to the Articles of Confederation, they gave the central government some critical powers, such as the right to coin money, to regulate commerce, to raise an army, to make treaties, and to declare war.

DEBATE AND COMPROMISE

The delegates were adherents of Montesquieu's concept of the balance of power in politics. This principle was supported by colonial experience and strengthened by the writings of John Locke. Under these influences, they conceived of a central government with three equal and coordinate branches of government. It was reasoned that if one branch tried to become too powerful, it could be immediately checked by the other two. Legislative, executive, and judicial powers were to be so balanced that no one could ever gain complete and absolute despotic control.

The delegates also decided that the legislative branch, like the colonial legislatures, should consist of two houses. And there the debate began. Representatives of the states with small populations, such as New Jersey, objected to any Congress that would be based on population. On the other hand, representatives of large states, like Virginia, argued for "one man, one vote," seeing that as the only fair way to represent the people. This debate went on endlessly until Roger Sherman came forward with the obvious compromise: representation according to population in the House of Representatives, and two senators per state in the Senate. It was instantly adopted, and one of the major stumbling blocks to creating the new national government was removed.

Each succeeding question raised new problems, which had to be resolved with new compromises. The Northern states did not want the slaves counted when determining the number of seats a state would have in the House of Representatives. The compromise was that the House of Representatives would be apportioned by counting each slave as three fifths of a person.

Some delegates, such as Roger Sherman and Elbridge Gerry, remembering Shays's Rebellion, did not trust the mass of people to govern themselves, and did not want any branch of the federal government to be elected directly by the people. The compromise was that the state legislatures would appoint the Senators, and the representatives would be popularly elected (this was later changed by constitutional amendment, after the people proved themselves capable of governing themselves). Likewise, the president is not chosen directly by the people, but by the electoral college.

There were no serious differences on such national economic questions as paper money, laws concerning contract obligations, or the role of women, whom everyone (that is, the male delegates) agreed must be excluded from politics (this was later to be changed by constitutional amendment).

The weather was hot, humid, and miserable in Philadelphia that summer. It would be many years before anyone would invent air conditioning. Philadelphia offered little, if any, relief, even at night. To escape the stifling temperature, Washington rode out of town to Valley Forge to go fishing. The next day, with a string of trout hanging from his saddlebags, he returned to the city, and back to the job of writing the Constitution.

Laboring through an extremely hot and miserable Philadelphia summer in 1787, the Constitutional Convention finally finished the draft, which incorporated in a surprisingly brief document the organization of the most complex government yet devised, a government supreme within a clearly defined and limited sphere, but without complete and absolute power. Such a government had never before been attempted in world history.

In conferring powers, the Convention gave the federal government the power to levy taxes, borrow money, establish uniform duties, levy excise taxes, coin money, fix weights and measures, grant patents and copyrights, establish and run post offices, and build post roads (the first interstate highway system). The national government also had the power to raise and maintain an army and navy, regulate interstate commerce, manage Indian affairs, conduct foreign policy, and declare war. It could pass laws for naturalizing foreigners, it controlled all public lands, and it could admit new states that were totally and completely equal to the original 13 states.

The principle of three branches of government had already been tested in the state constitutions and had proved sound. Therefore, the Convention set up a governmental system with separate legislative, executive, and judiciary branches, each of which was held in check by the other two. For example, laws passed by Congress required the approval of the president. The president could appoint officials and make treaties, but they had to be approved by the Senate. Congress had the power to impeach the president, and remove him from office, for misconduct (tried twice in history, both unsuccessfully, once with Andrew Johnson, and once with Bill Clinton). The Supreme Court could invalidate any law passed by Congress, but the justices were appointed by the president, and could be impeached by Congress. In effect, each branch had its own separate powers, and it also had the power to thwart the actions of other branches.

JUST A MINUTE

In the entire history of the United States, only six amendments have passed Congress, only to fail to be ratified by the states. The most notable of these failed amendments is the Equal Rights Amendment, which was not ratified by the states within the required seven-year time period.

The delegates were concerned that the Constitution would not be powerful, and provide for a strong central government, if it could be easily altered. To protect the Constitution from such changes, Article Five stated that amendments to the Constitution would require a two-thirds vote by both houses of Congress, followed by ratification by three fourths of the states.

JUST A MINUTE

The small number of amendments to the Constitution are a testament to the excellent job done by the Founding Fathers. Only 27 amendments have been added to the Constitution. If you discount the first 10, the Bill of Rights, which were passed as a group almost simultaneously with the Constitution, it has only been amended 17 times. It you remove the one implementing Prohibition (no drinking), and the one repealing Prohibition (which cancel each other out), the current Constitution really has only 15 amendments. Not a bad summer's work.

The final issue facing the Constitutional Convention, perhaps the most important problem of all, was how the new government should enforce its powers. Under the Articles of Confederation, the national government had possessed, on paper, significant powers, which the states routinely ignored.

Many delegates thought that the use of force was the answer. But how could a government endure if it was at war with its own states? Civil war could destroy the country. The solution was direct and forthright: The national government would not act upon the states, but upon the people within the states. They would legislate for each and every individual citizen in the country, with a system of national laws. To implement this concept, the Convention adopted two short but very important clauses:

> Congress shall have power ... to make all laws which shall be necessary and proper for carrying into execution the ... powers vested by this Constitution in the Government of the United States. (Article I, Section 7)

> This Constitution and the laws of the United States, which shall be made in pursuance thereof, and all treaties made, or which shall be made, under the authority of the United States, shall be the supreme law of the land, and the judges in every State shall be bound thereby, anything in the Constitution or laws of any State to the contrary notwithstanding. (Article VI)

In one bold stroke, the laws of the United States became enforceable not only in its own national courts, through its own judges and marshals, but also in the state courts, through state judges and state law officers.

The Founding Fathers were products of the Enlightenment, and they designed a government that, they believed, would promote individual liberty and public virtue. Whether they envisioned that their work would endure for so many centuries, or whether they foresaw that the country they created would one day be the sole superpower on the planet, cannot be ascertained, but that is what they accomplished that long, hot summer in Philadelphia.

RATIFICATION AND THE BILL OF RIGHTS

After 16 weeks of deliberation, the finished Constitution was signed by the delegates. The Convention over, the delegates "adjourned to the City Tavern, dined together, and took a cordial leave of each other." Yet a critical step remained to be accomplished. The new Constitution, which they had not even been authorized to create, now had to be ratified by the states.

QUOTABLE QUOTES

Franklin, pointing to the half-sun painted in brilliant gold on the back of Washington's chair, said: "I have often in the course of the session … looked at that [chair] behind the president, without being able to tell whether it was rising or setting; but now, at length, I have the happiness to know that it is a rising, and not a setting, sun."

The Convention had decided that the Constitution would take effect upon ratification by 9 of the 13 states, but in reality, they needed unanimous consent. When they reached the required nine states, the two largest states, Virginia and New York, still had not yet ratified. Without the support of these two states, there was a real danger that the Constitution would not be honored.

The argument over the new Constitution, and the strong central government which it created, raged between the Federalists, who favored a strong central government, and the Anti-Federalists, who preferred a weak national government made up of strong and independent states. Arguments on both sides were voiced in the press, in the state legislatures, and at the state conventions who were considering ratification.

Virginia Anti-Federalists were led by Patrick Henry, who became the chief spokesman for those who feared the powers of the new central government. The Anti-Federalists didn't even like the opening phrase of the Constitution: "We the People of the United States," which suggested that all the power of the states was being stripped away. In New York, Federalists

Alexander Hamilton, John Jay, and James Madison pushed for the ratification of the Constitution in a series of essays known as *The Federalist Papers*.

Hostility toward a strong central government was only one concern among those opposed to the Constitution. Many feared that the Constitution did not sufficiently protect individual rights and freedoms. George Mason, author of Virginia's 1776 Declaration of Rights, was one of three delegates to the Constitutional Convention who refused to sign the final document because it did not enumerate individual rights. Together with Patrick Henry, he campaigned vigorously against ratification of the Constitution by Virginia. Indeed, five states, including Massachusetts, only ratified the Constitution on the condition that such amendments be added immediately.

FYI James Madison took extensive notes at the Constitutional Convention, but he would not allow these annotations to be published until the last of the delegates had died. As a result, no other delegate was ever able to challenge his version of the proceedings.

When Congress convened for the first time in September 1789, they were buried under amendments to protect individual rights. Congress quickly adopted 12 of these amendments, and by December 1791, enough states had ratified 10 of them to make them part of the Constitution. Collectively, they are known as the Bill of Rights, which include freedom of speech, press, religion, the right to assemble peacefully, protest and demand changes; protection against unreasonable searches, seizures of property and arrest; due process of law in all criminal cases; right to a fair and speedy trial; and protection against cruel and unusual punishment.

Anti-Federalist delegates were finally persuaded and joined with the Federalists to ratify the Constitution.

HOUR'S UP!

QUIZ

1. After the Constitutional Convention adjourned, the delegates went:
    A. Home
    B. To a bar
    C. On tour
    D. To sleep

2. Which of the following is not one of the three branches of the federal government:

    A. President

    B. Supreme Court

    C. Congress

    D. Internal Revenue Service

3. Of the following, who did not have an original colony and state named after them?

    A. Sir Thomas West (Lord De La Warr)

    B. Duke of York

    C. Queen Elizabeth I (The Virgin Queen)

    D. Lord Leroy Massachusetts

4. Which one of the following was not one of the original 13 colonies:

    A. New York

    B. New Hampshire

    C. New Jersey

    D. New England

5. All of the following are in the Bill of Rights, except:

    A. Right to assemble

    B. Right to protest

    C. Right to a speedy trial

    D. Right to life

PART II

Expansion from Sea to Shining Sea

HOUR 7

A National Government

LESSON PLAN:

In this hour, you will learn about the conflict over the national bank, how we almost went to war with France, and how we did go to war with England and come close to becoming colonies again.

You will also learn ...

- Why George Washington was chosen to be the first president of the United States.
- Why Hamilton and Jefferson did not get along.
- All about the Louisiana Purchase, the best land deal in history.
- All about the War of 1812, including the year it started.

The United States experienced growing pains during its early years. The two-party system grew out of the fundamental differences between the founding fathers on the very nature of the new country. On one side were aligned those such as Jefferson who believed that the individual states were sovereign. Others, such as Hamilton, were convinced that the new federal government was paramount, and that the colonies, in forming the United States, were no longer free to make their own policy in disregard of the other states. As the country acquired new territory, and expanded westward, this controversy would continue.

PRESIDENT WASHINGTON

The last act of the Confederation was to arrange for the first presidential election. There was really only one candidate, the ever-popular George Washington, and he was unanimously elected on April 30, 1789. In words spoken by every president since, Washington pledged to "preserve, protect, and defend the Constitution of the United States."

When Washington took office, the new Constitution enjoyed neither a long-standing tradition, nor the full backing of the public. Moreover, the new government had yet to set up its bureaucracy. No taxes were coming in. With no judges or courts, laws could not be enforced. The Army was miniscule. What ships the Navy had built during the revolution had long since rotted away at their moorings.

FYI Many of the myths that pervade the life of George Washington can be attributed to Parson Weems, who published what purported to be George Washington's biography. For example, the story of Washington and the cherry tree is pure fiction. According to the story, Washington, when a little boy, received a new hatchet, and cut down one of his father's valuable cherry trees. When confronted with his deed, little Washington boldly stated to his father, "I can not tell I lie. I did it." His father was so impressed with his forthright honesty, he didn't punish the errant youth.

Congress immediately created the Department of State, with Thomas Jefferson at the helm, and Treasury, with Alexander Hamilton as the secretary. They established the Supreme Court, with 1 chief justice and 5 associate justices, 3 circuit courts, and 13 district courts. Because Washington's leadership style was only to make decisions after consulting with those men whose judgment he valued, he created the presidential Cabinet, consisting of the heads of all the executive departments.

Meanwhile, European immigration was increasing. The lure of owning a farm on the frontier was a strong inducement to people who were working the land for another person. Native Americans and new emigrants alike were moving west: New Englanders and Pennsylvanians into Ohio, Virginians and Carolinians into Kentucky and Tennessee. Good farms were to be had, and the rich valleys of upper New York, Pennsylvania, and Virginia soon became major wheat-growing areas.

Although the average household produced most of what it needed, the Industrial Revolution was beginning to change that. The Industrial Revolution was to add the phrase "sweat shop" to the language, a factory in which workers are employed for long hours at low wages and under unhealthy and inhumane conditions. Massachusetts and Rhode Island, with their swift rivers for power, were becoming important textile centers; Connecticut was gaining a reputation for turning out tinware and clocks; and New York, New Jersey, and Pennsylvania were producing paper, glass and iron. The United States was now second only to Britain in the shipping business. American ships were even traveling to China to sell furs and bring back tea, spices, and silk.

JUST A MINUTE

 During Washington's term as president, three more states were admitted into the Union. Vermont (1791) is from the French *vert mont,* meaning "green mountain." Kentucky (1792) is from the Iroquois word *Ken-tah-ten,* which means "land of tomorrow." Tennessee (1796) is named after the Cherokee villages, the ***Tanasi.***

Washington's leadership was crucial, as his vast prestige could silence almost any dissent and implement almost any policy. His stature brought stability to the weak and struggling new country, which could ill withstand any internal dissension in its formative years.

HAMILTON VS. JEFFERSON

In the 1790s, the conflict continued between the Federalists and the Anti-Federalists. The Federalists, led by Alexander Hamilton, represented the urban mercantile interests of commerce and industry, while the Anti-Federalists, led by Thomas Jefferson, spoke for the rural and agricultural interests. The controversy continued to center on the power of the central government versus that of the states, with the Anti-Federalists the champion of states' rights.

Hamilton, in response to the call of the House of Representatives for a plan for the "adequate support of public credit," knew that America must have credit for industrial development, commercial activity, and the operations of government. There were many who wished to repudiate the national debt, or only pay 10 cents on the dollar. Hamilton, however, insisted upon full payment and also upon a plan by which the federal government took over the unpaid debts of the states incurred during the Revolution. He realized that only then would the central government have the full trust of not only the people, but of foreign governments.

QUOTABLE QUOTES

John Laurens, like Alexander Hamilton, was an aide-de-camp to General Washington in the war. His father, Henry Laurens, was president of the Continental Congress. Hamilton wrote a series of what are sometimes referred to as "love letters" to Laurens. History books often ignore this portion of the statesman's written legacy. In one letter, he says, "I wish, my dear Laurens that it might be in my power, by action rather than words, to convince you that I love you."

Hamilton also devised the idea for a Bank of the United States, with branches throughout the country. He established a national mint, and argued in favor of tariffs, arguing that the "infant industries" needed temporary protection while they were growing, protected from foreign competition. These measures placed the credit of the federal government on a firm foundation and provided it with revenues to operate, while at the same time it encouraged commerce and industry, and created a solid phalanx of businessmen with a financial interest in supporting a strong national government.

Jefferson, on the other hand, advocated a decentralized agrarian republic. Even though he recognized the need for a strong central government in foreign relations, he did not want it strong in any other respect. Hamilton's great aim was more efficient organization, whereas Jefferson once said, "I am not a friend to a very energetic government." Hamilton sought to avoid anarchy and thought in terms of order; Jefferson feared tyranny and thought in terms of personal freedom.

An important clash between them occurred shortly after Jefferson took office as secretary of state. When Hamilton introduced his bill to establish a national bank, Jefferson objected, on the grounds that there was nothing in the Constitution that gave the central government the power to establish a bank. The Constitution expressly enumerates all the powers belonging to the federal government, and reserves all other powers to the states. Since a bank was not mentioned as a national power, it must be a state power, and, therefore, not authorized.

Hamilton argued that Congress was authorized to "make all laws which shall be necessary and proper" for carrying out other powers specifically granted. Since the Constitution authorized the national government to levy taxes, pay debts, and borrow money, the creation of a national bank was necessary to carry out these functions. Congress, therefore, was entitled, under its implied powers, to create a national bank. Washington and Congress accepted Hamilton's interpretation, and set an important Constitutional precedent for the interpretation of the federal government's authority to make laws.

CITIZEN GENET AND FOREIGN POLICY

The cornerstone of Washington's foreign policy was to preserve peace, to give the country time to recover from the devastation of war, to create a strong central government, and to allow the national integration of the individual states into one country. In April 1793, events in Europe threatened to embroil the fledgling country in war. France declared war on Great Britain, Holland, and Spain. The French Revolution had just executed King Louis XVI on the guillotine, and all the monarchs of Europe were afraid the republican fervor would spread to their country.

According to the Franco-American Treaty of Alliance of 1778, the United States and France were perpetual allies, and America was now obliged to enter the war on the side of France, who would expect the United States to help defend their possessions in the West Indies. However, the United

States was at that time militarily and economically a very weak country, and was in no position to become involved in a war with major European powers. On April 22, 1793, Washington abrogated the terms of the Franco-American treaty. He proclaimed the United States to be "friendly and impartial toward the belligerent powers." With a stroke of the pen, Washington ended the relationship that had made American independence possible in the first place.

A new French envoy, Edmond Charles Genet, known as Citizen Genet, was sent as ambassador to the United States. When Genet arrived, he was cheered by the citizens, but Washington and his government treated him with cool formality. Angry at receiving the official snub, he violated a promise not to outfit a captured British ship as a privateer. Then, Genet threatened to take France's cause around the government, and directly to the American people. Immediately, the United States requested his recall by the French government.

FYI Genet was afraid to return to France because he knew that Madame Guillotine could be waiting for him, and he could lose his head for doing a bad job in America. He married a daughter of Governor Clinton of New York, and stayed in America. Ironically, his great-great-grandson, Edmond Charles Clinton Genet, fought with the Lafayette Escadrille in World War I, a squadron of the French air force made up entirely of Americans.

Relations with Great Britain were also strained. British troops still occupied some of their pre-war forts in the West, property stolen by British soldiers during the Revolution had not been restored or compensated, and the British navy was seizing American ships bound for French ports. To settle these matters, Washington sent John Jay to London as a special envoy, where he negotiated a treaty securing withdrawal of British soldiers from western forts, and a promise to pay damages for Britain's seizure of ships and cargoes. Because the United States was not in a very strong position, the treaty also placed limitations on American trade with the West Indies. Jay was also forced to acknowledge the British view that naval stores and war materiel were contraband that could not be conveyed to enemy ports by neutral ships.

Jay's Treaty touched off a storm of disagreement in the Senate over foreign policy between the Anti-Federalists (who had now adopted the name Republicans), and the Federalists. The Federalists were pro-British, because their commercial interests were tied to trade with Britain. By contrast, the Republicans favored France, mainly for ideological reasons, and disliked the

Jay Treaty, as it was regarded as being too favorable to Britain. After great debate, however, it was ratified by the Senate.

Washington retired in 1797, firmly declining to serve for more than eight years as the nation's head, and created a two-term tradition that continued unbroken until FDR. In what was to become a first in world history, the transition to the new government was bloodless. In his Farewell Address, Washington warned the nation to "steer clear of permanent alliances with any portion of the foreign world." This advice influenced American isolationist attitudes toward the rest of the world for generations.

ADAMS TAKES CHARGE

Washington's vice president, John Adams of Massachusetts, was elected the new president. France, angry over the Anglo-British treaty, and the fact that the United States had severed their mutual defense treaty, broke off diplomatic relations. By 1797 France had seized more than 300 American ships. When Adams sent three commissioners to Paris to negotiate, agents of the French government (whom Adams labeled X, Y, and Z in his report to Congress) informed the Americans that negotiations could only begin if the United States were to loan France $12 million, in addition to the amount required to bribe the appropriate officials of the French government. American's were incensed. The XYZ Affair led Congress to vote appropriations to build up the virtually nonexistent U.S. Navy.

QUOTABLE QUOTES

The XYZ Affair contributed to American patriotic legend in the reply of Charles Cotesworth Pinckney, minister to France, to the French request for money. He said, "millions for defense, sir, but not one cent for tribute."

In 1799, after a number of sea battles with the French, war between the two countries seemed certain. Adams, heeding the advice of Washington, wanted to avoid war at any cost, and sent three new commissioners to France. Napoleon had just come to power, and he realized that the last thing that France needed was another country against it. He encouraged the negotiation of the Convention of 1800, which formally released the United States from its 1778 mutual-defense alliance with France. However, because his treasury was empty, and realizing there was little danger of them actually declaring war, France refused to pay any compensation for the American ships taken by the French navy.

Being treated in such a fashion did not sit well with Congress, and in retaliation they passed the Naturalization, Alien, and Sedition Acts. The Naturalization Act, which changed the requirement for citizenship from 5 to 14 years, was targeted at French immigrants suspected of supporting the Republicans. The Alien Act, which by its terms was only to last for two years, gave the president the power to expel or imprison aliens in time of war. The Sedition Act prohibited writing, speaking, or publishing anything of "a false, scandalous and malicious" nature about the president or Congress.

The acts did not go down well with the American people. Only a few paltry convictions were obtained under the Sedition Act, and they only served to create martyrs to the cause of civil liberty, and to arouse support for the Republicans. Jefferson and Madison sponsored the passage of the Kentucky and Virginia Resolutions, which declared that the states could "interpose" their views on federal actions and "nullify" them.

 FYI The doctrine of nullification, which was created by Jefferson and Madison, would later be used by the Southern states to justify their position on slavery.

A New Broom

By 1800 the American people were ready for a change. Under Washington and Adams, both Federalists, the United States had established a strong central government, but it was often at the expense of the personal freedoms that each and every American, and especially the Republicans, held sacred. The Federalists' alienation of large parts of the electorate laid the stage for the election of Jefferson as president.

Jefferson was popular because of his appeal to American idealism. At the first inauguration to be held in the new capital of Washington, he promised "a wise and frugal government" to preserve order among the inhabitants, but one that would "leave them otherwise free to regulate their own pursuits of industry, and improvement."

FYI Albert Gallatin, born in Geneva, Switzerland, into an aristocratic family, commanded a battalion on the British side at the battle of Yorktown. He immigrated to America, and gained citizenship after nine years of residency, while teaching French at Harvard University. He engineered the financial details of the Louisiana Purchase, helped plan the Lewis and Clark Expedition, and at the age of 70 wrote a monumental treatise describing all known Native American tribes, including those of Mexico and Central America. At 81 he founded the American Ethnological Society. For all that, soon after his death in 1848, his name faded from popular history, and he became "America's forgotten statesman."

Adams had acted in a regal manner while president. However, Jefferson's presence in the White House produced a more democratic approach to government. He instructed his subordinates to regard themselves as merely the peoples' trustees. He encouraged agriculture and westward expansion. Believing America to be a haven for the dispossessed and the oppressed, he urged a liberalization of the naturalization law. By the end of his second term, his brilliant secretary of the treasury, Albert Gallatin, had reduced the national debt to less than $560 million. Swept away by Jeffersonian democratic fervor, state after state abolished property qualifications for the ballot, ensuring that every citizen would have the right to vote, regardless of his station in life.

THE LOUISIANA PURCHASE

As a result of the Seven Years' War (called the French and Indian War in America), France had ceded to Spain all of its territory west of the Mississippi River. This included the port of New Orleans, at the juncture of the Gulf of Mexico and the Mississippi River, which was indispensable to the shipment of American products that came down the river from the Ohio and Mississippi valleys. Napoleon had forced the Spanish government to cede this great tract of land in North America back to France. The move greatly alarmed the United States. If the French were successful in creating a large colonial empire west of the United States, this would frustrate the American ideal of "manifest destiny," under which Americans sought to push their dominion all the way to the Pacific, and also threaten the trading rights and security of those Americans who lived in the interior and relied on the great river for transportation. Jefferson realized that if France took possession of Louisiana, "from that moment we must marry ourselves to the British fleet and nation."

JUST A MINUTE

The United States made the best land deal in history. The "Louisiana Purchase" wasn't just the present day state of Louisiana, it was everything west of the Mississippi and east of the Rockies. It was 500 million acres for $15 million, or about 3 cents an acre.

In reality, Napoleon had no real interest in America, his goals all centered on his conquest of Europe. Knowing that another war with Great Britain was impending, Napoleon decided to sell the Louisiana territory to the United States, a course of action that would both fill his treasury and at the same time put Louisiana beyond the reach of the British.

This opportunity provided a constitutional dilemma for Jefferson: There was no express power in the document to authorize the central government to purchase new lands. At first he thought he should amend the Constitution, but his advisers didn't want to wait for years until enough states had ratified the amendment. In the meantime, almost anything could happen, Napoleon might change his mind, or perhaps the British would invade and seize the territory. They convinced him, in spite of his conviction that the Constitution should be narrowly construed, that the power to purchase territory was inherent in the power to make treaties. Jefferson relented, rationalizing that "the good sense of our country will correct the evil of loose construction when it shall produce ill effects." In effect, Jefferson had abandoned all of his lofty principles in the interests of expediency.

FYI Louisiana was named for King Louis XIV of France. Ironically, with all of the excesses of the French Revolution, no one had thought to rename the colony after something other than a king they had toppled off the throne.

Despite having just helped to inflate the war coffers of Napoleon with the Louisiana Purchase, in 1805 Jefferson declared America neutral during the war between Great Britain and France. Although both sides sought to restrict neutral shipping, British control of the seas made its interdiction and seizure much more serious than any actions by France.

THE IMPRESSMENT ISSUE

The British had a massive navy, more than 700 warships manned by 150,000 sailors and marines. The navy controlled the sea lanes, blockaded French ports, protected British commerce, and maintained the crucial link to Britain's lifeline, her colonies. However, the men of the British fleet lived under such harsh and cruel conditions, it was impossible to obtain crews by free enlistment. Sailors deserted at the first opportunity, and often found a new job on U.S. vessels. Knowledgeable of this fact, and because they had the power, British officers routinely would stop American ships, and take off anyone they suspected of being a British subject. In addition, because Americans could easily be mistaken in those days for Brits, they often impressed not only English subjects, but American citizens as well. The Americans found this situation to be intolerable.

To help remedy this situation, Jefferson issued an executive order directing British warships to leave U.S. territorial waters. The British reacted by impressing even more sailors. Jefferson, knowing that the U.S. Navy was no match for the British, decided to try economic pressure as a way to force the British to back down. In December 1807, Congress passed the Embargo Act, forbidding all foreign commerce. It was ironic that the Republicans, the champions of states rights, personal freedom, and limited government, had passed a law that increased the powers of the national government. In a single year American exports fell off to one fifth. Shipping interests were rendered almost worthless, and merchants and seamen in New England and New York were irate. Even agricultural interests were hard hit, for Southern and Western farmers had no way to export their cash crops of cotton and tobacco.

The thought that the entire British empire could be brought to its knees by removing American trade was illusory. The United States was hard hit, but not England. As domestic discontent grew, Jefferson tried a different tack. In early 1809, he signed the Non-Intercourse Act, permitting commerce with all countries except Britain and France.

James Madison became president that same year. Relations with Great Britain continued to deteriorate, and the two countries drifted toward war. The president went before Congress with a report that detailed thousands of cases of British impressment of American citizens. Further fueling the desire for war were the settlers of the northwestern frontier, who blamed repeated Indian attacks on the British in Canada. They believed that an American conquest of Canada would eliminate British influence among the Indians and open up new lands for colonization. This desire to annex Canada, coupled with the deep resentment over impressment of American sailors, generated war fervor, and in 1812 the United States declared war on Britain.

THE WAR OF 1812

The declaration of war had been made with little regard for the actual military strength of the United States. There were fewer than 7,000 regular soldiers, and they were already committed to guard duty at forts on the coast, at the Canadian border, and in the remote interior. The only other forces available were the state militias, which were not well equipped, and whose training had been largely neglected since the Revolution.

Actual hostilities began with an American invasion of Canada, which was badly planned and executed. After its failure, the British invaded the United States, and captured Detroit. The only bright spot in the early part of the war was the action of American privateers, who captured 500 British vessels during the fall of 1812 and the winter of 1813.

The year 1813 went better for the Americans. On September 12, Commodore Oliver Hazard Perry annihilated the British fleet on Lake Erie. Then, General William Henry Harrison led an army of militia, volunteers, and regulars north from Kentucky, recaptured Detroit, and pushed into Canada, defeating the retreating British and their Indian allies on the Thames River.

FYI Not only was William Henry Harrison president, but his father, Benjamin Harrison, was a signer of the Declaration of Independence, and his grandson, also named Benjamin Harrison, was also president.

A year later, Commodore Thomas Macdonough won a naval battle against a large British flotilla on Lake Champlain, in upstate New York. This was the naval support for a British invasion force, which numbered more than 10,000. But without their logistical support, they were forced to retreat back to Canada.

On the East Coast, the British fleet was harassing shipping. On the night of August 24, 1814, an expeditionary force, which had been landed from the fleet, marched to Washington, D.C. The government was forced to flee, and the British burned the capital.

The British burning of Washington shocked and enraged Americans in the same way as the attacks at Pearl Harbor and the World Trade Center would enrage later generations.

FYI The hero of the burning of Washington was the wife of the president, Dolley Madison. While everyone else was running, she calmly loaded up valuable government papers and antiquities from the White House, leaving behind her own clothes and furniture, and spirited them safely out of town.

Peace negotiations had been dragging on, but nothing conclusive was accomplished until the British learned of Macdonough's victory on Lake Champlain. The Duke of Wellington, who was faced with a British treasury depleted by the heavy cost of the Napoleonic Wars, instructed his negotiators to agree to the Treaty of Ghent in December 1814. It ended the hostilities, and provided for a commission to settle boundary disputes.

 FYI Because of the snails pace of communications in those days, a major battle was fought at New Orleans, Louisiana, after the peace treaty was signed. Led by General Andrew Jackson, the Americans scored the greatest land victory of the war over British regulars.

HOUR'S UP!

QUIZ

1. The crime that Parsons Weems said Washington committed as a boy was:

 A. Witchcraft

 B. Stealing hemp from his father's barn, which was grown on the plantation for rope making, and smoking it

 C. Cutting down his father's cherry tree

 D. Getting one of his father's slaves pregnant

2. The state of Louisiana was named after:

 A. Louis Armstrong

 B. Saint Louis, a famous Cardinal

 C. King Louis, a French king

 D. Louisa May Alcott

3. Hamilton and Jefferson did not get along for all of the following reasons, except:

 A. Hamilton was a Federalist, and Jefferson was a Republican.

 B. Hamilton favored the farmers and the rural agrarian interests, while Jefferson favored the urban mercantile interests.

    C. Hamilton wanted a national bank, and Jefferson didn't.

    D. Hamilton believed in a strong central government, and Jefferson believed in states rights.

4. Under the Franco-American Treaty of Alliance of 1778, the United States and France were to be allies, and to defend each other forever. However, the United States abrogated the treaty:

    A. During the French Revolution, because we supported Lafayette, who was an aristocrat

    B. At the beginning of World War I, because we didn't want to go "Over There"

    C. Before World War II, because we were afraid of the Nazis

    D. Because the United States didn't have a navy that floated

5. During the War of 1812, the British invaded the United States and burned down the city of:

    A. Philadelphia

    B. Boston

    C. Washington

    D. Encino

HOUR 8

The New Country

CHAPTER SUMMARY

LESSON PLAN:

In this hour, you will learn about the Second Great Awakening, how the Supreme Court finally got some respect, why slavery kept spreading, and a little bit about the rise of political parties.

You will also learn ...

- That the cotton gin was not an early American mixed drink.

- That the Monroe Doctrine had nothing to do with the Catholic Church.

- That there weren't 15 miles on the Erie Canal, but 363, something you would know, if you'd ever navigated on the Erie Canal.

By the beginning of the nineteenth century, two centuries of life in the American colonies had erased the religious fervor which had driven their ancestors to come to the new land. In reaction to the secularism of the age, a religious revival occurred. New religious denominations, such as the Baptists and the Methodists, arose to challenge the old traditional religions.

This was also the period when sectional strife over the issue of slavery began to tear the country apart. This came to a head with the Nullification Crisis, in which South Carolina tried to assert that it had the right to disregard or "nullify" any federal law with which it disagreed. This rebellion against federal authority was quickly put down by a show of military force by President Jackson, the military hero of the War of 1812. However, thirty years later, South Carolina would follow the same path of rebellion against federal authority when it seceded from the Union.

THE GREAT AWAKENING, THE NEXT GENERATION

By 1800, many educated Americans were becoming secular. In reaction to this trend, there arose the second great religious revival. In contrast to the First Great Awakening, these revivals were notable for the absence of hysteria and emotional outbursts. Unbelievers were awed by the "respectful silence" of those bearing witness to their faith.

In New England, this renewed interest in religion inspired a wave of social activism, giving rise to abolition groups, the Society for the Promotion of Temperance, and groups to reform prisons and care for the handicapped and mentally ill. Missionary societies were formed to evangelize the West. These missionaries not only acted as apostles for their faith, but as educators, civic leaders, and exponents of Eastern, urban culture. Publication and education societies, such as the American Bible Society, promoted religious education.

The revival in western New York was largely the work of Charles Gradison Finney, a lawyer who had experienced a religious epiphany. He preached in the *Burned-Over District* throughout the 1820s and the early 1830s. His revivals were characterized by careful planning, showmanship, and advertising. Charles Gradison Finney ultimately moved to Ohio, where he became president of Oberlin College.

STRICTLY DEFINED

> The area from Lake Ontario to the Adirondack Mountains where Finney preached the Gospel had been the scene of so many religious revivals in the past that it was known as the **Burned-Over District.** Two other important religious denominations in America, the Mormons and the Seventh-Day Adventists, also got their start in the Burned-Over District.

In Appalachia, the center of the revival was the camp meeting, a "religious service of several days length, for a group that was obliged to take shelter on the spot because of the distance from home." Pioneers in isolated areas looked to the camp meeting as a refuge from the lonely life on the frontier. The sheer exhilaration of participating in a religious revival with hundreds and perhaps thousands of people inspired dancing, shouting, and singing, making it in this way a close associate of the first Great Awakening. Baptist and Methodist ministers were there, and the revival meeting became a major mode of expansion and recruitment for these denominations.

These two denominations both had a structure that helped them recruit on the frontier. The Methodists depended on ministers, known as circuit riders, who sought out people in remote frontier locations. The circuit riders were themselves common people, unlike the Ivy League educated ministers of the traditional eastern religions, and as a result they had a natural rapport with the frontier families they hoped to convert. The Baptists had farmer-preachers, people who received "the call" from God, studied the Bible on their own, founded their own church, and then were ordained by their flock. Using this method, the Baptists became dominant throughout the border states and most of the South.

FYI These Protestant religions, while dominant, were not the only religious groups in the country. As early as 1654, for example, Jews arrived in New Amsterdam (now New York) from Brazil on board the ship the St. Charles, otherwise known as the "Jewish *Mayflower*."

During the Second Great Awakening, the numerical strength of the Baptists and Methodists rose relative to that of the older denominations dominant in the colonial period, the Anglicans, Presbyterians, and Congregationalists. America was becoming a more diverse nation in the early to mid-nineteenth century, and the growing differences within American Protestantism reflected and contributed to this diversity.

BUILDING UNITY

The War of 1812 was, in a sense, a second war of independence from Great Britain. After the war, the United States was finally accorded equality in the family of nations. National government under the Constitution brought a balance between liberty and order. With a low national debt and an empty continent to explore and settle, the people were enthusiastic about the prospect of peace, prosperity, and social progress.

The war had cut off the flow of foreign goods, and convinced many that it was vital to protect and develop American manufacturing until it could stand alone against foreign competition. They realized that economic independence was as important as political independence. Congressional leaders such as Henry Clay of Kentucky and John C. Calhoun of South Carolina urged a policy of protectionism, with restrictions on imported goods to encourage the development of American industry.

It was a favorable time to raise the customs tariff. Sheep men in Vermont and Ohio wanted protection against the competition of English wool. A new industry in Kentucky of weaving hemp into cotton bagging needed protection from the Scottish bagging industry. Pittsburgh iron men wanted to keep British and Swedish iron suppliers from driving down the price. In 1816, Congress enacted a tariff high enough to give manufacturers real protection.

Westerners had their own agenda. They wanted a national federal system of roads and canals to link them with the Eastern cities and ports. However, they were unsuccessful in pressing their demands for federal dollars for road and canal building because of opposition from New England and the South. Roads and canals remained the province of the states until the passage of the Federal Highways Act in 1916, but it was not until after World War II, in 1956, that the federal government finally created the Interstate Highway System that we know today.

In 1817, governor Dewitt Clinton of New York convinced the state legislature to authorize $7 million for construction of a canal 363 miles long, 40 feet wide, and 4 feet deep, from Albany to Buffalo. Eight years later, on October 26, 1825, Clinton set out from Buffalo in the canal boat *Seneca Chief* to open the Erie Canal.

THE SUPREMES GET SOME RESPECT

John Marshall, a committed Federalist, was chief justice from 1801 until 1835. During his administration, he took the court from the weakest branch of the government and transformed it into a powerful tribunal, taking a rightful place alongside Congress and the president.

Marshall did this by never deviating from one cardinal principle: The Constitution was paramount, and neither Congress nor the President could violate it. During Marshall's tenure, the court decided nearly 50 constitutional cases. In *Marbury* v. *Madison* (1803), he decisively established the right of the Supreme Court to review the constitutionality of any law of Congress or of a state legislature, and to invalidate it if it did not pass constitutional muster. In *McCulloch* v. *Maryland* (1819), which dealt with the recurring question of the implied powers of the government under the Constitution, he stood boldly in defense of Alexander Hamilton's theory that the Constitution gives the government powers beyond those expressly stated.

SLAVERY GOES WEST

In the early years of the republic, when the Northern states were passing laws for the gradual emancipation of their slaves, many leaders had thought that slavery would slowly die out, for it certainly was not an economical way to do business. In 1786, George Washington wrote that he wished some plan might be adopted "by which slavery may be abolished by slow, sure and imperceptible degrees." Jefferson, Madison, Monroe, and other leading Southern statesmen also made such statements. The Northwest Ordinance of 1787 had banned slavery in the Northwest Territory. The Constitution banned the slave trade twenty years after its adoption. As late as 1808, when the international slave trade was abolished, there were many Southerners who thought that slavery was in decline, and would soon fade away.

FYI Eli Whitney thought that a machine to clean the seed from cotton would make its inventor rich. He filed an application for a patent on June 20, 1793; and in February 1794 he deposited a working model at the Patent Office. Whitney's gin brought the South prosperity, but the unwillingness of the planters to pay for its use and the ease with which the gin could be pirated put Whitney's company out of business by 1797. When Congress refused to renew the patent when it expired in 1807, Whitney concluded that 'an invention can be so valuable as to be worthless to the inventor.' He went on to invent more machines, but he never patented another one.

The belief that slavery was in its death-throws was premature, however, as new economic factors made slavery far more profitable. Chief among these was the rise of a great cotton-growing industry in the South, stimulated by the introduction of new strains of the cotton plant, and by Eli Whitney's invention in 1793 of the cotton gin, which mechanized the difficult process of separating the seeds from cotton. At the same time, in the North, the Industrial Revolution, which made textile manufacturing a large-scale operation, vastly increased the demand for raw cotton. As the country moved west, the new lands greatly extended the area available for cotton cultivation. The business of cotton moved rapidly from the Tidewater states on the East Coast, through the lower South, into the delta region of the Mississippi, and then into Texas.

Sugarcane, another labor-intensive crop, also contributed to slavery's extension. The rich, hot lands of southeastern Louisiana proved ideal for growing sugarcane. By 1830, half the nation's sugar was coming from that region. Another great crop suited to slave labor was tobacco, and the money to be made from that crop also drove slavery farther westward.

As the slave society of the South spread west, a rough equality was maintained between the number of slave and free states. When Alabama was admitted to the Union, 11 states permitted slavery and 11 states prohibited it. However, because population was growing faster in the North, the Northern states had a clear majority in the House of Representatives. But equality between the North and the South was maintained in the Senate, because each state had 2 senators, putting 22 Senators on each side of the slavery issue.

FYI Two presidents died on the same day, exactly 50 years after they had written the Declaration of Independence, and it was on July 4! John Adams, the second president, and Thomas Jefferson, the third president, both died on July 4, 1826. As if that wasn't strange enough, five years later, James Monroe, the fifth president, died on July 4, 1831. Three out of the first five presidents, therefore, died on July 4!

In 1819, Missouri, which had 10,000 slaves, applied to enter the Union as a slave state, and the North rallied to oppose it. Congress, especially the Senate, was deadlocked, until Henry Clay proposed the Missouri Compromise: Missouri and Maine would come in together, one slave, one free. In addition, slavery would be banned in all new states created north of Missouri's southern boundary. The controversy was temporarily resolved, but Thomas Jefferson wrote to a friend that "this momentous question like a fire-bell in the night awakened me with terror. I considered it at once as the death knell of the Union."

THE MONROE DOCTRINE

Ever since the English colonies had won their independence, the Spanish colonists of Central and South America had also wanted their independence. Napoleon's conquest of Spain in 1808 provided the catalyst for revolution in Latin American, because the mother country was too preoccupied to worry about its colonies. By 1822, led by Simon Bolivar, Francisco Miranda, José de San Martin, and Miguel Hidalgo, all the colonies of Hispanic America had fought revolutions and obtained their independence.

The people of the United States took a deep interest in what was happening to the south, for these countries had followed the Americans' democratic lead, and it confirmed their own belief in the government they had created. In 1822, President James Monroe, under powerful public pressure, recognized the new countries of Latin America, and exchanged ministers. This recognition by the United States helped to confirm their status as independent countries.

Russia, Prussia, and Austria, monarchies that were concerned about the spread of democracy and revolution, formed the Holy Alliance. The Alliance, which sometimes included France, hoped to prevent, by united intervention, the spread of revolution into their dominions. This policy, of course, was the antithesis of everything Americans believe about freedom, democracy, and self-determination.

The Alliance announced that it was going to restore to Spain its former colonies. Americans were alarmed, for they did not want to see the new democracies crushed, nor did they want European powers to enter the hemisphere. Britain did not want Spain to regain its empire, because they had built a profitable trading relationship with the new countries. London wanted to join with Washington in reassuring Latin America that they would guarantee their sovereignty, but Secretary of State John Quincy Adams convinced Monroe to act unilaterally.

QUOTABLE QUOTES

John Quincy Adams, in urging that the United States act alone in keeping foreign countries out of the Western Hemisphere, stated: "It would be more candid, as well as more dignified, to avow our principles explicitly to Russia and France, than to come in as a cock-boat in the wake of the British man-of-war."

Although he acted alone, Monroe made his announcement knowing that the British navy would back him up, and help him to defend Latin America from the Holy Alliance. President Monroe used his annual message to Congress to announce the "Monroe Doctrine":

> The American continents ... are henceforth not to be considered as subjects for future colonization by any European powers. We should consider any attempt on their part to extend their [political] system to any portion of this hemisphere as dangerous to our peace and safety. With the existing colonies or dependencies of any European power we have not interfered and shall not interfere. But with the governments who have declared their independence and maintained it, and whose independence we have ... acknowledged, we could not view any interposition for the purpose of oppressing them, or controlling in any other manner their destiny, by any European power in any other light than as the manifestation of an unfriendly disposition toward the United States.

The Monroe Doctrine expressed solidarity between the United States and the newly independent republics of Latin America. These nations, for the most part, had based their new constitutions on the North American model. Democracy now held sway over almost the entire Western Hemisphere, while monarchies still ruled virtually all of Europe.

THE NEW POLITICS

The presidency of James Monroe (1817–1825) was termed the "era of good feelings," and acknowledged the total political triumph of the Republican Party over the Federalist Party, which disappeared as a result.

The demise of the Federalists brought disarray to the system of choosing presidents. Because state legislatures could nominate candidates, in 1824, Tennessee and Pennsylvania chose war hero Andrew Jackson, Kentucky selected Speaker of the House Henry Clay, Massachusetts put forward favorite son Secretary of State John Quincy Adams, and a congressional caucus nominated Treasury Secretary William Crawford.

As expected, they won the electoral votes in the regions from which they were nominated. Adams garnered electoral votes from New England and New York; Clay won Kentucky, Ohio, and Missouri; Jackson took the Southeast, Illinois, Indiana, the Carolinas, Pennsylvania, Maryland, and New Jersey; and Crawford won Virginia, Georgia, and Delaware. With such fragmentation, no candidate could muster a majority in the Electoral College. In that situation, provided for in the Constitution, the election is thrown into the House of Representatives. In the House, Clay supported Adams, who became president.

FYI Jackson was the first candidate of the new Democratic Party. Ironically, it was the successor to a party called the Republican Party, which had been founded by Jefferson, Madison, and Monroe. This earlier Republican Party had absolutely nothing to do with the present-day Republicans, who only date back to Abraham Lincoln. Nor did it have anything to do with the party founded by Adams, which was called the National Republicans, and which later changed its names to the Whigs.

John Quincy Adams was not a popular president. His years in office appeared to be one long campaign for reelection, and his coldly intellectual temperament did not win him friends or influence people. In the next election, Adams was defeated by Jackson by an overwhelming electoral majority.

Jackson, famous as an Indian fighter and hero of the Battle of New Orleans during the War of 1812, was immensely popular. He drew his support from the little people, the small farmers of the West, and the workers, artisans, and small merchants of the East. He took their side against the rising commercial and manufacturing interests of the Industrial Revolution.

One reason for the election of Jackson was that the common people were increasingly winning the right to vote, and he was the popular candidate of the people. The election of 1828 was a significant benchmark in the trend towards universal male *suffrage*, with which Vermont had entered the Union. Tennessee permitted suffrage for the vast majority of taxpayers. New Jersey, Maryland, and South Carolina had all abolished property and tax requirements by 1810. States entering the Union after 1815 either entered with universal white male suffrage, a preference on the frontier, or a very low requirement to be a taxpayer and thus qualified to vote. By the year 1821, Connecticut, Massachusetts, and New York had all abolished their property requirements. In 1824, members of the Electoral College were still selected by six state legislatures, but by 1828, this was reduced to just two, Delaware and South Carolina.

STRICTLY DEFINED

Suffrage is the right to vote. In the early years of the United States, not every person had the right to vote. Today, every citizen 18 years of age or older has the right to vote, without any regard to race, religion, social status, gender, or national origin.

NULLIFICATION CRISIS

In South Carolina, business and farming interests had hoped that Jackson would use his presidential power to modify tariff laws they had long opposed. They believed that all of the benefits of the protective tariff were going to Northern manufacturers, and that while they grew richer, South Carolina grew poorer, because the planters had to bear the burden of higher prices caused by the tariffs.

John C. Calhoun, the vice president, in his *South Carolina Exposition and Protest,* had advocated the principle of nullification. South Carolina dealt with the tariff by adopting the Ordinance of Nullification, which declared both the tariffs of 1828 and 1832 null and void within the borders of South Carolina. The legislature also authorized raising a military force, and appropriations for arms and equipment, to support their stance with the federal government, if necessary.

 In the early years of the United States, the presidential candidate with the second largest number of electoral votes became vice president. John C. Calhoun ran for president in the 1824 election against John Quincy Adams and Andrew Jackson. However, Calhoun withdrew from the race, due to Jackson's support, ran for vice president unopposed, and, thus, in 1824, he became vice president under Adams. In the next election, in 1828, he was reelected as vice president under Andrew Jackson, thus becoming the only person in history to serve as vice president under two different presidents.

There had been other state challenges to the authority of the federal government since the founding of the republic. The Kentucky and Virginia Resolutions of 1798, for example, had defied the Alien and Sedition Acts. In the Hartford Convention, New England had voiced its opposition to President Madison and the war against the British. But no state had previously gone to the extreme of arming their militia, and declaring that they would defy the federal government with armed men.

In response to South Carolina's declaration, Jackson sent a show of force, seven naval vessels and a man-of-war, to Charleston harbor in November 1832. On December 10, he issued a thinly veiled threat to the nullifiers. South Carolina, the president declared, stood on "the brink of insurrection and treason." He appealed to the people of the state to reassert their allegiance to the Union for which their ancestors had fought.

Senator Henry Clay, a great advocate of protection, and a political rival of Jackson, introduced a compromise bill in Congress. Clay's tariff bill, which was quickly passed to avert the crisis, specified that all duties in excess of 20 percent were to be reduced in stages, so that by 1842, the duties on all articles had returned to the lower tariff levels of 1816.

FYI This episode with South Carolina was a precursor to the Civil War. South Carolina would be the first one of the states to secede from the Union and join the Confederacy, and also the first to fight, when they fired on Fort Sumter.

The Clay compromise knocked the wind out of South Carolina's sails. In addition, South Carolina had expected the support of other Southern states, but no other state had sided with them; instead, they had all unanimously declared South Carolina's course unconstitutional. South Carolina was forced to back down, and a crisis that could have resulted in revolution or civil war was defused.

HOUR'S UP!

QUIZ

1. The Erie Canal:

    A. Is part of the inner ear

    B. Was really, really spooky

    C. Is named after Lake Erie

    D. Was later renamed the Love Canal

2. Eli Whitney was the inventor of:

    A. Cotton candy

    B. Cotton gin

    C. Sloe gin fizz

    D. Gin rummy

3. The Monroe Doctrine was all of the following, except:

   A. Written by Marilyn Monroe

   B. Created during the administration of president James Monroe

   C. Declared that North and South America could no longer be colonized by any European power

   D. Instituted to counteract the Holy Alliance

4. The Whigs were replaced in American politics by:

   A. Republicans

   B. Democrats

   C. Black Panthers

   D. Greenpeace

5. The following persons died on July 4:

   A. Thomas Jefferson

   B. John Adams

   C. James Monroe

   D. George M. Cohan

HOUR 9

Westward Expansion

CHAPTER SUMMARY

LESSON PLAN:

In this hour, you will learn more about banks, reform movements, women's rights, and political parties.

You will also learn ...

- Why Tippecanoe needed Tyler, too.
- Why Davy Crockett went to Texas.
- What makes an Indian cry.
- Why women weren't allowed to vote.

In the early days of the colonies, everyone but the Indians had been a recent immigrant. But after more than two centuries of immigration, distinctions began to arise between the "original" settlers, and the newer immigrants. There were also ethnic differences, especially between the Irish, who were Catholic, and the founders of the country, who had been predominately Protestant. This lead to the formation of political parties such as the Know-Nothings, whose platform focused on the prevention of unrestricted emigration.

There was one group in early America who had been there since the original settlers, and still did not have equal rights, and that was the women. By this point in history, universal male suffrage for all freemen had become a reality. However, women were still denied this basic right of citizenship. Starting in the 1840s, women began to organize and start their slow advance toward full equality under the law.

THE ALL-NEW BATTLE OF THE BANK

The first Bank of the United States had been established in 1791, under Alexander Hamilton, for a 20-year period. Though the government held some of its stock, it was not a government bank, rather, it was a private profit-making corporation answerable to its stockholders. It had been designed to stabilize the currency and to stimulate trade, but it was resented by Westerners and working people who believed that it was a "monster" granting special favors to a few powerful men. When its charter expired in 1811, this popular opinion prevented it from being renewed.

Without a federal bank, the banking business was left in the hands of state-chartered banks, each of which issued their own currency, and in excessive amounts, creating confusion and fueling inflation. It became increasingly clear that multiple state banks could not provide the country with a uniform currency, and in 1816, a second Bank of the United States was chartered for a new term of 20 years.

Once again, Westerners and the less-affluent working people aligned against the Bank. They claimed the bank possessed a virtual monopoly over both the country's credit and its currency and only represented the interests of the wealthy.

The bank's charter came up for renewal during Jackson's presidency. Although it was well managed and rendered valuable service, Jackson, elected as the popular champion of those aligned against it, vetoed the bill to authorize the new charter. He denounced monopoly and special privilege, saying "our rich men have not been content with equal protection and equal benefits, but have besought us to make them richer by act of Congress." Congress was unable to muster the votes to override the veto.

In the next election, the bank question was the source of controversy between the merchant, manufacturing, and financial interests on one hand, who were creditors who favored tight money and high interest rates, and the laborers and farmers, who were often in debt to banks and, therefore, favored an increased money supply and lower interest rates.

FYI Andrew Jackson was orphaned during the Revolution and grew up dirt poor. He was the first president to arise from "the people" instead of from the aristocracy. As voter requirements disappeared, he aimed his campaign at these newly enfranchised masses. He created a new style of political campaign, aimed at the common people, with plenty of barbecues, parades, bands, and even campaign buttons. Politics were never to be the same again.

Jackson was elected to a second term, which he saw as a clear mandate from the people to shut down the bank, even before its charter expired. He found a way to do this in the bank's own charter, which authorized the president to remove public funds. In September 1833, he ordered that no more government money be deposited in the bank and that checks should be written against the money already on deposit to meet the ordinary expenses of government, so that the United States would gradually remove all of its money from the bank.

To replace the federal bank, a number of carefully selected state banks were designated to substitute for the federal bank. For the next generation, the United States would lurch forward with a system of state banks. They helped to fuel westward expansion by providing cheap credit, but periodically depositors would be wiped out in panics. It was not until the Civil War, and the requirement to finance a massive war effort, that the United States would once again charter a national banking system.

A WHIG CAN ALSO BE A PARTY

With Jackson's Democrats now the only political party in the country, it was necessary for those who hoped to oust him from office to create an opposition party. All of the diverse and dissatisfied citizenry organized themselves into a party that they named the Whigs. However, it was more than a decade before they were able to hammer out their differences and create a coherent platform, mainly through the brilliant leadership of Henry Clay and Daniel Webster. Unfortunately, in the 1836 election, the Whigs were still too divided to unite behind a single man or upon a common platform. As a result, the Democratic candidate, and Jackson's vice president, Martin Van Buren of New York, won the election.

Van Buren's administration was plagued by an economic depression, although no one would have looked good in the office after the flamboyant and popular Jackson. Van Buren lacked the personal magnetism and flair for leadership that might have produced a more successful administration. With the election approaching, the Democrats were stuck in that no-win political situation where the country is in a depression, times are hard, and the people are going to vote for a change of political parties, in the hopes that that will make things better.

The Whig candidate for president was William Henry Harrison of Ohio. Like Jackson, he was popular as an Indian fighter, had been successful as a general in the War of 1812, and was regarded as a man of the people and a representative of the democratic West. He probably could have swept the election on his own, but his vice presidential running mate, John Tyler, made the slate even more popular by balancing the ticket: He was a Virginian whose views on states' rights and a low tariff were popular in the South. They won by a landslide.

"Tippecanoe and Tyler, Too" was Harrison's slogan for the 1840 presidential campaign. In 1811, General William Henry Harrison led an army against the Indians on the Tippecanoe River in Indiana. Harrison was successful in defeating the Indians before Chief Tecumseh could succeed in uniting the Indian tribes into an unbeatable force.

Inauguration day was cold and rainy, and, ironically, the 68-year-old Harrison, a veteran of many years of rough campaigning, caught a cold, and died. Tyler thus became the first vice president to succeed to the office of president on the death of the incumbent. Because Tyler's beliefs differed from those of Clay and Webster, the influential leaders of the party, there became an open break between the president and the party that had elected him.

Americans, however, found themselves divided in a more significant way than the simple partisan politics of the Whigs and Democrats. The large influx of Catholic immigrants in the years before the Civil War, primarily Irish and German, was of great concern to the native-born Protestant Americans.

FYI MYTH: Signs began to appear, which said "Help Wanted. No Irish need apply" (NINA). FACT: The fact that Irish vividly "remember" seeing these signs is a curious historical puzzle. Only Irish Catholics could see the sign: No historian, archivist, or museum curator has ever located one, no photograph or drawing exists. No Protestant or Jew ever saw a NINA sign. The business literature, both published and unpublished, never mentions NINA. The newspapers and magazines, as well as the courts, are likewise silent. There is no record of an angry Irish youth tossing a brick through the window that held such a sign. The sign appears to be an Irish Catholic urban legend.

A SHOW ABOUT "KNOW-NOTHINGS"

More important than their religion, immigrants did what immigrants always do—as soon as they arrived, they competed with the native-born Americans for the jobs in the cities. In addition, under the new laws (which encouraged universal male suffrage), they weren't long off the boat before they were voting. Last, the Catholic Church refused to endorse the temperance movement, and many people were convinced that Rome was trying to subvert the United States through alcohol.

Alcoholism was a widespread problem in the nineteenth-century America, and on payday workers would often drink up the wages needed by their families to survive. The Temperance Movement sought to encourage abstinence by these men from the use of the intoxicating drink. At the Temperance rallies, men were encouraged to sign "pledges" in which they promised to never again let liquor touch their lips. These pledges were often quickly forgotten and disregarded once the excitement of the Temperance meeting was over, and a new payday had arrived.

Native-born, American-only organizations were soon being organized in reaction to the perceived Catholic immigrant threat, and one of the most powerful was the *Know-Nothings*, whose Grand Council was headquartered in New York City. Among the chief aims of the Know-Nothings was a revision of the period required for naturalization from 5 to 21 years, and the exclusion of those who were foreign-born or Catholic from public office. By 1855, they had control of the legislatures in New York and Massachusetts, and 90 U.S. congressmen were affiliated with the party.

STRICTLY DEFINED

When members of the Order of the Star Spangled Banner, a secret society founded in 1849, refused to identify themselves, they were swiftly labeled the **Know-Nothings.**

What ultimately destroyed the ability of the Know-Nothings to play a major role in national politics, however, was their failure to reach agreement on the slavery issue. The Know-Nothings of the South were in favor of continuing slavery, while Northern members were abolitionists. At their national convention in 1856 to nominate candidates for president and vice president, 42 Northern delegates walked out when a motion to support the Missouri Compromise was tabled, and the party disappeared as a national force shortly thereafter.

STIRRING UP REFORM

American society was changing, and the reform movement, an outgrowth of the Second Great Awakening, was beginning to achieve significant gains.

Labor organizations in Philadelphia, Pennsylvania, succeeded in reducing the old "dark-to-dark" workday to a 10-hour day. New Hampshire, Rhode Island, Ohio, and California were to pass similar reforms.

California was admitted to the Union in 1850, and it was the only state in the Union which did not border any other state, since statehood for Arizona (1912), Nevada (1864), Utah (1896), and Oregon (1859) were in the future.

With the advent of universal suffrage, the ruling classes in America (having observed the excesses of the uneducated peasants during the French Revolution), realized that an ignorant, illiterate electorate was their worst enemy. In addition, the unions of organized labor were becoming potent political forces, controlling important politicians such as DeWitt Clinton in New York, Abraham Lincoln in Illinois, and Horace Mann in Massachusetts, and these labor unions were demanding free, tax-supported schools which were open to their children, the children of working class families. Gradually, state by state, legislation was enacted to provide for state-supported schools. These school systems quickly became commonplace in the north, which already had the tradition of the village schoolhouse. But in other parts of the country, the battle for public education was to drag on for years.

Another force for reform that emerged during this period was the Temperance Movement, the goal of which was to prevent the sale and use of liquor. Reformers realized the ruinous effects of alcohol, and the violence, abuse, and suffering that women and children experienced at the hands of heavy-drinking husbands and fathers. In 1826, ministers in Boston organized the Society for the Promotion of Temperance, which in turn formed the American Temperance Union. The Union's agenda was to persuade the state legislatures to ban the production and sale of liquor. By 1855, they had been successful in thirteen states, although the laws were subsequently struck down in court in some states. In the years before the Civil War, the Temperance Movement was successful in reducing Americans' overall per-capita consumption of alcohol.

 FYI Dorothea Dix led the campaign to reform the treatment of the insane, who were often just locked up in state prisons to get them out of the way. She was successful in the establishment of hospitals for the insane around the country.

WESTWARD HO THE WAGONS

Native-born and immigrant alike, people were moving west. In New England, the lifeless soil and the abundance of rocks drove farmers to give up and take advantage of the rich interior lands of the continent. In the backcountry of the Carolinas and Virginia, people without any roads or canals to get their goods to the seaports, who were tired of the political dominance of the aristocratic Tidewater planters, also packed up and headed west. By 1800, the Mississippi and Ohio river valleys beyond the Appalachians were filling up with settlers.

Nicknamed the "Prairie Schooners," these massive wagons held all the worldly possessions of the pioneers as they moved westward.

QUOTABLE QUOTES

"Hi-o, away we go, floating down the river on the O-hi-o," was the song of thousands of migrants. It wasn't The Beatles, but at least it rhymed.

The westward flow of population led to the creation of new states in the new territories. As they were admitted to the union, the political map stabilized east of the Mississippi River. From 1816 to 1821, three free states, Indiana, Illinois, and Maine, were admitted, as were three slave states, Mississippi, Alabama, and Missouri.

QUOTABLE QUOTES

One English traveler named Fordharn described frontier settlers as "a daring, hardy race of men, who live in miserable cabins. They are unpolished but hospitable, kind to strangers, honest and trustworthy. They raise a little Indian corn, pumpkins, hogs, and sometimes have a cow or two. The rifle is their principal means of support."

When a settler found a place on which he wanted to stay, he would rapidly clear the land of timber, burning the wood for potash and pulling the stumps. He would build a comfortable log house with glass windows, a chimney and partitioned rooms, dig a well, grow his own grain, vegetables and fruit, range the woods for deer, wild turkeys and honey, fish the nearby streams, and feed his cattle and hogs. As he grew more established, he would build a large barn and a brick or frame house and acquire better livestock.

Farms in those early days of the country were cheap and easy to acquire. Government land after 1820 could be bought for $1.25 an acre. After the 1862 Homestead Act, land was free, and all you had to do was move in, stake your claim, make some improvements, and the land was yours.

This was a time in the history of the country, when, according to journalist Horace Greeley, young men should "go west and grow with the country." The farmers, as they established towns on the frontier, were followed by doctors, lawyers, storekeepers, editors, preachers, mechanics, and politicians. They erected flour mills, sawmills, and distilleries. They laid out highways, and built churches and schools. The transformation of the western wilderness was incredibly swift. For example, Chicago was merely a small trading village in 1830, but long before its original settlers had died, it had become one of the largest and richest cities in the nation.

FYI In 1819, in return for assuming the claims of American citizens to the amount of $5 million, the United States obtained from Spain both Florida and Spain's rights to the Oregon country in the Far West.

The Far West beyond the Mississippi was still relatively unsettled, although it was inhabited by fur trappers, traders, and Indians. As in the days of French exploration in the Mississippi Valley, the trader and the trapper were the pathfinders for the settlers who would later venture beyond the Mississippi. The French and Scots-Irish trappers explored the great rivers and their tributaries, and discovered the passes through the Rocky Mountains and the high Sierras, which would make possible later the occupation of the interior, and the migration to the West Coast.

The population grew from 7.25 million to more than 23 million from 1812 to 1852, and the land available for settlement increased by almost the entire size of Europe.

The Indian Removal

Repeatedly, expansion brought settlers into conflict with the Indians. During the War of 1812, Andrew Jackson, in charge of the Tennessee militia, put down an uprising of Creek Indians in lower Alabama, and forced them to cede two thirds of their land to the United States. Later, Jackson was put in charge of routing bands of Seminole Indians from their sanctuaries in Spanish-owned Florida.

In 1830, Congress passed the Indian Removal Act, and voted funds to transport the eastern tribes to a special Indian territory to be set up in Oklahoma. In all, the tribes signed 94 treaties during Jackson's two terms, in which they ceded millions of acres to the federal government, and agreed to relocate from their ancestral homelands to these reservations west of the Mississippi.

QUOTABLE QUOTES

 "I would sooner be honestly damned than hypocritically immortalized," said Davy Crockett, Congressman from Tennessee, who fought valiantly against the "Indian Removal Act." Although many Americans were against the act, it passed anyway. His political career was destroyed by his support of the Cherokee, so Crockett left Washington, D.C., and headed west to Texas, where he was to die defending the Alamo.

Perhaps the most unfortunate chapter in the history of the Indian removals concerned the Cherokees, whose lands in western North Carolina and Georgia had been guaranteed by treaty since 1791. Even though they were the most progressive of the eastern tribes, and were integrating into the white culture as fast as any of the newly arriving immigrants, the Cherokees' fate was sealed when gold was discovered on their land in 1829. They even appealed their removal to the Supreme Court, who agreed with them, but even this did nothing to stop their removal by the government. The Cherokees were forced to make a long and cruel trek to Oklahoma. Many died of disease and starvation along the way, in what has gone down in history as the "Trail of Tears."

WOMEN HAVE RIGHTS, TOO

While women enjoyed many of the same legal rights as men, when they married they lost their separate identities in the eyes of the law. In addition, women were not permitted to vote, and their education in the seventeenth and eighteenth centuries was limited largely to reading, writing, and the skills of music, dancing and needlework.

Frances Wright, a Scottish lecturer and journalist, publicly promoted the idea of women's rights throughout the United States in the 1820s. Even though women were often forbidden to speak in public, Wright not only spoke, but shocked audiences with her views on birth control and divorce.

Ernestine Rose, a Polish immigrant, was instrumental in pushing through a law in New York that allowed women to keep their property in their own name after marriage. The Married Women's Property Act encouraged the legislatures in other states to enact similar laws.

WOMEN DECLARE THEIR INDEPENDENCE

Elizabeth Cady Stanton found an ally in Lucretia Mott when the two met at an antislavery conference in London. It was immediately apparent to them that female delegates were not welcome. Barred from speaking, in fact from even appearing on the convention floor, Cady Stanton and Mott protested by leaving the convention hall, taking the other female delegates with them. It was then that they decided to hold the first women's rights convention, to address the social, civil, and religious rights of women.

At that meeting in 1848, Cady Stanton presented a "Declaration of Sentiments," based on the Declaration of Independence, and listed her grievances against men. For example, a married woman could not keep her children if she left an abusive husband or sought a divorce. If a woman was granted a divorce, the only occupation open to her was teaching. A woman could not testify against her husband in court. Married women who worked in factories were not entitled to keep their earnings; they had to turn them over to their husbands. When a woman married, any property she had as a single woman automatically became her husband's. Single women who owned property were taxed without the right to vote for the lawmakers imposing the taxes, the very reason why the American colonies had broken away from Great Britain.

QUOTABLE QUOTES

In 1869, Ernestine Rose, Elizabeth Cady Stanton, and Susan B. Anthony founded the National Woman Suffrage Association (NWSA) to advocate a constitutional amendment for women's right to vote. Describing her partnership with Susan B. Anthony, Cady Stanton would say, "I forged the thunderbolts and she fired them."

The resolutions passed unanimously, except for women's suffrage. Only after a speech by Frederick Douglass, the black abolitionist, did the suffrage resolution pass. Still, the majority of those in attendance found it hard to accept the concept of women voting, even though they were themselves women.

By awakening women to the injustices they faced, Seneca Falls laid the foundation for future change. It led to other women's rights conventions, where a growing number of women advocated the need for political and social equality.

FYI Run by the National Park Service, Women's Rights National Historical Park is located in Seneca Falls, New York. Historic sites in the park include: the 1840s Greek Revival home of Elizabeth Cady Stanton, organizer and leader of the women's rights movement; the Wesleyan Chapel, site of the First Women's Rights Convention; Declaration Park, with a 100-foot-long water-wall engraved with the Declaration of Sentiments and the names of the signers of the Declaration; the Hunt House, home of Jane and Richard Hunt, the site where the idea for the First Women's Rights Convention was conceived; and the M'Clintock House, home of MaryAnn and Thomas M'Clintock, where the Declaration of Sentiments was drafted.

HOUR'S UP!

1. The Know-Nothings are all of the following, except:

    A. They hated Catholics.

    B. They hated immigrants.

    C. They were a political party.

    D. They were intelligent.

2. President William Henry Harrison's nickname was:

    A. Old Yeller, because of his cowardly war record

    B. Old Tippecanoe

    C. Tyler Two

    D. Tyler's Tutu

3. Davy Crockett did all of the following, except:

    A. Born on a mountain top in Tennessee

    B. Killed him a bear when he was only three

    C. Sided with the Indians

    D. Win the battle of the Alamo

4. People believe that the following signs were posted in early America:

    A. Help Wanted. No Danish Need Apply.

    B. Help Wanted. No Polish Need Apply.

    C. Help Wanted. No Irish Need Apply.

    D. Help Wanted. No Finnish Need Apply.

QUIZ

5. The Cherokees were all of the following, except:

    A. Originally from Georgia and North Carolina

    B. Even though their land was guaranteed by a treaty with the United States, they lost their case in the United States Supreme Court to prevent their removal

    C. Forcibly removed by the federal government to Oklahoma on a cruel overland trek that is known as the "Trail of Tears"

    D. Their descendants got their revenge when oil was discovered on their new land in Oklahoma

Slavery Divides the Country

CHAPTER SUMMARY

LESSON PLAN:

In this hour, you will learn about the problems with slavery, the war with Mexico, and westward expansion to California.

You will also learn ...

- That the Underground Railroad isn't the name of the subway in Washington.
- Why all the gold was rushing to California.
- Why Texans remember the Alamo.
- Why Abolitionists wanted to free the soil.

In the 1840s and 1850s, slavery became the most important source of controversy in America, centering around two distinct issues. The first problem was the frontier. As the country moved westward, acquiring immense new territories such as Texas, Louisiana, and California, those in the North wanted to ensure that these territories were admitted to the Union as free states, while the South wanted slavery to be legal in these new lands. Since each side realized that a new slave or free state would affect the balance of power in the Senate, this became a bitter source of conflict.

The second great debate surrounding slavery was the movement towards complete abolition. The Abolitionists not only wanted to prevent the spread of slavery into new states, they were dedicated to the complete eradication of the practice throughout the country. This enraged the Southern states, who believed in "states rights," the right of each state to control their internal affairs, free from outside intervention from the federal government. This debate had been the basic dichotomy between the two political parties since the foundation of the country, when the Federalists had advocated a strong central government, and the Anti-Federalists had stood for the proposition that the states did not surrender their sovereignty when they allied together to create the United States.

Two Americas

French writer and political theorist Alexis de Tocqueville, after traveling to the United States, wrote *Democracy in America*. First published in 1835, it is an insightful look into American social and political practices of the time. Although he was critical of many things, his verdict was fundamentally positive. Tocqueville was concerned with whether equality could survive in the face of a growing factory system that threatened to create divisions between the industrial workers and the new business elite.

QUOTABLE QUOTES

 America began to attract a steady stream of foreign visitors. One historian noted: "What had been a somewhat obscure, occasionally romanticized backwater of colonial exploitation became, virtually overnight, a phenomenon to be investigated, a political and moral experiment to be judged."

Travelers marveled at the growth and vitality of the country. Everywhere there was evidence of prosperity, and rapid progress in agriculture, commerce, and great public works. America in the nineteenth century generated expectations and passions that often did not agree with a reality that was more mundane and complex. Its size and diversity created many contradictions, it was both a freedom-loving and a slave-holding society, it was a nation of great and undeveloped frontiers, as well as of cities of commerce and industrialization.

QUOTABLE QUOTES

 One skeptic of the American experiment was English novelist Charles Dickens, who first visited the United States in 1841 and 1842. "This is not the Republic I came to see," he wrote in a letter. "This is not the Republic of my imagination .... The more I think of its youth and strength, the poorer and more trifling in a thousand respects, it appears in my eyes. In everything of which it has made a boast, excepting its education of the people, and its care for poor children, it sinks immeasurably below the level I had placed it upon."

The Land of Milk and Honey

New England and the Middle Atlantic states were the main centers of manufacturing, commerce, and finance. They turned out textiles, lumber, clothing, machinery, and leather. Ships flying the American flag were in every ocean, engaged in trading, fishing, and whaling.

JUST A MINUTE

By 1850, the national territory stretched across the entire continent and included a population of 23 million people in a union comprising 31 states.

The South continued to depend on agriculture. Tobacco was important to the economies of Virginia, Maryland, and North Carolina. In South Carolina, rice was the major crop, and the climate and soil of Louisiana were good for sugar. But it was cotton that came to dominate the South. Slave labor was critical to all these crops.

JUST A MINUTE

By 1850, cotton accounted for 63 percent of the South's exports. The textile mills of Great Britain made up one half of the market. By 1860, the South produced three fourths of the world's cotton. Most slaves were owned by plantation owners, with 25 percent of the owners owning 75 percent of the slaves. Twenty-five percent of the people in the South had only one slave.

The Midwest, with its great prairies, was rapidly becoming a major supplier of wheat and meat products to the eastern seaboard and Europe. The introduction of labor-saving machines like the McCormick reaper made it possible for the individual farmer to increase his farm production.

An important stimulus to the west was the improvement in transportation: Railroads were a quantum leap in technology. Before the Civil War, the Appalachian Mountains were crossed by five railway lines, which linked the Midwest and the East. These railroads were mainly in the north; it was not until the late 1850s that the first continuous railroad line ran through the mountains and connected the lower Mississippi River region with the Atlantic seaboard.

SLAVERY DIVIDES THE COUNTRY AGAINST ITSELF

Slavery, more than any other issue, defined the differences between the North and the South. Northerners believed that slavery was inherently evil, and it was that inherent wickedness that was responsible for the region's backwardness. Southerners, on the other hand, pointed to the immense fortunes amassed by Northern businessmen from marketing the cotton crop, and also from the resulting textiles that they produced in their mills. While the Southerners might stand on the backs of the slaves, they contended that the North in turn stood on their backs.

JUST A MINUTE

The South had another word for slavery, they called it that "peculiar institution." Southerners were convinced that only black slaves could do the work of planting and harvesting the cotton, that only Africans could stand the heat and the backbreaking labor of the cotton fields. In reality, it was impossible to get white men to do the work, at any price.

Sectional lines had been steadily hardening on the slavery question since the 1830s. In the North, abolitionists grew more and more politically powerful. An allied organization was the "free-soil" movement, who vigorously opposed the extension of slavery into those Western territories not yet admitted as states. To Southerners before the Civil War, slavery was an ancient tradition, in some regions of the United States it had existed for more than 200 years. For them, it wasn't a subject for discussion or debate, it simply existed, an integral part of their social structure and economy.

The "poor whites," or "white trash," those who lived on the absolute lowest rung of Southern society, were uneducated and poor, and did not have any slaves. However, they also supported slavery, for a very basic and rationale reason: They realized that if the slaves were freed, they would themselves sink to the lowest rung of society. As long as there were slaves, it didn't matter how poor you were, there was someone below you in social structure. In addition, they realized that once the slaves were free, they would want land, education, and jobs. Willing to work for low wages, they would soon make it hard for any white man to make a decent living.

JUST A MINUTE

Only a minority of Southern whites owned slaves. In 1860 there were a total of 46,274 planters throughout the slave-holding states, with a planter being defined as someone who owned at least 20 slaves. More than half of all slaves worked on plantations. Some of the yeoman farmers, 70 percent of whom held fewer than 20 acres, had a handful of slaves, but most had none.

Political leaders of the South, the professional classes, and most of the clergy did not apologize for slavery—they championed it. Southerners insisted that slavery was much more humane than life in the northern factories, where immigrants were exploited under horrible working conditions and miniscule wages, and lived on the brink of starvation in dark, dank tenement houses full of rats, lice, and disease. On a plantation, every slave family had their own home, fresh air, and plenty to eat.

Slavery, whether the south wanted to admit it or not, was in transition, itself a victim of the industrial revolution. It had started as a paternalistic system, in which each slave worked under the direct supervision of their master. Personal contacts between labor and management, therefore, were immediate. There was only so far that a master could push his slaves when they were in daily and personal contact. However, as the dictates of the cotton industry resulted in larger plantations with massive production, fore-men, called overseers, were hired to manage more and more facets of the plantations management. Their pay, in many cases even their entire tenure, was tied to the efficiency of their workers, and their total production. Under such motivations, the overseers raised quotas, and the entire system of slavery, like a modern corporation, became impersonal and increasingly ruthless.

However, no matter how it was conducted, no matter whether your master was a remote, heartless figure intent on pinching the last penny out of his investment, or a kind paternalistic soul who took an intense interest in the lives of his slaves, there was a common problem with the entire institution of slavery that could never be eradicated. They were slaves. This was a vio-lation of every human being's inalienable and God-given right to be free, and a violation of the basic tenants of the Constitution.

THE ABOLITIONISTS

An earlier antislavery movement, which sought to abolish the slave trade with Africa, won its final victory in 1808, when Congress outlawed the slave trade. After that great victory, the only voice that continued to be raised in opposition to slavery was the Quakers. Although they kept complaining, their protest was quite ineffectual and went largely ignored. While the nation slept, the cotton gin and the expansion westward of the cotton plan-tations into the Mississippi delta region was creating an increasing demand for slaves.

This situation was radically changed by the emergence of a new abolitionist movement, tied neither to the Quakers nor to the earlier groups who had ended the slave trade. These new abolitionists were militant and combative, uncompromising in their outlook, and insistent upon an immediate end to slavery. These new abolitionists found a leader in William Lloyd Garrison, a young man from Massachusetts with the crusading zeal of a demagogue.

On January 1, 1831, William Lloyd Garrison published the first issue of his newspaper, *The Liberator,* which bore the following declaration of principles: "I shall strenuously contend for the immediate enfranchisement of our slave population. On this subject I do not wish to think, or speak, or write with moderation. I am in earnest, I will not equivocate, I will not excuse, I will not retreat a single inch AND I WILL BE HEARD."

Garrison awakened Northerners to the evil among them, an institution many had long come to regard as permanent and unchangeable. His position was unequivocal: He demanded an immediate end to slavery. He held up to public gaze the most repulsive aspects of slavery, and castigated slave holders as torturers and traffickers in human life. He recognized no financial rights for the masters, he acknowledged no compromise, and he tolerated no delay. He even reproached those of his fellow abolitionists who believed that reform could be accomplished by legal and peaceful means. Garrison was joined by another powerful voice, that of Frederick Douglass, an escaped slave who galvanized Northern audiences as a spokesman for the Massachusetts Anti-Slavery Society. He later was to edit his own abolitionist weekly newspaper, the *Northern Star.*

Another group of activist abolitionists were those who ran the *Underground Railroad,* which helped runaway slaves escape first to the North, and then over the border into Canada, where slavery was completely and totally illegal. Once in Canada, the slave was free, and would not be returned, since the U.S. fugitive slave laws did not apply in Canada. By the 1830s, the railroad was firmly established in all parts of the North, but was most successful in Ohio, Indiana, and Illinois, where the route to Canada was shorter. In Ohio alone, in the thirty years before the Civil War, more than 40,000 fugitive slaves crossed the state to freedom.

STRICTLY DEFINED

The **Underground Railroad,** although it was called a "railroad," was really an elaborate network of secret routes. The system received its name around 1831, in honor of the newly invented steam railroads. The system even used terms used in railroading: The homes and businesses where fugitives would rest and eat were called "stations" and "depots" and were run by "stationmasters," those who contributed money or goods were "stockholders," and the "conductor" was responsible for moving fugitives from one station to the next.

In 1835, an angry mob destroyed abolitionist literature in the post office in Charleston, South Carolina, which is federal property. When the postmaster, a southerner, announced he would not enforce delivery of abolitionist material, a bitter debate ensued in Congress. Many argued that this issue had nothing to do with slavery, it concerned the cause of civil liberties for whites, and their right to federal services. Many thought that the federal government should intervene, to ensure that no group of private citizens could deprive others of their constitutional rights.

Another issue was a ban on slavery in the District of Columbia. Because it was not a state, such an issue had to be decided by Congress, and abolitionists decided to flood Congress with petitions calling for the ban. In 1836, the House of Representatives, tired of the debate required whenever such a petition arrived, voted to table them automatically, thus effectively killing any further debate on the issue. Former President John Quincy Adams, who had been serving in the House of Representatives since 1830, thought this "gag rule" was a violation of the First Amendment. The House finally repealed the gag rule in 1844.

Despite all the hoopla, the average person in the North knew or cared little about slavery, and certainly would never have gone to war over the issue. Some, in fact, were actively opposed to the abolitionist movement. For example, in 1837, a mob attacked and killed the antislavery editor Elijah P. Lovejoy in Alton, Illinois.

REMEMBER THE ALAMO!

Americans, in their westward movement, had settled in large numbers in the Mexican province of Texas, and some had even received large land grants from the Mexican government. However, their increasing numbers, which showed no signs of abating, soon alarmed the authorities in Mexico City, and in reaction they prohibited further American immigration.

However, it was when the government of Mexico was taken over by General Antonio Lopez de Santa Anna, and he set himself up as dictator, that the Texans revolted. Although Santa Anna completely destroyed the rebels who were defending the Alamo in early 1836, the remaining Texas revolutionaries rallied under Sam Houston. They destroyed the Mexican army and captured Santa Anna at the Battle of San Jacinto, and declared their independence. Texas, as an independent republic, petitioned for admittance to the Union, and was admitted as the twenty-eighth state in 1845.

FYI The Alamo was an abandoned Spanish mission on the outskirts of San Antonio that was fortified by a band of 189 Texas volunteers in defiance of Santa Anna's invading army. These patriots defied the 7,000-man Mexican army for "13 days of glory," a siege that lasted from February 23 to March 6, 1836. Finally overwhelmed, the Alamo defenders died to the last man, including such famous figures as William Travis, the commander, Davy Crockett, the Congressman and explorer, and adventurer Jim Bowie, the inventor of the Bowie knife. The defenders sold their lives dearly, the cost to the Mexican forces was dreadful. Colonel Juan Almonte, an aide to Santa Anna, privately noted: "One more such glorious victory and we are finished."

Although Mexico broke off relations with the United States over the issue of Texas statehood, the most contentious issue was the new state's border. Texas claimed the Rio Grande River, Mexico argued that the border stood far to the north along the Nueces River. Meanwhile, settlers were flooding into the territories of New Mexico and California at a time when many Americans claimed that they had a "manifest destiny" to expand the boundaries of the United States westward all the way to the Pacific Ocean.

The United States approached Mexico with an offer to purchase the New Mexico and California territories, but they were rebuffed. When Mexican and U.S. troops clashed along the Rio Grande, the United States declared war in 1846. While the U.S. army, supported by the navy, invaded Mexico, the settlers in California, Hispanic and Americans alike, rose up in revolt against the despotic Mexican rule. General Zachary Taylor won victories at Monterey and Buena Vista, and then General Winfield Scott landed near Vera Cruz on Mexico's east coast, and after a series of heavy engagements, captured the capital at Mexico City. With the resignation of Santa Anna, peace was established with the Treaty of Guadalupe Hildago.

JUST A MINUTE

At the end of the Mexican War, the United States gained new territory encompassing the present-day states of Arizona, Nevada, California, Utah, and parts of New Mexico, Colorado, and Wyoming. Even though the territory had already been conquered, in the peace treaty the United States went ahead and paid Mexico for it, at a cost of $15 million.

The war proved to be a training ground for officers who would later fight on both sides in the Civil War. Both Ulysses S. Grant and Robert E. Lee, as well as many others who would be generals during the Civil War, served as junior officers in Mexico.

YET ANOTHER COMPROMISE

The new territories created a new problem. Until 1845, the Missouri Compromise of 1820 had ensured that slavery would be confined to the areas where it already existed. The new territories made the renewed expansion of slavery a real likelihood.

Northerners believed that if slavery were contained, and not allowed to spread, it would ultimately decline and fade away. To justify their opposition to adding new slave stars to the American flag, they pointed to the antislavery statements of Washington and Jefferson, who had already become icons in American folklore, and to the Ordinance of 1787, which had forbid slavery in the Northwest Territory.

Southerners considered the expansion of slavery a necessity, because cultivating cotton rapidly exhausted the soil, and the plantation owners needed new and fertile lands. Moreover, to protect their "peculiar institution," the South believed it needed additional slave states to offset the admission of new free states, to keep their balance of power in the Senate.

Texas, which had permitted slavery as a republic, was allowed to enter the Union as a slave state. But California, New Mexico and Utah did not have slavery. Extremists in the South urged that all the lands acquired from Mexico be thrown open to slave holders. Antislavery Northerners, as was to be expected, demanded that all the new regions be closed to slavery.

Another compromise was clearly necessary. One group of moderates suggested that the line of the Missouri Compromise be extended to the Pacific, with free states to the north and slave states to the south. Another group proposed that the question be left to "popular sovereignty," permitting the settlers to vote for themselves as to whether to organize the region as a slave or a free state.

Southern opinion, following their belief in states rights, held that all the territories had the right to determine for themselves whether to permit slavery. The North, which always ran contrary on this issue, asserted that no territories had the right to make this decision. The border state regions of Maryland, Kentucky, and Missouri, reflecting their mixed populations, were divided on the issue.

JUST A MINUTE

In 1848, nearly 300,000 men voted for the candidates of the Free-Soil Party, who declared that the best policy was "to limit, localize and discourage slavery."

The discovery of gold in California accelerated the issue, as more than 80,000 "forty-niners" arrived in the territory in 1849, making them qualified for statehood immediately. California was a crucial question, for clearly Congress had to determine the status of this new region before any organized government could be established. Everyone looked to Senator Henry Clay, who twice before in times of crisis had come forward with the necessary compromise.

Henry Clay's Compromise of 1850, as finally passed by Congress, provided that California would be admitted with a free state constitution; that the remainder of the new annexation, the territories of New Mexico and Utah, would be organized without any mention of which way they would go on the slavery issue; that more effective procedures would be established for apprehending runaway slaves and returning them to their masters; and that the buying and selling of slaves would be abolished in the District of Columbia.

The compromise seemed to once again settle the slavery problem. However, the new Fugitive Slave Law was a great point of contention with many in the North, who did not want to have anything to do with the catching and returning of slaves. In direct defiance of the new law, Northerners continued to help fugitives escape via the Underground Railroad.

A NATION DIVIDED AGAINST ITSELF

In 1852, Harriet Beecher Stowe published *Uncle Tom's Cabin*, a novel she was provoked to write by the passage of the Fugitive Slave Law. Its publication caused a sensation, and more than 300,000 copies were sold the first year, as the presses ran day and night to keep up with the demand.

The front piece in the original edition of Uncle Tom's Cabin.

Although overly sentimental in places, and full of stereotypes, *Uncle Tom's Cabin* portrayed the cruelty of slavery, and the fundamental differences between free and slave societies. Voters in the North were deeply stirred by the work, and it inspired widespread support for the antislavery cause.

The Compromise of 1850, barely three years old, was already falling apart. New territories, Kansas and Nebraska, were being settled more rapidly then anyone had foreseen, and pressure was increasing for the establishment of territorial governments.

Under the terms of the Missouri Compromise of 1820, Kansas was closed to slavery. However, Missouri was a slave state, and it objected to being bordered by three free-soil neighbors, Illinois, Iowa, and Kansas. They feared that their state would eventually be forced to become a free state as well. Missourians in Congress, backed by the Southern states, blocked all efforts to organize the region.

Stephen A. Douglas, the Democratic senior senator from Illinois, proposed the Kansas-Nebraska Act. Douglas argued that the Compromise of 1850, which had left Utah and New Mexico free to resolve the slavery issue for themselves, superseded the Missouri Compromise. Therefore, Kansas should also be free to makes its own decision. His plan called for two territories, Kansas and Nebraska, into which settlers could bring slaves. The inhabitants themselves would then determine whether they should enter the Union as free or slave states, in the same manner as Utah and New Mexico.

The bill enraged the free-soil supporters. Those in the north accused Douglas of looking for southern votes in the upcoming presidential race in 1856. The free-soil press violently denounced it. Northern clergymen assailed it. Businessmen who had previously been friendly to the South did an abrupt about-face.

FYI Douglas should never have introduced the Kansas-Nebraska Act. When he subsequently went to Chicago, to speak in his own defense, the ships in the harbor lowered their flags to half-mast, the church bells tolled for an hour, and a crowd of 10,000 hooted so loudly that he could not make himself heard.

Despite the violent backlash, the Kansas-Nebraska Act managed to pass and be enacted into law. The flow of Southern slave holders and antislavery families into Kansas resulted in armed conflict, and soon the territory was being called "bloody Kansas."

The Kansas-Nebraska Act signaled the death-knell of the Whig Party, which had never been able to take a stand against slavery. Its place in the two-party system of American politics was taken by a powerful new organization, the

Republican Party, who stood firmly on the position that slavery be excluded from all the territories. In 1856, this new party nominated John Fremont, who was famous for his expeditions into the Far West. Although Fremont lost the election, the new Republican Party took most of the Northern states, and had positioned itself as a powerful new force in American politics.

WHAT DRED HATH SCOTT WROUGHT?

Dred Scott was a Missouri slave who had lived with his master for 20 years in Illinois and Wisconsin, states where slavery had been banned by the Northwest Ordinance. When his master took him back to Missouri, Scott sued for his freedom on the ground that he had resided on free soil.

The Supreme Court, which was dominated by Southerners, decided that Scott did not have the right to even bring the action because he was not a citizen, that the laws of Illinois had no effect on his status because he was a resident of Missouri, and that slave owners could take "property" anywhere and they would still remain slaves.

That should have been enough to find against Scott and end the case, but they went on and also stated that Congress did not have the power to restrict the expansion of slavery. The Supreme Court, in one really bad decision, invalidated the entire history of compromises by which Congress for a generation had sought to control the tempestuous slavery issue. The Dred Scott decision stirred fierce resentment throughout the North. Never before had the Supreme Court been so bitterly condemned.

HOUR'S UP!

1. The Alamo was all of the following except:

    A. It was not originally built as a fort, but as a Spanish mission

    B. The battle in which Jim Bowie and Davy Crockett were both killed

    C. For 13 days, the 189 defenders of the Alamo fought a Mexican army of 7,000

    D. A great victory for Texans in their fight for independence from Mexico

2. *Uncle Tom's Cabin* was all of the following except:

    A. Written by Harriet Beecher Stowe

    B. Portrayed the cruelty of slavery

C. Inspired by the passage of the Fugitive Slave Law

D. Published right after the end of the Civil War

3. The California "Gold Rush" was:

　A. A really, really groovy high you get from a drug called "Gold Dust"

　B. A San Francisco counterculture band

　C. The original name for the "Solid Gold" dancers

　D. Miners, forty-niners, and their daughter, Clementine

4. "Abolitionists" wanted to:

　A. Abolish the income tax

　B. Prevent illegal immigration

　C. End slavery

　D. Prohibit both the importation and the consumption of alcohol

5. In the "Dred Scott" Supreme Court decision, all of the following is true except:

　A. The Supreme Court was packed with Southerners.

　B. The court held that a slave was property and did not have the right to bring a lawsuit.

　C. Congress did not have the right to limit the spread of slavery into new states.

　D. As a slave, Dred Scott did not have the right to travel on the Underground Railroad.

Hour 11

Sectional Conflict

Chapter Summary

LESSON PLAN:

In this hour, you will learn what pushed the South to finally secede from the Union, the major battles and campaigns of the Civil War, and explore the peace movements and draft riots of the Civil War.

You will also learn ...

- Who ran at Bull Run.
- Why John Brown is moldering in his grave.
- Who besides Lincoln was at his Gettysburg Address.
- What happened at Appomattox Courthouse.

The struggle over slavery and states rights, which had been a contentious issue between the North and South ever since the conclusion of the Revolution, finally erupted into open warfare in 1861, with the election of Abraham Lincoln, the Republican candidate. The Civil War was a long and bloody conflict, made all the more tragic because it was a war of brother against brother, American against American. The North had the advantage of a greater population from which to recruit an army, and the majority of the country's industrial capacity. The South had the advantage of fighting a defensive war, and a long military tradition that gave it a decided edge in the early years of the conflict. However, in the end, the overwhelming superiority of the North was sufficient to drive old Dixie down, and to preserve the Union.

Lincoln and Douglas Debate

Abraham Lincoln had long regarded slavery as an evil. In a speech in Peoria, Illinois, in 1854, which thrust him into the national spotlight for the first time, he declared that all national legislation should adhere to the principle that slavery must be first restricted and then gradually abolished. He rejected the principle of popular sovereignty for the new Western states because slavery was not only the concern of the local citizens but affected the entire country.

Abraham Lincoln, during his debates with Douglas, said, "A house divided against itself cannot stand. I believe this government cannot endure permanently half slave and half free. I do not expect the Union to be dissolved, I do not expect the house to fall, but I do expect it will cease to be divided."

In 1858, Lincoln ran for the senate in Illinois against Stephen A. Douglas. They engaged in a series of seven well-publicized debates during the course of the campaign. Senator Douglas, known as the "Little Giant," had a great reputation as an orator and debater, but he had met his match in Lincoln, who challenged Douglas's concept of popular sovereignty. Although Douglas ultimately won the election, Lincoln in the process became a national figure, who would be on everyone's mind at the next Republican national convention.

JOHN BROWN'S BODY

John Brown was a militant antislavery fanatic who three years before had captured and killed five proslavery settlers in "bloody" Kansas. He firmly believed that he had been ordained as an instrument of God to smite those who engaged in slavery. On the night of October 16, 1859, John Brown led a band of followers in an attack on the federal arsenal at Harper's Ferry, in what is now the state of West Virginia. His goal was to seize the weapons and use them to arm slaves in an uprising against their masters. After two days of fighting, Brown and his surviving men were taken prisoner by a force of U.S. Marines commanded by Colonel Robert E. Lee.

FYI During a visit to Washington, D.C., in the autumn of 1861, poet Julia Ward Howe attended a public parade and review of Union troops. On her way back to Willard's Hotel her carriage was delayed by marching regiments. To pass the time, she and her cohorts in the carriage sang a few of the war songs so popular those days, among them, "John Brown's Body," which contained the provocative words, "John Brown's body lies-a-moldering in the ground. His soul is marching on." The morning after hearing the song, Julia Ward Howe wrote her own words to the tune. Soon after, it was published in the *Atlantic Monthly* as "The Battle Hymn of the Republic," and did indeed become the anthem of the Union Army.

John Brown's attempt to start a revolution, while thwarted, seriously shocked the nation. Southerners saw in the abortive uprising their worst fears of a slave revolt realized. Northerners were also alarmed, seeing it as an assault on law and order. He was tried for conspiracy, treason and murder, and was hung on December 2, 1859. Antislavery zealots hailed Brown as a martyr to the great cause.

THE WAR BETWEEN THE YANKEES AND THE AMERICANS

In 1860, the Republican Party nominated Abraham Lincoln as its candidate for president. The party was united behind a platform that called for an end to the spread of slavery, a tariff for the protection of industry, and free homesteads to settlers in the West. The Democrats were not so united, as the party split North and South. The southern Democrats nominated Vice President John C. Breckenridge of Kentucky for president. The northern Democrats nominated Stephen A. Douglas. The Whigs, who had virtually disappeared as a party, formed into the Constitutional Union Party, and nominated John C. Bell of Tennessee.

JUST A MINUTE

Today we call it the Civil War, but in those days both sides had their own name for it. The North called it the War of the Rebellion, the South called it the War for Southern Independence, or the War Between the States. If they couldn't agree on the name of the war, it was obviously impossible for them to agree on the subject of slavery. Granny Clampett (on TV's *Beverly Hillbillies*) called it the war between the Yankees and the Americans.

Lincoln won only 39 percent of the popular vote, but carried all 18 free states, and with them a clear majority of 180 electoral votes. Even though he had the second highest number of popular votes, Douglas received very few electoral votes. The other two candidates split the south: Bell won Tennessee, Kentucky, and Virginia, while Breckenridge took the other slave states except for Missouri, which was won by Douglas.

South Carolina had been waiting for an event that would unite the South. When Lincoln was elected, South Carolina declared "that the Union now subsisting between South Carolina and other states under the name of the 'United States of America' is hereby dissolved." Following their lead, by February 1, 1861, six more Southern states adopted similar resolutions of secession. Uniting together, these seven states, calling themselves the Confederate States of America, adopted their own constitution.

On March 4, 1861, Abraham Lincoln was sworn in as the new president of the United States. In his inaugural address, he called the secession of the seven states "legally void." Under the Constitution, states could join the union, but once admitted, they could not legally leave. He appealed for the states to voluntarily come back into the Union, and nullify their resolutions of secession. However, that was a futile appeal, as events had progressed beyond such a solution. On April 12, the Southerners opened fire on the federal troops stationed at Fort Sumter in the harbor of Charleston, South Carolina.

JUST A MINUTE

More Americans would die in the Civil War than any other war in United States history, primarily because Americans died on both sides of the conflict. The Union lost twice as many men as the Confederacy, the high cost of fighting an offensive war. It is unlikely that this country will ever again see a conflict as costly as the War Between the States.

Events progressed quickly. Jefferson Davis became the president of the Confederate States of America. Virginia seceded, followed by Arkansas, Tennessee, and North Carolina, bringing the total of states in revolt to 11. The decision was especially difficult in Virginia, which had looked upon the United States as their own creation, and the vote actually split the state. Virginia joined the Confederacy, and those counties who voted against secession split off and formed the new state of West Virginia.

Still hanging in the balance were the border states. Delaware, Maryland, Kentucky, and Missouri all had slavery, and thus strong ties to the Southern cause, but that segment of the population was never dominant enough to take control of the state, and they remained loyal to the Union. Despite remaining in the Union, however, Maryland, Kentucky, Missouri, and West Virginia still raised regiments for the South, with the result that these borders states had regiments fighting in both the Union and Confederate armies.

JUST A MINUTE

The North had the decided advantage. The North had 23 states with a population of 22 million, while the South only had 11 states with a population of 9 million.

Each side had advantages. The Union had industrial superiority, with factories for manufacturing arms and ammunition, uniforms, and other war supplies. They also had a far better network of railways. The Confederacy had the advantage of fighting a defensive war on its own territory, and had a stronger military tradition, with more experienced military leaders.

RUN BULL, RUN

The first large battle of the war, near Washington, D.C., at Bull Run, Virginia, made it clear that it was going to be a long and bloody war. It was a decided Confederate victory, with the Union army retreating in confusion back toward Washington. It was to be the first in a long line of Southern victories, which unfortunately never translated into a decisive military advantage.

The Union needed a clear plan for victory. The first part of that strategy was a blockade of the Southern ports. Most of the Navy was in Union hands, and Secretary of the Navy Gideon Welles immediately embarked on a program to expand the Navy. Although the effect of the blockade was at first negligible, by 1863 it had virtually stopped the shipment of cotton to Europe, and also halted the importation of munitions, clothing, and medical supplies that were critical to South victory.

The Union had two great naval victories under Admiral David Farragut. In the first, he took a Union fleet into the mouth of the Mississippi River and captured the city of New Orleans, which put into Federal control the mouth of the Mississippi River. In the second, he captured a Confederate ironclad vessel at Mobile Bay, Alabama, and sealed up the port.

QUOTABLE QUOTES

Admiral Farragut uttered his famous words at the battle of Mobile Bay, "Damn the torpedoes! Full speed ahead!"

In the Mississippi valley, the Union army began by taking the important Mississippi River port of Memphis, which gave them effective control of western Tennessee. General Ulysses S. Grant's army advanced quickly through Tennessee until they were stopped at the battle of Shiloh. However, the arrival of federal reinforcements allowed him to ultimately defeat the Confederates, and continue their advance into the South.

JUST A MINUTE

The total number of those killed, wounded, and missing as a result of the two days of fighting at Shiloh numbered more than 24,000, a casualty rate that shocked both nations. But it was only the beginning.

In Virginia, the Union forces attempted a succession of bloody campaigns in an attempt to capture Richmond, the Confederate capital, but they were repeatedly defeated. The Confederates had a geographical advantage, they were fighting a defensive war, and numerous streams which crossed the road between Washington and Richmond provided excellent bastions. In addition, Robert E. Lee and Thomas J. ("Stonewall") Jackson were excellent generals. In 1862, the Union commander, George McClellan, made a slow, cautious attempt to seize Richmond. But in a succession of battles between June 25 and July 1, the Union troops were stopped, and both sides suffered terrible losses.

The Tomb of the Unknown Soldier at Arlington Cemetery is watched over day and night by the elite 3rd U.S. Infantry, known as the "Old Guard."

 FYI The property that is now Arlington Cemetery was originally Arlington Plantation, the home of General Robert E. Lee. Because it overlooked Washington, D.C., it was seized by the Union army, and the plantation house became a Union hospital. As soldiers died, they were buried on the grounds. After the war, the Lee family sued for return of their property, and won in the Supreme Court. However, with thousands of burials, it was only fit to be a federal cemetery, and the Lee family ultimately sold it to the federal government for $150,000.

Lee scored another Confederate victory at the Second Battle of Bull Run, crossed the Potomac River, and invaded Maryland. McClellan moved slowly and with hesitancy to meet him, even though he knew that Lee had split his army and was heavily outnumbered. The Union and Confederate armies finally clashed at the Battle of Antietam, near Sharpsburg, Maryland. However, McClellan failed to break Lee's lines or press the attack, and Lee was able to successfully retreat across the Potomac with his army intact. Furious at the escape of the rebel army, Lincoln fired McClellan.

JUST A MINUTE

One day at Antietam, September 17, 1862, was the single bloodiest day of the war. More than 4,000 died on both sides and 18,000 were wounded.

Although Antietam was inconclusive in military terms, its consequences were disastrous for the Confederacy. Both Great Britain and France had been on the verge of recognizing the new country. They now once more equivocated, and ultimately, neither would ever recognize the rebel government. Without that diplomatic recognition, aid from Europe that the Confederacy desperately needed never materialized.

THE EMANCIPATION PROCLAMATION

In December 1861, Congress had formed the Joint Committee on the Conduct of the War, which was bent on finding someone to blame for the poor performance of the Union army at Bull Run and other battles. The committee was soon dominated by radical Republicans, and they began to push Lincoln toward emancipation.

Lincoln had been waiting for a Union victory to issue the Emancipation Proclamation, and Antietam was close enough. The proclamation declared that all the slaves in the 11 states that were in rebellion were set free. Of course, it did not really set them free, because the North did not have the control of the Confederate states that it needed to enforce its proclamation. Contrary to popular belief, the proclamation did not free the slaves in the border states. However, it now made the abolition of slavery a stated war aim of the Union. Previously, the United States had fought the war solely on the principle of preserving the Union.

Lincoln issued a second Emancipation Proclamation on January 1, 1863. Previously, the Union army did not know what to do with escaped slaves who came into their lines. Their only official status had been as "contraband of war," which technically meant that they were still slaves, only now the property of the federal government. Following the first Emancipation Proclamation, they were free, but they still could not join the army. This new proclamation authorized the recruitment of blacks into the Union army, which abolitionist leaders such as Frederick Douglass had been trying to implement since the beginning of the war. The Union army now set about recruiting and training regiments of black soldiers. Ultimately, more than 178,000 African Americans served in the United States Colored Troops, and 29,500 blacks served in the Union navy.

The Emancipation was far from universally accepted in the North. In both Indiana and Illinois, for example, the state legislatures passed laws calling for peace with the Confederacy and the retraction of the "wicked, inhuman and unholy" proclamation.

Caught in the Draft

The Union army, in order to conduct an offensive war and to conquer the South, was going to have to be more than twice the size of the Confederate army. Although there were many volunteers, as the war progressed, it was obvious that many more men were going to be needed. This resulted in the first compulsory draft in U.S. history. Passed in 1863, the draft was another source of complaint by the Peace Democrats, and dissent was particularly strong among the *copperheads* of Pennsylvania, Ohio, Indiana, and Wisconsin. Federal troops had to be called out in those states to enforce compliance with the draft law.

STRICTLY DEFINED

In 1861, Republicans started calling antiwar Democrats **copperheads,** likening them to the poisonous snake, biting the Union in the neck. By 1863, the Peace Democrats had accepted the label, but for them the copper "head" was the likeness of Liberty on the copper penny, and they proudly wore pennies as badges.

In the summer of 1863, resistance to the draft took a violent turn. New York City was a stronghold for the Peace Democrats, and several draft officials had already been killed that year. In July, a group of blacks were brought into the city, under police protection, to replace striking Irish longshoremen, at the same time that officials were holding a lottery for the unpopular draft. These two events, occurring together, sparked a 4-day riot in which a number of black neighborhoods, draft offices, and Protestant churches were destroyed, and at least 105 people were killed. It was necessary to bring Union regiments, from the recent battle at Gettysburg, to the city to restore order.

 FYI A man who was drafted could buy his way out for $300, the annual income in those days for an unskilled laborer. This added to the impression, which was also believed by nonslave-owning Confederate soldiers, that this was a "rich man's war and a poor man's fight."

Peaceniks and Copperheads

The Union was far from united behind President Lincoln and the war effort. Throughout his presidency, Lincoln faced serious opposition to both his political and wartime policies. The war was costly, both in men and material, and many in the North thought that the country was well rid of the South.

This antiwar movement, known as the Peace Democrats, was headed by Stephen Douglas, the former Democratic candidate for president. Even though this was only the northern half of the party, they were still the party of "popular sovereignty," and believed that full-scale war to preserve the Union was not only not justified, but violated the rights of the Southern states to determine their own destiny.

In addition, Peace Democrats were opposed to the emancipation of the slaves. In 1862, for example, virtually every Democrat in Congress voted against eliminating slavery in the District of Columbia, and from prohibiting it in the territories. This opposition to emancipation came from the working poor, particularly Irish and German Catholic immigrants, who feared a massive migration of free blacks to the North. In 1862, race riots erupted in several Northern cities.

Opposition from the Peace Democrats was interfering with the war effort, and in September 1862, Lincoln imposed martial law and suspended the writ of habeas corpus for those who interfered with recruitment or gave aid and comfort to the rebels. Secretary of War Edwin Stanton enforced martial law vigorously, and many thousands of Southern sympathizers and Democrats were arrested. This abrogation of civil law, although constitutionally justified during times of national crisis, gave the Peace Democrats yet another reason to criticize Lincoln.

GETTYSBURG AND VICKSBURG

The North's military prospects in the east remained bleak as Lee's Army of Northern Virginia continued to defeat the Union Army of the Potomac, first at Fredericksburg, Virginia, in December 1862 and then at Chancellorsville, Virginia, in May 1863.

FYI Although one of Lee's most brilliant military victories, Chancellorsville, Virginia, was also one of his most costly. Stonewall Jackson, one of the Confederate army's most valuable generals, was mistakenly shot by his own men.

Emboldened by his victory at Chancellorsville, Lee marched his army northward into Pennsylvania, in July 1863, with the hopes of forcing the Union to sue for peace. He almost reached the state capital at Harrisburg, when he encountered the Union army at Gettysburg. In a three-day battle, the largest of the Civil War, the Confederates tried to break the Union lines. After a final attempt with a charge by Pickett's division failed, Lee's army retreated back to the Potomac.

JUST A MINUTE

More than 3,000 Union soldiers and almost 4,000 Confederates died at Gettysburg; wounded and missing totaled more than 20,000 on each side.

Vicksburg was critical to the Union control of the Mississippi. The Confederates had strongly fortified themselves on high bluffs overlooking the river, which were too high for naval attack. Grant put the city under siege, and after six weeks of fighting, on July 4, he captured the city, together with the strongest Confederate army in the West. The Mississippi River was now entirely under Union control, and the Confederacy was thereby broken in two. It was now impossible to supply the Confederacy from either Texas or Arkansas.

The Northern victories at Vicksburg and Gettysburg in July 1863 marked the turning point of the war. After those two battles, it was clear that the South was defeated, although the war would drag on for more than a year.

QUOTABLE QUOTES

On November 19, 1863, Lincoln dedicated a new national cemetery at Gettysburg with perhaps the most famous address in U.S. history. He concluded his brief remarks with these words: "... we here highly resolve that these dead shall not have died in vain, that this nation, under God, shall have a new birth of freedom, and that government of the people, by the people, for the people, shall not perish from the earth."

THE PRESIDENTIAL RACE

Despite the Union victories at Vicksburg and Gettysburg in July 1863, Peace Democrats continued to play on the nation's misfortunes and racial sensitivities. Their campaign was so successful, that Lincoln was convinced he would lose his bid for reelection in November 1864.

The Peace Democrats 1864 candidate for president was George McClellan, a general that Lincoln had removed as commander of the Army of the Potomac. However, McClellan refused to endorse his own party's platform of negotiating an end to the war. In addition, by 1864, most in the North realized that the South was defeated, even if they would not themselves admit it, and that a Union victory was inevitable. Lincoln easily defeated McClellan in November, taking every Northern state except New Jersey and Delaware.

TOWARD APPOMATTOX

Lincoln realized that he only had one general who was winning battles, so he brought Grant east and made him commander in chief of all Union forces in 1864. In May, Grant advanced deep into Virginia and met Lee, for the first time, in the Battle of the Wilderness. Losses on both sides were heavy, but unlike Union commanders in the past, Grant refused to retreat. He was determined to outflank Lee, and pounded away with artillery and infantry attacks, all the while trying to maneuver around him, which stretched the Confederate line to its limit. "I propose to fight it out along this line if it takes all summer," Grant said at the battle of Spotsylvania.

QUOTABLE QUOTES

Grant was a notorious consumer of Kentucky bourbon whiskey, and he was accused of being drunk during his great battles. Responding to that criticism, at the height of the war, Lincoln supposedly said, in speaking of Grant, "Find out what brand of whiskey the man drinks, and send a case of it to each of my generals." (Grant is said to have favored Old Crow.)

Union forces gained control of Tennessee in the fall of 1863 with victories at Chattanooga and Lookout Mountain. General William T. Sherman was now poised to invade Georgia. He outmaneuvered several smaller Confederate armies, burned the state capital at Atlanta, and then marched straight to the Atlantic coast, systematically destroying railroads, factories, warehouses, and any other Confederate facility that could support the war effort. Cut off from their normal supply lines, the army was forced to live off the land, and as a result the regiments ravaged the countryside in search of food. Once he reached the Atlantic seaboard, he turned his army northward, and by February 1865, he had taken Charleston, South Carolina. Although the South always perceived of "Sherman's March to the Sea" as merely the North's revenge on the South for starting the war, Sherman's real intent was to crush the South's spirit, realizing that would lead to victory as surely as winning any battle. He was right; after his infamous march, the South's will to fight was gone.

While Sherman was devastating Georgia, Grant was laying siege to Petersburg, Virginia. In March 1865, Lee was forced to abandon both Petersburg and the Confederate capital of Richmond. He tried to retreat south, but his troops were in rags, they were starving, and ammunition was running out. Surrounded by massive Union armies, Lee realized that it was hopeless, and that any further fighting would only result in needless slaughter. He surrendered to Grant at Appomattox Courthouse. Although it would take several months for the other Confederate armies to finally surrender, the Civil War was over.

Grant, infamous for his nickname, "Unconditional Surrender," was generous in his terms at Appomattox. The men were allowed to retain their weapons and their horses. When his troops complained, Grant quieted the complaints by stating, "The rebels are our countrymen again." The war for Southern independence was over, but it would become forever enshrined in Southern folklore as the "glorious lost cause."

HOUR'S UP!

1. At Bull Run:
   A. Soldiers wearing red handkerchiefs ran with the bulls.
   B. The Union advance was slowed by bulls with the runs.
   C. Abraham Lincoln, in his famous Bull Run speech, declared he was bullish on America.
   D. The Confederates discovered that the Union army was full of bull.

2. The Emancipation Proclamation did all of the following except:
   A. Freed the slaves in the North
   B. Proclaimed the end of the Civil War
   C. Freed the slaves in the South
   D. Made the abolition of slavery a goal of the Union army

3. The Gettysburg Address was:
   A. Very important, because Lincoln wasn't getting his mail
   B. Actually in Altoona, Pennsylvania
   C. Named after John Paul Getty
   D. A speech given to dedicate the federal cemetery

4. At Appomattox Courthouse:
   A. Ulysses S. Grant was convicted of DWI, lost his license for a year, and had to pay a $1,500 fine.
   B. Robert E. Lee finally got his long-awaited divorce settlement, which included title to the Arlington Plantation.

C. Lee successfully sued the federal government for the return of his plantation, Arlington, which had been turned into a cemetery.

D. Grant and Lee signed a stipulation, in which they agreed to quit fighting.

5. The New York City Draft Riots were caused by all of the following except:

A. The first compulsory draft law in the history of the United States, passed to provide troops for the Union army

B. Black workers being brought in to New York to break a strike by Irish longshoremen

C. Students getting deferments from the draft to attend college

D. Rich kids being exempted from the draft by paying $300

QUIZ

HOUR 12

Reconstruction and Growth

CHAPTER SUMMARY

LESSON PLAN:

In this hour, you will learn about the end of the Civil War, the assassination of Abraham Lincoln, the Reconstruction of the South, and how new industries and technologies began to change the face of America.

You will also learn ...

- How an actor made things even worse for the South.

- How the victorious North went about "reconstructing" the defeated South, and brought them back into full partnership in the Union.

- How the Democrats recovered as a party after trying to tear the United States into two countries.

- How the railroad helped to open up the West.

- How new inventions and the industrial revolution turned an agricultural country of rural farmers into an industrial country of great cities.

The North had won the war, but it was now incumbent upon them to win the peace. With the Union preserved, it was Lincoln's aim to heal the wounds between North and South, but after his assassination, more radical forces in the North gained control, determined to impose a radical reconstruction on the South. The South was placed under the control of the army, and it was a number of years before the chastened Confederate states were finally able to regain their independent status as self-ruling states.

WITH MALICE TOWARD SOME

Abraham Lincoln was determined to weld the Union back together, not by force and repression but by fairness, justice, and forgiveness. In 1864, he had been elected for a second term as president, defeating his Democratic opponent, George McClellan, the general Lincoln had fired after the battle of Antietam.

QUOTABLE QUOTES

Lincoln's second inaugural address closed with these words:

> With malice toward none; with charity for all; with firmness in the right, as God gives us to see the right, let us strive on to finish the work we are in; to bind up the nation's wounds; to care for him who shall have borne the battle, and for his widow and his orphan ... to do all which may achieve and cherish a just and lasting peace among ourselves and with all nations.

On April 14, 1864, barely a month into his second term, the president and his wife attended a performance of the popular play "Our American Cousin" at Ford's Theater in Washington, D.C. While attending the theater, he was shot by John Wilkes Booth, an actor who wasn't even in the play. The next morning, Lincoln died in a downstairs bedroom of a house across the street. Several days later, while trying to escape the nationwide manhunt, Booth was killed in a shootout in a barn in the Virginia countryside. The remainder of his accomplices in the plot, including Mary Suratt, were captured and later executed.

QUOTABLE QUOTES

Poet James Russell wrote about Lincoln: "Never before that startled April morning did such multitudes of men shed tears for the death of one they had never seen, as if with him a friendly presence had been taken from their lives, leaving them colder and darker. Never was funeral panegyric so eloquent as the silent look of sympathy which strangers exchanged when, they met that day. Their common manhood had lost a kinsman."

Lincoln was succeeded by his vice president, Andrew Johnson, a Southerner who had remained loyal to the Union, had risen to become a general in the Union army, and then had become a national hero at the battle of Nashville. Lincoln had put a Southerner on the ticket as part of his reconciliation policy, and now, by a twist of fate, the Southerner was the president.

Johnson was determined to follow the policy that Lincoln had set for the reconstruction of the South. Lincoln had taken the view that the people of the Southern states had never legally seceded, instead, they had been misled by some disloyal citizens into a defiance of federal authority. Thus, in 1863, Lincoln had signed a proclamation, offering any state, if 10 percent of the voters formed a government loyal to the U.S. Constitution and acknowledged the supremacy of Congress and the president over their state, official recognition as the legal government of their state. However, Congress not only rejected this plan, but challenged Lincoln's right to even make the offer. Many members in Congress wanted to see the seceded states punished for what they had done.

Despite lack of support from Congress, Johnson proceeded to carry out Lincoln's vision for reconstruction. He used his power of presidential proclamation to appoint a governor for each of the former Confederate states, and used presidential pardons to restore political rights to large numbers of Southern citizens. The governors that he appointed convened special conventions to reorganize their state government. Johnson called upon each convention to invalidate the secession, to abolish slavery, to repudiate all debts incurred by the Confederacy, and to ratify the 13th Amendment. By the end of 1865, most states had completed this task.

In March 1865, Congress took one of its first steps to deal with the serious problem of the freed slaves, when it established the Freedmen's Bureau. Its mission was to ensure that the new citizens could learn to support themselves. To make sure there was no confusion as to the status of the freed slaves, Congress ratified the 13th Amendment to the U.S. Constitution, which abolished slavery.

 FYI   During Sherman's march to the sea, he signed an order authorizing that each slave be given "forty acres of land, and an army mule," to get them started on their new life as a free person. When they established the Freedmen's Bureau, it was thought that the "forty acres and a mule" would be continued, but instead, Congress gave all the land back to the white owners who had been in revolt.

RADICAL RECONSTRUCTION

Johnson realized that Congress had the right to deny Southern legislators their seat in the U.S. Senate or House of Representatives, under the clause of the Constitution that says "Each house shall be the judge of the ... qualifications of its own members." Northern Congressmen, lead by Thaddeus Stevens, and known as "Radical Republicans," refused to seat the South's senators and representatives. Then, Congress proceeded to implement a plan for the reconstruction of the South quite different from that envisioned by Lincoln and Johnson.

Congress had already passed the 13th Amendment to the Constitution, freeing the slaves, and now, remembering the Dred Scott decision, which had denied slaves their right of citizenship, they passed the 14th Amendment, to ensure that there would be no question as to the legal status of former slaves. The 14th Amendment states, "All persons born or naturalized in the United States and subject to the jurisdiction thereof, are citizens of the United States and of the states in which they reside."

All the states in the South, except Tennessee, refused to ratify the 14th Amendment. In some states, the vote against the amendment was unanimous. In addition, Southern state legislatures began passing the "Black Codes." The codes differed in their particular language and provisions from state to state, but they all had the same basic purpose. In order to get a job and work, blacks had to sign an annual labor contract, which included severe penalties for any violation. Children who worked were required to enter into an apprenticeship, and were subject to corporal punishment by their masters. In addition, vagrants could be sold into private service if they could not pay severe fines. In effect, these "Black Codes" were just another form of slavery, clothed in language to make the "slaves" look like employees.

Those in the North were enraged, and it seemed that only radical measures against the Southern states would result in equal treatment for all the freed slaves. Congress passed the Reconstruction Act of March 1867, which invalidated the governments that had been organized in the Southern states, divided the South into five military districts, and placed them under the army. These states would only be released from military rule, and allowed to establish civil governments, if they took an oath of allegiance, ratified the 14th Amendment, and adopted black suffrage.

This was followed by the 15th Amendment, which was ratified in 1870, and which ensured that the slaves, who were now citizens, would be able to vote. It provided that, "The rights of citizens of the United States to vote shall not be denied or abridged by the United States or any state on account of race, color or previous condition of servitude."

The Radical Republicans in Congress were slowly getting their way on the Constitutional amendments to ensure black citizenship and suffrage, but President Johnson was using his veto on provisions designed to punish former Confederate leaders, such as depriving them of the right to hold office. Congressional antagonism to Johnson reached such a fever pitch, that for the first time in American history, Congress began impeachment proceedings to remove him from office.

FYI Since the adoption of the Constitution, only two presidents, Andrew Johnson and Bill Clinton, have been brought to trial in the Senate on charges voted by the House. The Senate failed by one vote to convict Andrew Johnson in 1868. In December 1998, the full House voted to impeach President Bill Clinton on charges of perjury and obstruction of justice arising from his relationship with Monica Lewinsky. Clinton's trial by the Senate began in January 1999. On February 12, he was acquitted by a vote of 55–45 on the first charge and 50–50 on the second.

The leaders in Congress were in search of a legal charge they could bring against Johnson, and they found one in his alleged violation of the Tenure of Office Act, which required Senate approval for the removal of any office-holder the Senate had previously confirmed. Johnson had removed the secretary of war from his cabinet, and they alleged that this violated the act. However, many senators realized that they were treading on delicate Constitutional ground, and it would be a dangerous precedent if Congress could remove a president just because he disagreed with the Senate. In addition, it was obvious that if the actual appointment of a cabinet member was done by the president, he inherently had the right to fire them as well. The attempted impeachment therefore failed to muster enough votes, and Johnson continued in office until the end of his term.

Congress, by the end of June 1869, in conformance with the Military Reconstruction Act, had readmitted to the Union Arkansas, North Carolina, South Carolina, Louisiana, Georgia, Alabama, and Florida. In these seven reconstructed states, the majority of the governors, representatives, and senators were *carpetbaggers*. In the legislatures of Louisiana and South Carolina, African Americans actually gained a majority of the seats. The remaining three Southern states, Mississippi, Texas, and Virginia, finally accepted the reconstruction terms, and were readmitted to the Union in 1870.

STRICTLY DEFINED

Carpetbaggers was an epithet used in the South after the Civil War to describe Northerners who went to the South during Reconstruction to make money. Although regarded as transients because of the cheap bags made of carpet in which they carried their possessions (hence the name carpetbaggers), most intended to settle in the South and to take advantage of speculative and commercial opportunities there. With the support of the black vote, the carpetbaggers played an important role in the Republican state governments. The corrupt activities of some later made the term carpetbagger synonymous with any outsider who meddles in an area's political affairs for his own personal financial benefit.

Southern whites, having failed by legal means to resubjugate their former black slaves, and seeing their political and social dominance threatened, turned to illegal and violent means to prevent blacks from gaining equality. In 1870, increasing disorder led to the passage of the Enforcement Act, designed to punish severely those who attempted to deprive black freedmen of their civil rights.

THE END OF RECONSTRUCTION

In May 1872, Congress passed a general Amnesty Act, restoring full civil and political rights to all but several hundred leading Confederate officers and officials. With the former Confederates once more enfranchised, the Southern states began electing members of the Democratic Party to office, ousting carpetbagger governments, and intimidating blacks from voting or attempting to hold public office. Four years later, the Republicans remained in power in only three Southern states.

The South had ejected the federal troops and regained control of their own state governments, but it was still a region devastated by war, burdened by debt, and demoralized by a decade of racial warfare. The Southern states now began to institute new and even more humiliating methods of discrimination against freed blacks. The last quarter of the nineteenth century saw a profusion of *Jim Crow laws* implemented in the Southern states. These laws segregated public schools, limited black access to many public facilities, such as parks, restaurants and hotels, and effectively denied blacks the right to vote by the imposition of poll taxes and literacy tests.

STRICTLY DEFINED

Jim Crow laws were statutes enacted by Southern states that legalized segregation between blacks and whites. The term originated in a song, "Jim Crow," popularized by Thomas Dartmouth "Daddy" Rice. Rice overheard an old black slave singing the song, and in 1828 he appeared on stage as "Jim Crow," an exaggerated, highly stereotypical black character. Rice, a white man, was one of the first performers to wear blackface makeup. His Jim Crow song-and-dance routine was an astounding success around the country, and he also performed to great acclaim in London and Dublin. "Jim Crow" became a stock character in minstrel shows, along with Jim Dandy and Zip Coon. White audiences loved portrayals of blacks as singing, dancing, grinning fools. By 1838, the term "Jim Crow" was being used as a derogatory collective racial epithet for African Americans.

The North failed completely to address the economic problems faced by the freedmen. Efforts such as the Freedmen's Bureau proved inadequate to the desperate needs of former slaves for institutions that could provide them with political and economic opportunity, let alone protect them from violence and intimidation. Blacks needed the North to protect them from white Southerners, who united into organizations such as the Ku Klux Klan. These groups intimidated blacks and prevented them from exercising their rights. Without economic resources of their own, Southern blacks were forced to become tenant farmers on land owned by their former masters. This pushed them into a cycle of poverty that would continue well into the twentieth century.

During the period of Reconstruction, the Republican governments did make real gains in rebuilding the devastated Southern states, expanding public services, and establishing tax-supported, free public schools for blacks and whites. However, as soon as the Democratic Southerners recovered their power, they set about reversing most of the gains achieved by the freedmen. The failure of Reconstruction meant that the African American struggle for equality and freedom, which many had thought had been accomplished by the Civil War, would not occur for another century.

TECHNOLOGY CHANGES THE WORLD

The Civil War, like most wars, stimulated manufacturing and industry, science and invention. As early as 1844, Samuel F. B. Morse had invented electrical telegraphy, which quickly linked the continent with its first communications network. In 1876, Alexander Graham Bell invented the first telephone, and within half a century, 16 million telephones would quicken the social and economic life of the nation.

The growth of business was speeded by the invention of the typewriter in 1867, the adding machine in 1888, and the cash register in 1897. The linotype machine, invented in 1886, in conjunction with the rotary press and paper-folding machinery, made it possible to print 240,000 eight-page newspapers in an hour. Thomas Edison's invention of the incandescent lamp would light up millions of homes. The talking machine, or phonograph, was also perfected by Edison, who, in conjunction with George Eastman, helped develop the motion picture. Science and invention resulted in a new level of productivity in every field.

JUST A MINUTE

Americans are inventors. Before the Civil War, 36,000 patents were granted; in the next 30 years, 440,000 patents were issued, and in the first quarter of the twentieth century, the number reached nearly a million.

Industry was also on the move. The nation's most basic industries, iron and steel, forged ahead, protected from foreign competition by a high tariff. Previously concentrated in the Eastern states, especially Pittsburgh, the iron industry moved west with the discovery of new ore deposits, particularly the great Mesabi Iron Range at the head of Lake Superior. This ore was on the surface and inexpensive to mine. Virtually free of chemical impurities, it could be processed into steel of superior quality at about one tenth the previously prevailing cost, and this area was soon one of the largest iron producers in the world.

THE MAN OF STEEL

Andrew Carnegie was the man most responsible for the great advances in steel production. Carnegie, who had come to America from Scotland as a child of 12, had worked at a variety of jobs to support himself, such as bobbin boy in a cotton factory, and telegrapher for the Pennsylvania Railroad.

Before he was 30 years old, through a series of shrewd and farsighted invest-ments, he had organized or had stock in companies making iron bridges, rails, and locomotives. Ten years later, the steel mill he built on the Monongahela River in Pennsylvania was the largest in the country.

Carnegie was intent on acquiring total vertical control of the steel business. He not only acquired mills, but also coke and coal properties, iron ore from Lake Superior, a fleet of steamers on the Great Lakes, a port town on Lake Erie and a connecting railroad. His business, allied with a dozen others, could demand and receive favorable terms from both railroads and shipping lines. Nothing comparable in vertical integration and industrial growth had ever been seen in America.

FYI Andrew Carnegie made a lot of money, and one place he spent it was on his well-known Carnegie libraries. Like everything else about the man, this was not outright philanthropy, it was a business deal. Carnegie gave the town enough cash to build the library, but the town had to agree to shell out an amount equal to 10 percent of that gift each year for upkeep, utilities and books. Unlike benefactors today, Carnegie did not demand naming rights. His preference was to place "over the entrance, a representation of the rays of the rising sun, and above 'LET THERE BE LIGHT.'" Carnegie built 2,811 free libraries. Of these, 1,946 were in the United States, 660 in Britain and Ireland, and 156 in Canada. A handful of the free libraries are also scattered in places like New Zealand, the West Indies, and even Fiji.

Even though Carnegie dominated the industry, and realized the value of the synergy of total vertical integration combined with a complete monopoly, he never achieved his goal of complete and total control over the natural resources, transportation, and industrial plants needed to make steel. In the 1890s, new companies emerged to challenge his position, but Carnegie, now an old man, instead of fighting these challengers, was persuaded to merge his holdings, and thereby to create an organization that would include most of the important iron and steel properties in the nation. In the end, Carnegie only saw his vision realized through the merger which created the United States Steel Corporation, called U.S. Steel.

Big Business and Smoggy Cities

U.S. Steel, which resulted from this 1901 merger, was symptomatic of a trend in American business which had been under way for 30 years: the combination of smaller, independent industrial enterprises into large central-ized corporations. This process had begun during the Civil War, spurred by the demand for increased industrial output to arm, clothe, and feed the mammoth Union army. After the war, the trend toward larger corporations gathered momentum as businessmen looked to find ways to hedge against overproduction, which inevitably led to declining prices and falling profits. They realized that if they could control both production and the markets, they could bring competing firms into a single organization. The "corporation" and the "trust" were developed to achieve just those ends.

Corporations changed the way that Americans did business. Previously, most businesses were small and family run, and thus were extremely vulnerable to changes in the business environment. Corporations, operating with large amounts of capital, were able to withstand downturns in sales, and in reaction to market changes, they could retool, reorganize, and continue to make handsome profits. Such qualities attracted more investors, who realized that their investment was relatively safe, because of the size of the corporation. Additional capital from these investors meant even more expansion, more stability, and more profits.

Trusts were an extension of this concept taken to a higher level. Trusts were combinations of corporations, managed by a board of trustees, which by definition were even more capital intensive, more stable, and able to garner even more profits. Such trusts made possible economies of scale, large-scale combinations, centralized control and administration, and the pooling of patents. Their great capital resources enabled expansion, made it possible for them to compete with foreign business organizations, and to drive hard bargains with organized labor, which was beginning to become a potent force of its own. Such large organizations could also exact favorable terms from railroads, and through their lobbyists obtain favorable legislation.

FYI Rockefeller, like Carnegie, liked a cooperative and conditional system of philanthropy, in which he would supply part of the sum needed for a particular project, if the others interested in it would also provide substantial financial support. It was on such a basis that Rockefeller participated in the founding of the University of Chicago. Rockefeller offered to give $600,000 of the first $1 million for endowment, provided the remaining $400,000 was pledged by others within 90 days. You can take the man out of business, but you can't take the businessman out of the man.

The Standard Oil Company, founded by John D. Rockefeller, was one of the earliest examples of the large corporation. Other industries soon followed his example, and such large organizations were created in the cottonseed oil, lead, sugar, tobacco, and rubber industries. Four great meat packers, two of whom were Philip Armour and Gustavus Swift, created a beef trust. Cyrus McCormick made a better reaper, and gained control of the reaper business.

A survey taken just after the turn of the century showed that more than 5,000 corporations had been consolidated into just 300 industrial trusts.

Western Union, the earliest communications company, was followed by the Bell Telephone System and the American Telephone and Telegraph Company. Cornelius Vanderbilt began by consolidating 13 separate railroads into a single line connecting New York City and Buffalo. He then proceeded to acquire lines to Chicago, Illinois, and Detroit, creating in the end the New York Central Railroad. Other railroad consolidations were also occurring, and soon the nation was organized into a handful of trunk lines.

The city arose out of this new industrial order, in fact the two went hand in hand. The modern city brought together the various economic forces needed to make the large corporations and trusts work: massive accumulations of capital, business and financial institutions, railroad yards, factories, and hordes of factory workers. These cities were magnets that drew people from Europe, and from the countryside with the promise of higher paying jobs and a more exciting life than was possible in rural villages. There was no city in America before the Civil War with a population of one million, but 30 years later New York, Chicago, and Philadelphia could claim populations of that size or larger.

JUST A MINUTE

In 1830, only 1 of every 15 persons lived in communities of 8,000 or more; in 1860 the ratio was nearly 1 in every 6; and in 1890, 3 in every 10.

HOUR'S UP!

1. Abraham Lincoln was assassinated during a performance of the play *Our American Cousin*. He was shot by John Wilkes Booth, an actor:

    A. Who was playing a doctor

    B. Who was playing a lawyer

    C. Who was playing an Indian chief

    D. Who wasn't in the play

2. Alexander Graham Bell was:

    A. Inventor of the doorbell

    B. Inventor of the Graham cracker

    C. Inventor of the telephone

    D. The lead singer in Alexander's Ragtime Band

3. All of the following were men of steel, except:

    A. Superman

    B. Clark Kent

    C. Andrew Carnegie

    D. John D. Rockefeller

4. Thomas Edison invented all of the following except:

    A. Record player

    B. Light bulb

    C. Motion pictures

    D. Internet

5. The Freedmen's Bureau was:

    A. A chest of drawers owned by Dred Scott and later acquired by Frederick Douglass

    B. Later renamed the Freedmen's Bureau of Investigation and is today more commonly referred to as the FBI

    C. The brainchild of Rabbi Elliott Freedman

    D. Promised the former slaves "Forty Acres and a Mule"

PART III

One Nation, No Longer Divided

HOUR 13

Growth and Transformation

The rapid settlement of the West after the Civil War was spurred by the transcontinental railroad, which moved both eastern citizens and newly arrived immigrants in record time. However, this westward migration was not without its cost, especially in the impact that it had on the Native American population. Whereas in previous centuries the increase in European population had been relatively gradual in the settlement of the east coast, the movement west, aided by the new technology of the railroad, was frenetic, and its impact upon the lifestyle of tribes such as the Apache in the southwest, and the Sioux in the Dakotas, was dramatic. However, their attempts to delay the inevitable westward movement were futile, and by the end of the century, the United States not only held unquestioned dominion over its 48 continental states and territories, but it was already expanding beyond the North American continent, to such far flung climes as Hawaii, Asia, South America, and the Caribbean.

RAILROADS KEEP ON ROLLIN'

Railroads were the largest and most important corporations of the nineteenth century. As they became an increasingly important part of the expanding nation, unfair railroad practices increased. Rail lines extended cheaper rates to large shippers in the form of rebates, which operated to the disadvantage of smaller shippers.

CHAPTER SUMMARY

LESSON PLAN:

In this hour, you will learn about the growth of railroads, government regulation of the big trusts, the growth of agriculture, the continued problems of the South, the expansion westward, the Indian wars, and the Spanish-American War.

You will also learn ...

- Why trusts were good, and then they were bad.
- Why cowboys were driving those cattle all over the place.
- Who was left standing at Custer's Last Stand.
- Why everyone was charging up San Juan Hill.

Railroads charged arbitrarily higher rates to some shippers between certain points, regardless of the distance, especially when they held a monopoly on that route. Thus, it cost less to ship goods from Chicago to New York than to places a few hundred miles from Chicago. In addition, some competitors would set rates between two points where they both had rail lines, and then divide the freight business generated by both of them according to a pre-arranged scheme that ensured that which ever way the shipper turned, he would pay high rates, and the two competitors would share the profit.

Obviously, such practices were widely unpopular with the public. The individual states attempted to regulate the problem, but rail lines ran across many state borders, and national regulation was really necessary. The burning resentment of the people was heard loud and clear in Congress, who realized that they had to take action. In response to this problem, in 1887, President Grover Cleveland signed the Interstate Commerce Act, which made pools, excessive charges, rebates, and rate discrimination illegal. It also created the Interstate Commerce Commission (ICC) to take action against those who violated the act. However, the railroads hired very high priced lawyers, who managed to thwart virtually all of the ICC's attempts at regulation.

Another problem was the excessively high tariffs, which had originally been passed during the Civil War, but which like all taxes, once passed, have a way of not being rescinded, by a government who always finds a way to spend the excess revenue. Since it had been passed by the Republicans, the Democrats decided to make it a political issue, and blamed excessive tariffs for the increase in the cost of living and for the rapid development of trusts. The tariff became the main issue of the presidential election campaign in 1888, and Republican candidate Benjamin Harrison, a defender of protectionism, and thus the tariff, won on that issue. To fulfill his campaign promises, in 1890, the administration passed the McKinley tariff bill, which was designed to protect established industries as well as to help and encourage "infant industries." The new tariff had even higher rates, and contributed to high retail prices.

The large trusts were under attack throughout the 1880s by political reformers such as Henry George and Edward Bellamy, and the fate of the trusts became a hot political topic. In response to the public outcry, Congress decided in 1890 to break up these monopolies, and passed the Sherman Antitrust Act. This new law made illegal all combinations in restraint of interstate trade, and ensured enforcement by incorporating severe penalties for violating the act.

FYI Theodore Roosevelt did not want to eliminate corporations but he did dislike trusts and thought they should be crushed. He used the Sherman Antitrust Act of 1890 to attack trusts by filing suits in court against these organizations, including the meat, oil, steel, sugar, and tobacco trusts. In all he filed 44 antitrust suits. He made such effective use of its provisions that he earned the nickname "Trust-Buster."

AGRICULTURE GROWS THROUGH INVENTION AND EDUCATION

The industrial revolution affected not only factories, but also agriculture, as machines began to play more and more of a part in farming. As a result, farming transitioned from a family-operated, family-subsistence business to a commercial agricultural system. Farming, like every other industry, was becoming big business.

JUST A MINUTE

Between 1860 and 1910, the number of farms in the United States tripled, increasing from 2 million to 6 million, while the area farmed more than doubled from 80 million acres to 175 million acres.

After the Civil War, the cultivation of such commodities as wheat, corn, cotton, beef, pork, and wool increased dramatically. The population was also growing at a fast pace, helped along by a dramatic flow of immigration from Europe. Even though an increasingly higher proportion of the people were living in cities, the American farmer's productivity was increasing at such a rate that they could supply not only their own families, but also feed and clothe those in the cities.

As farmers and immigrants flooded into the vast new farming lands of the Midwest, machinery was one of the factors that helped the farmer to dramatically increased his output. In 1840, Cyrus McCormick invented one of the most important of these machines, the McCormick Reaper, which was able to dramatically increase the amount of grain that a farmer would cut and harvest in a day.

For example, the reaper required only two people for operation, a person to ride the horse and a man to rake the cut grain from the platform. The reaper cut as much grain in one day as it took 4 to 5 men using cradles or 12 to 16 men using reaping hooks.

McCormick built a factory in the fast growing young prairie town of Chicago, and by 1860 he had sold a quarter of a million reapers. A hundred other inventions followed, including the automatic wire binder, the threshing machine, the combine, mechanical planters, cutters, huskers, shellers, cream separators, manure spreaders, potato planters, hay driers, and poultry incubators.

The Morrill Land Grant College Act was passed to encourage establishment of agricultural and industrial colleges, by allotting federal land in each state for the exclusive use of education. These colleges were not only to serve as educational institutions, but also as centers for research in scientific farming.

 FYI On television, Johnny Carson made a national joke out of the fact that his show was broadcast from "beautiful downtown Burbank." Luther Burbank was born in Lancaster, Massachusetts, on March 7, 1849, and his agricultural research was so important, that in California his birthday is celebrated as Arbor Day, and trees are planted in his memory. However, it was a sheep ranching dentist from Los Angeles, Dr. David Burbank, that put his name on the city. He purchased more than 4,000 acres near Los Angeles in 1867, and ran an extremely successful sheep ranch, which ultimately was subdivided into the suburban city which is today Burbank.

In addition to the colleges, Congress also appropriated funds to establish agricultural experimental stations throughout the country, as well as appropriating funds for the Department of Agriculture to conduct research. With such a large number of well-funded organizations at work on agricultural problems, it wasn't long before science was helping farmers to increase their yields. In California, Luther Burbank produced new strains of fruits and vegetables; in Wisconsin, Stephen Babcock created a test for determining the butterfat content of milk; in Alabama, at the African American Tuskegee Institute, George Washington Carver found hundreds of new uses for the peanut, sweet potato, and soybean.

FYI Mark Carleton was a Department of Agriculture scientist who was sent to Russia, where he found disease- and drought-resistant winter wheat. Brought back to the United States, it soon accounted for more than half the wheat crop. Marion Dorset conquered hog cholera, and George Mohler put an end to hoof-and-mouth disease. From around the world, Americans brought back improved strains: from North Africa came Kaffir corn; from Turkestan, yellow-flowering alfalfa.

THE DIVIDED SOUTH

In the years after the Civil War, the South tried hard to attract industry, with various inducements offered to investors to build steel, lumber, tobacco, and textile factories in the region. However, despite all these efforts, by the turn of the century the South's share of the nation's industrial capacity was about the same as before the Civil War. The price for this industrialization was high: Southern mill towns were as exploitative as those in the North, if not worse.

The South remained poor, overwhelmingly agrarian, and economically depressed. In such a society, without affluence, it was difficult for any sort of social change to gestate. As a result, southern society retained the traditional system of a rigid social segregation of blacks from whites. White Southerners found ways to use the powers of the state to maintain white dominance.

Supreme Court decisions helped this system by upholding the sovereignty of the states, and restricting the power of the federal government to intervene in the internal affairs of the states. In 1873, the Supreme Court found that the 14th Amendment, which had been passed to ensure that the new citizens arising from slavery would be accorded all of their rights as citizens, only offered limited protection. In 1883, it ruled that the 14th Amendment did not prevent individuals, as long as they were acting on their own behalf, and not as state officials, from practicing discrimination. And in *Plessy* v. *Ferguson* (1896) the Court found that the "separate but equal" system of public accommodations for African Americans did not violate the Constitution.

With the Supreme Court supporting the principle of "separate but equal," it was soon to be found in every facet of Southern life, including railroads, restaurants, hotels, hospitals, and schools. Faced with institutionalized discrimination, African Americans took one of two approaches. That advocated by Booker T. Washington, a most prominent black leader, was for African Americans to ignore the discrimination, and to improve their financial and intellectual position by whatever peaceful means they could devise. The other position, advocated by W.E.B. DuBois, attempted to challenge the policy of racial segregation through political action. However, his efforts attracted little support in either political party, and these laws remained on the books in the South until the Civil Rights movement in the 1960s was finally able to successfully challenge the entire system of racial segregation.

WEST, THE FINAL FRONTIER

At the end of the Civil War, the vast plains of the West, the prairie that stretched to the foothills of the Rocky Mountains, was virtually empty of settlers. The immense inland region was primarily populated by Native Americans: the Great Plains tribes of the Sioux, Blackfoot, Pawnee, and

Cheyenne, and the Indian cultures of the Southwest, including the Apache, Navajo, and Hopi.

FYI One of the laws responsible for this rapid settlement of the West was the Homestead Act of 1862, which granted free farms to citizens who would occupy, improve, and farm the land. Unfortunately, much of this Western land was more suitable for cattle ranching than farming, and as these farmers failed, the land eventually fell into the hands of cattlemen and the railroads.

The days of the wagon trains were over, and access to the West was much easier with the completion of the transcontinental railroad. To accomplish this miracle in such a short time, and to help hold California in the Union during the Civil War, Congress had voted a charter to two railroad companies, one would build east from California, the other would build west from Iowa. Going westward was the Union Pacific Railroad, using mostly newly arrived Irish. Going eastward was the Central Pacific Railroad, relying heavily on Chinese immigrants. The two railroads finally met on May 10, 1869, at Promontory Point in Utah. Previously, travel to California required months of arduous travel on a wagon train; now it could be accomplished in six days, in the relative comfort of a sleeper, or "Pullman" car. The continental rail network grew rapidly, and soon there were four great railroads linking the Atlantic with the Pacific.

Miners were some of the first to permanently settle in the west. The first great movement was the California Gold Rush in 1848. Other gold and silver strikes brought miners to Colorado and Nevada 10 years later, to Montana and Wyoming in the 1860s, and to the Black Hills of the Dakota country in the 1870s. Miners established rough and tumble mining camps which had to be fed, and the capacity of these areas for farming and cattle was such that in the end, the real precious find in Montana, Colorado, Wyoming, Idaho, and California turned out to be the land itself.

FYI John Chisum was an early cattleman, who created the famous Chisum Trail that the cowboys used to get their beef to the rail head. During the Lincoln County wars, he employed Billy the Kid as one of the men to protect his interests. To settle things down, President Rutherford B. Hayes appointed Lew Wallace, a former army general, as governor of New Mexico, and he pardoned Billy.

Cattle-raising had early on been important in Texas. After the Civil War, enterprising cattlemen realized they could drive their Texas longhorn cattle north, across the open public land, feeding for free as they went. The cattle arrived, fatter than when they started, in frontier cow towns like Abilene, Kansas, which were on the rail lines, and from which the cattle could easily be shipped to the huge meat packing plants in Chicago. Soon these cattle drives were a regular event, and, for hundreds of miles, the trails were covered in herds of cattle moving north. Between 1866 and 1888, more than six million head of cattle were driven up from Texas. The long cattle drives reached their zenith in 1885, when the railroads began to reach all the way into Texas. Soon cattle ranches were established in other parts of the West, especially Colorado, Wyoming, Kansas, Nebraska, and the Dakotas.

Not far behind the rancher came the farmers with their families, draft horses, cows and pigs. They fenced in the lands with barbed wire, built towns, and brought in "civilization." Ranchers were excluded from the lands they had once roamed without legal title. Soon the romantic "Wild West" of legend had ceased to be.

In less than a century after the Declaration of Independence, 13 colonies hugging the eastern seaboard had managed to expand west across the entire continent.

CUSTER'S LAST STAND

Expansion into the plains and mountains of the West by miners, ranchers, and settlers led to increasing conflicts with the Indians. Although tribes such as the Utes, the Nez Perces, and the Apaches fought wars with the United States, it was the Sioux of the Northern Plains that provided the most significant opposition to frontier advance.

Ironically, the culture of the Plains Indians had already undergone massive change even before the westward migration of settlers led to conflict and war. For example, this painting reflects the change in the culture of the plains Indians brought about by their adoption of the horse, which had been introduced to America by the Spaniards.

Conflict with the Sioux began in 1862 and continued through the Civil War. In 1876, the last serious Sioux war erupted, sparked by the influx of gold miners into the Black Hills of Dakota. The Army was ordered to keep the miners off Sioux hunting grounds, but they were largely ineffective, and conflict between the Sioux and the miners increased. Led by leaders such as Red Cloud and Crazy Horse, the Sioux were particularly skilled at high-speed mounted warfare.

The army was ordered in, to force the Indians back onto their treaty lands, and to protect the miners. One of the commanders in the field was General George Armstrong Custer, a Civil War hero turned Indian fighter. He located the main encampment of Sioux on the Little Big Horn River. Custer had been successful in fighting the Indians for years, and thought that he could surprise the Indians, and disperse them, without waiting for his reinforcements to move up. He was wrong. In an engagement now referred to as Custer's Last Stand, he and his entire command were completely annihilated.

FYI In 1890, the Sioux thought that the "ghost dance" would bring them final victory over the white men. A ghost dance ritual on the Northern Sioux reservation at Wounded Knee, South Dakota, led to an uprising, followed by the arrival of the U.S. Cavalry, a last, tragic encounter that ended in the death of hundreds of Sioux men, women, and children.

The Indian victory at Little Big Horn was short lived. The massacre of Custer and his men only focused national attention on the Indians, and more men and material were devoted to the task of removal and containment. Government policy ever since the Monroe administration had been to move the Indians beyond the white frontier. As the settlers came to occupy the entire country, the reservations were forced to become smaller and more crowded. Conditions on the reservations became intolerable, and many whites began to protest the government's treatment of the Indians. Helen Hunt Jackson wrote A Century of Dishonor (1881), which like Uncle Tom's Cabin (1852) for an earlier generation, struck a chord in the nation's conscience.

However, rather than trying to save the Indian culture, most reformers of the day believed the Indian should be assimilated into the dominant white culture. In 1887, Congress passed the Dawes Act, an attempt to break up the tribes, and to make each Indian a productive, self-sufficient farmer. The tribal lands, which had been held on a communal basis, were divided up, and each Indian family was given his own farm. Like the Homestead Act before it, and on which it was modeled, the land belonged to the government for the first 25 years. The Indian could not sell the land, but if he remained on it, farmed and improved it, at the end of the period the owner won full title and citizenship. This policy, well intentioned in its inception, proved disastrous. Its assault on the communal organization of the tribes caused disruption of their traditional culture. Ultimately, land speculators were able to grab a large percentage of the land. Realizing the failure of this approach, in 1934 Congress passed the Indian Reorganization Act, and tried to protect the communal way of life on the remaining reservations.

THE CHARGE UP SAN JUAN HILL

European countries, along with an emerging new Asian superpower, Japan, were dividing up the world between them. Many Americans felt that to safeguard its own security, the United States had to stake out spheres of influence as well. That view was supported by a powerful naval lobby, which wanted an expanded fleet and a network of overseas ports. On the other side of the issue were the anti-imperialistic forces, especially the Northern Democrats and reform-minded Republicans. Because there was no clear-cut consensus of public opinion, the American empire was acquired piecemeal and half-heartedly.

America's first venture beyond the continental limits of the United States was the purchase of Alaska from Russia right after the conclusion of the Civil War. Most Americans thought this acquisition of what they perceived as a land of snow and ice near the North Pole to be a colossal waste of money, and it was called "Seward's Folly" and "Seward's Icebox" after the Secretary of State who masterminded its purchase. However, when gold was discovered 30 years later in the Klondike, Americans rushed north, and the population increased. When Alaska joined the Union, it became the largest state.

By the 1890s, Spain's once vast empire had been reduced to Cuba and Puerto Rico in the Western Hemisphere, and the Philippines in the Pacific. Then, in 1895, Cuba declared its independence. As the United States watched the course of the revolution, many Americans were sympathetic with the Cubans, but President Cleveland was determined to stay neutral. Three years later, however, a new president, McKinley, was in office when the U.S. warship *Maine* suddenly and mysteriously blew up while lying at anchor in Havana harbor. More than 250 sailors were killed, and an outburst of indignation, fueled by sensational press coverage, swept the country.

The Spanish-American War, at four months long, was one of the shortest in American history. Theodore Roosevelt, then assistant secretary of the Navy, resigned and recruited a volunteer regiment he called the "Rough Riders." A week after the declaration of war, Commodore George Dewey proceeded with his fleet to the Philippines. He caught the entire Spanish fleet at anchor in Manila Bay and destroyed it without the loss of a single American life. In Cuba, American troops landed near Santiago, where, after winning a rapid series of engagements, including Teddy Roosevelt's famous charge up San Juan Hill, they fired on the Spanish ships in the port. Four armored Spanish cruisers steamed out of Santiago Bay and were promptly sunk.

Spain sued for peace, and the United States suddenly had its own overseas empire by acquiring Spain's. The treaty, signed on December 10, 1898, transferred Cuba to the United States, to administer until which time as Cuba would gain its independence. In addition, Spain gave up Puerto Rico and Guam in lieu of paying war reparations, and the United States received the Philippines in return for a payment of $20 million.

The United States was never comfortable running an empire. The entire concept ran contrary to the American system of self-determination, and therefore the new territories were encouraged to move toward democratic self-government. Unfortunately, while such a political system was part of the heritage of the English colonists, it was completely alien to the peoples of the former Spanish empire. By 1916, the Philippines was electing its own legislature, and in 1936 the Philippine Commonwealth was established. Independence was delayed by the Japanese invasion and occupation during World War II, but after the end of the war, the islands attained full independence.

The United States did not stay in Cuba long. By 1902, the troops had left, although the United States retained economic and political influence there until 1959, when Fidel Castro established a communist regime with close ties to the Soviet Union.

FYI On the southern end of Cuba is U.S. Naval Station Guantanamo Bay, where more than 3,000 U.S. military service members, civilians, and their families live. During the war in Afghanistan, it was used to house captured prisoners. Its origins go back to 1903, when the new Republic of Cuba leased to the United States the land on which the naval station is located, based on the following provision in the Constitution of the Republic of Cuba: "That to enable the United States to maintain the independence of Cuba, and to protect the people thereof, as well as its own defense, the government of Cuba will sell or lease to the United States lands necessary for coaling and Naval stations at certain specified points to be agreed upon by the President of the United States."

Puerto Rico, the third acquisition from the Spanish-American War, was initially supposed to follow a road toward independence like that of Cuba and the Philippines. However, the 1917 law in which the U.S. Congress granted Puerto Ricans the right to elect all of their legislators also created a different path for the island. It was made a U.S. territory, and its people became American citizens. In 1950, Congress changed direction again, and granted Puerto Rico complete freedom to chart its own future. In a 1952 referendum, the citizens voted to reject both statehood and total independence, and chose instead a commonwealth status. As American citizens, many Puerto Ricans have chosen to settle on the mainland.

The United States also became involved in the Hawaiian Islands, where Americans had been settling since the early 1800s, starting with missionaries from New England, and sailors from whaling ships. After the Civil War, Americans began to develop the islands' resources in earnest, and sugar cane and pineapples became important cash crops. When the Queen decided to end this American influence on the islands in 1893, American businessmen joined with influential Hawaiians in a bloodless revolution, deposed the Island's Queen, and installed a new government. This new government immediately requested annexation to the United States. Congress voted in July 1898 to annex the islands, and thereby also acquired an important naval base at Pearl Harbor. After World War II, Hawaii became the fiftieth state.

Hour's Up!

1. Congress passed the Sherman Anti-Trust Act because:

   A. Sherman was really annoying as long as he had that trust fund.

   B. The South hated Sherman after his "March to the Sea."

   C. They wanted to stop Bobby Sherman from singing.

   D. Trusts were getting too powerful.

2. The president's action in busting the trusts earned him the nickname:

   A. Buster Keaton

   B. Buster Brown

   C. Trust-Buster

   D. Dust Buster

3. Beautiful downtown Burbank was named in honor of:

   A. Commander Daniel Burbank, the NASA astronaut

   B. Truman Burbank, comedian Jim Carrey's character in the hit movie *The Truman Show*

   C. Dr. Luther Burbank, the agricultural research scientist from Santa Rosa, California

   D. Dr. David Burbank, the sheep-herding dentist

4. George Armstrong Custer was all of the following except:

   A. A hero of the Civil War

   B. Sent to the Dakotas to force the Sioux back onto their reservation

   C. Defeated Crazy Horse and Sitting Bull at the battle of the Little Big Horn

   D. Killed when his command was wiped out at Custer's Last Stand

5. Teddy Roosevelt was all of the following except:

   A. The person after whom they named the "Teddy Bear"

   B. Lead the charge up San Juan Hill during the Spanish American War

   C. Responsible for the United States building the Panama Canal

   D. The only Roosevelt to be elected president

QUIZ

HOUR 14

Discontent and Reform

CHAPTER SUMMARY

LESSON PLAN:

In this hour, you will learn about the Panama Canal, the intervention of the United States in South and Central America, the Open Door policy, the Good Neighbor policy, the Boxer Rebellion, the Granger Movement, sharecropping, the Populists, laissez-faire capitalism, the cross of gold speech, the struggles of labor, and the child labor laws.

You will also learn ...

- That the Good Neighbor Policy was not created by Mr. Rogers.
- How the United States created the country of Panama so they could put a canal in it.
- Why the sharecroppers didn't get much of a share of their crop.
- What kind of muck a muckraker would rake, if a muckraker could rake muck.

Although it would be the end of the twentieth century before the United States would stand supreme as the world's greatest superpower, even at the beginning of the century America was beginning to look and act like a world power. In imitation of the other superpowers, the United States was involved in the partition of China. It's first important unilateral action was the creation of the Panama Canal, an important sea lane linking the worlds two greatest oceans, and solely controlled by the United States. Not only did America create the nation of Panama, just so that it could have a route through which to carve the canal, but it began to use its immense power to intervene in other countries in the Western Hemisphere.

THE PANAMA CANAL

The need for a canal for sea trade, connecting the Atlantic and the Pacific, had long been recognized by the commercial nations of the world. As a result, the French had begun digging one in the late nineteenth century, but they were defeated by the disease endemic to the region. With the acquisition of the Philippines and Hawaii, and with significant coast on both the Atlantic and the Pacific, the United States had a military necessity for a canal that could provide for the fast movement of warships from one ocean to the other.

The best place to dig the canal was in Colombia's province of Panama, but the legislature of that country refused in 1903 to ratify a treaty giving the United States the rights in the country they needed to build it. As was usual in such situations in those days, the United States allied themselves with Panamanian revolutionaries, who promptly declared their independence from Colombia. To back them up, the U.S. Marines landed, the rebellion was a success, and Panama became an independent country. It was immediately recognized by President Theodore Roosevelt. There was only one step left: The new country signed a treaty with the United States, granting the United States the right to a "Canal Zone," the property on which the canal would be built.

 FYI Under the terms of the treaty, Panama granted the United States a perpetual lease to a 10-mile-wide strip of land between the Atlantic and the Pacific, in return for $10 million up front, and a yearly fee of $250,000.

Knowing that disease had defeated the French, the first order of business was the eradication of malaria and yellow fever in the tropical jungle, made possible by recent advances in medicine by researchers such as army doctor Walter Reed, who discovered that mosquito's carried the yellow fever. With the medical problem solved, there was still a major engineering feat to be accomplished. The completion of the Canal in 1914 was a huge triumph of engineering by Colonel George W. Goethals, who would later build the Goethals Bridge in New York City.

THE UGLY AMERICAN

Ever since the Monroe Doctrine, the United States had felt a special duty to the rest of the countries in the Americas. However, our protection and intervention was not always wanted, or appreciated, by the countries to the south. As early as 1867, the United States had pressured the French to remove troops supporting the emperor Maximillian from Mexico. Between 1900 and 1920, the United States intervened in six countries in the Western Hemisphere, established protectorates in Haiti and the Dominican Republic, and stationed U.S. Marines in Nicaragua. In 1917, the United States tried to influence the outcome of the Mexican revolution by sending an army into the northern part of the country to capture the elusive rebel Pancho Villa.

Not all U.S. actions involved sending in the Marines, however. In 1889, Secretary of State James G. Blaine proposed to join the 21 nations of the

Western Hemisphere into an early type of the United Nations for the Americas, dedicated to the settlement of disputes and to economic cooperation. The first Pan-American conference in 1890 created the Pan-American Union, which is today known as the Organization of American States (OAS).

 FYI Franklin D. Roosevelt repudiated the right of the United States to unilaterally intervene in Latin America at its own whim, announcing what he called the "Good Neighbor Policy," in an attempt to create better relations with the neighbors to the south.

THE OPEN DOOR POLICY

The United States, with the acquisition of Hawaii, the Philippines, and the West Coast, had definitely become a power in the Pacific, and trade with China was a natural result. However, since China's defeat by Japan (1894–1895), European nations had divided China into spheres of influence, secured monopolistic trade rights, and forced other concessions from the impotent giant. This was in direct contrast to America's foreign policy of equal commercial privileges for all countries. In 1899, Secretary of State John Hay announced an "Open Door Policy" for China, which called for equality of trading opportunities such as tariffs, harbor duties, and railway rates in the areas that the foreign powers controlled.

The people of China had had enough of being divided into occupation zones by foreign countries, and in 1900, these revolutionaries, called "Boxers," attacked the foreign legations in Peking. As the Boxer Rebellion raged, the United States announced that it would oppose any attempts by the Boxers to disturb the flow of trade. Once the rebellion was quelled, it required all of Secretary of State Hay's skill to maintain the Open Door policy and to protect China from being subjected to crushing indemnities by the other foreign countries. In October, Great Britain and Germany once more agreed they would adhere to the Open Door policy and the preservation of Chinese independence, and other nations soon followed.

 FYI Teddy Roosevelt received the Nobel Peace Prize in 1906 for helping to mediate an end to the Russo-Japanese War of 1904–1905.

HOME, HOME, ON THE GRANGE

The revolution in farming brought about great advances in farm production, in fact, it was too successful, and created overproduction. Not only did new advancements in science and machinery increase the yield per acre, but the amount of land available for farming grew rapidly as the expansion of the railroads and the removal of the Indians opened up new farmland for cultivation.

At the same time that lands were opening up in the United States, they were also expanding in Canada, Argentina, and Australia, adding even more farm production to the international market, and driving down prices. Adding to the farmers' economic problems were the railroads, on whom they were dependent to move their produce to market. As the years went by, the farmers fell more and more behind on their mortgages, and the result was increasing bank foreclosures on farms.

In the South, farmers had their own unique problems. The end of the Civil War had given rise to sharecropping, a system whereby tenant farmers, in return for the land, seed, and other essential supplies, would turn over a large percentage of their crop, sometimes as much as 50 percent, to the person who owned the land. Like the system of the "company store" in factory towns, under such a system the sharecropper fell further and further in debt every year. Around 80 percent of the black farmers and 40 percent of the white ones lived under this system. Because each sharecropper was trying to produce as much as he could on his parcel of land, this increased planting led to overproduction of cotton and tobacco, which not only depleted the soil, but also drove down the price and, thus, made it even harder to get ahead and make a living.

In response to these agricultural problems, in 1867 the employees of the U.S. Department of Agriculture started the *Granger* movement. The Granges at first focused on social activities to counteract the isolation faced by farm families. Encouraged by the participation of not only the farmers, but also their wives and farm children, the Grange had soon grown to more than 20,000 chapters with more than 1.5 million members.

STRICTLY DEFINED

The word *Grange* comes from the medieval Latin word *granica*, which is derived from the Latin word *granum*, which means "grain." The place where you stored the grain was called the grange, and later this evolved into the word granary. However, the archaic word grange also persisted.

To counteract the uneven balance between the individual farmer and the railroad, the Grange created their own stores, processing plants, factories, and cooperatives. They also became powerful political forces, and in some states were able to push through the legislature "Granger laws," aimed at limiting the fees charged by railroads and warehouses.

Other powerful farmers' organizations also developed. The Farmers' Alliances enrolled members from New York to California, and by 1890 there were more than 1.5 million members. There was an African American counterpart, the Colored Farmers National Alliance, which had over a million members. Unlike the Granges, which had begun as social organizations and evolved into political forces, the Farmers' Alliances were created as political organizations. From the beginning, their platform was to "unite the farmers of America for their protection against class legislation and the encroachments of concentrated capital." Their program called for the strict regulation of the railroads, the encouragement of inflation to provide debt relief, lowering of the tariff to drive down the price of manufactured goods, and establishing low-interest government loans.

Times became increasingly hard for the farmers. Droughts hit the Great Plains in the 1880s, just as they were to strike again during the Great Depression in the 1930s. By 1890, farmers were ready for a change.

Springing from political organizations that were already in place, such as the Grange and the Farmers' Alliance, came a third political force, the Populist Party. In the 1890 election, it was so successful that the farmers at last had Senators and Representatives in Washington to look after their interests, which included reform in transportation and finance. In the 1892 elections, their candidate for president, James B. Weaver, received more than a million votes.

QUOTABLE QUOTES

The platform of the Populists: "We are met, in the midst of a nation brought to the verge of moral, political and material ruin. Corruption dominates the ballot-box, the legislatures, the Congress, and touches even the ermine of the bench [courts]. From the same prolific womb of governmental injustice we breed the two great classes: tramps and millionaires."

The great political issue of the Populists was the coinage of silver. The farmers were convinced that their troubles could be traced to the shortage of money. They were of the opinion that increasing the amount of specie in circulation would raise the price of farm products and also drive up industrial wages. The surplus cash would cause inflation, and they could get out of debt by paying back their loans with inflated dollars. This was obviously a strategy for those who were poor, and heavily in debt. The rich and power-ful, however, did not want inflation, which would decrease the value of their assets. Thus, the affluent wanted a stable and inflation-proof gold standard, while the impoverished farmers wanted the unlimited coinage of silver.

In 1893, the country was on the verge of a great crisis. Banks failed, espe-cially in the South and Midwest, unemployment increased, and crop prices dropped. Supporters of silver went over to the Populists as the presidential elections of 1896 neared.

One of the most famous speeches in U.S. political history occurred at the Democratic convention in 1896. Pleading with the convention not to "cru-cify mankind upon a cross of gold," William Jennings Bryan, championing silver, swept the convention and won the Democrats' presidential nomina-tion.

QUOTABLE QUOTES

William Jennings Bryan: "If they dare to come out in the open field and defend the gold standard as a good thing, we will fight them to the uttermost. Having behind us the producing masses of this nation and the world, supported by the commercial interests, the laboring interests and the toilers everywhere, we will answer their demand for a gold standard by saying to them: You shall not press down upon the brow of labor this crown of thorns, you shall not crucify mankind upon a cross of gold."

In a rare political situation, William Jennings Bryan was not only the candi-date of the Democrats, but also the Populists. With the farmers solidly behind him, Bryan won the entire South, and all of the West except California and Oregon. However, Bryan failed to carry the industrial North, and its greater population (and electoral votes), resulted in a win for the Republican candidate, William McKinley.

The 1896 election was the high point for the Populist Party. In the next year, 1897, the discovery of gold in Alaska and the Yukon helped to prime the economy, and with it came increased prosperity. Gradually, the Populists faded from the scene.

THE STRUGGLES OF LABOR

Like the farmers, the workers also had their problems in the nineteenth cen-tury. Wages were low, the hours were long, and the working conditions were hazardous. The owners kept the majority of the wealth generated by their companies, very little of it ever trickled down to the average factory worker. Men were treated badly, women and children even worse. School was a luxury for urban children, while the majority were put to work for the paltry wages they could contribute to the family exchequer, at very young and tender ages.

Adding to the problems of the workers, ironically enough, were the constant mechanical improvements of the age. Each new machine reduced the need for unskilled labor, and the pool of such labor was constantly being increased by the vast hordes of European immigrants who were flooding into the country. As a result, there was great competition for the available jobs, further driving down wages for the urban poor.

At first, there were no labor laws on the books at all. Even women and children could be worked an unlimited number of hours a day, in conditions that were unbelievably squalid and dangerous. It was only in 1874 that laws began to appear, starting with a Massachusetts statute that limited the number of hours that women and children could work in a factory to 10 hours per day. Because the federal government saw such laws as the province of states, few statutes appeared on the books, since the massive corporations and trusts had much more clout in the state legislatures than the common factory workers.

Not only were the state legislatures of little help, but the courts were not sympathetic to the plight of the working class. They firmly adhered to the principles of *laissez-faire* capitalism, and to its literal meaning in French, which was "leave alone." The courts repeatedly backed big business, and ruled against the common man.

STRICTLY DEFINED

Laissez-faire, which in French means "leave alone," in economics and politics is a doctrine that holds that an economic system functions best when there is no interference by government. It is based on the belief that the natural economic order tends, when undisturbed by artificial stimulus or regulation, to secure the maximum well being for the individual and therefore for the community as a whole.

The human cost of survival of the fittest was high. For years, the United States had the highest job-related fatality rate of any industrialized nation in the world. Factory workers put in a 10-hour day, and this was 12 hours if you were in the steel industry. The paycheck of the father was not enough to live; only with the entire family, even the little children, in the factory could they hope to survive. Prospects for escaping such a life were slim. These people lived lives of quiet desperation—death often the only merciful escape.

John D. Rockefeller said: "The growth of a large business is survival of the fittest." He and other industrialists believed that any attempt to regulate business was the same as interfering with the natural evolution of the species.

In such an environment, the idea of organizing a union seemed the only answer. A labor organization would give power to the workers comparable to that held by management, and enable them to negotiate for better wages and working conditions. The first nationwide union was The Noble Order of the Knights of Labor, founded in 1869, a secret society organized by garment workers in Philadelphia. It was broad-based, being open to all workers, including blacks and women. The Knights' first great victory came in 1885 in a strike against Jay Gould, the railroad kingpin. Emboldened by this success, their ranks were quickly swelled by over a half a million new members.

Despite their success, it was soon overshadowed by another labor movement, the American Federation of Labor (AFL). Lead by Samuel Gompers, they employed a different philosophy of membership: The union was restricted to skilled workers. And unlike the earlier movements, which were more socialist in their conception, with their accompanying call for social leveling, the AFL was pure capitalism. They were the complete mirror image of the industrialists they were fighting. Their goals were simple: increase wages, reduce hours, and improve working conditions, leaving the social revolution to others.

The rise of labor was not a bloodless revolution, for the industrialists and robber barons were not about to passively allow their workers to share in their profits without a fight. It was only a matter of time before their skirmishes turned into outright warfare. The first significant conflict was the Great Rail Strike of 1877. The railroads tried to impose a 10 percent pay cut on all rail workers, and the workers immediately went on strike. When the owners tried to use strikebreakers, rioting broke out in a number of cities, including Baltimore, Chicago, Pittsburgh, Buffalo, New York, and San Francisco. To stop the widespread destruction, federal troops had to be sent in to restore order.

Like the Boston Massacre, the Haymarket Square bombing in Chicago in 1886 became a rallying cry for the rebels of labor. A bomb was thrown into a labor meeting being held during a strike at the McCormick Harvester Company in Chicago. Nine people were killed, and more than 60 were injured.

In 1892, there were riots at Carnegie's steel works in Homestead, Pennsylvania. Carnegie hired the Pinkerton Detective Agency to break the strike, but when they arrived, members of the Amalgamated Association of Iron, Steel and Tin Workers opened fire, and ten of the detectives were killed. The governor mobilized the National Guard, Carnegie hired nonunion strikebreakers, and the strike was broken.

The year 1894 brought the strike by the Pullman workers. The American Railway Union came out in sympathy, and soon most of the country's railroads were at a standstill. In an attempt to keep the railroads rolling, the U.S. Attorney General mobilized a force of more than 3,000 deputies, and obtained a federal court injunction against the unions. This resulted in riots, and President Cleveland sent in federal troops to restore order and break the strike.

Strong-arm tactics by the government and the industrial tycoons inevitably created even more militant unions. One of the most radical was the International Workers of the World (IWW), better known as the "Wobblies." They were primarily miners, and thus were hard, rough, and ready men from the get-go. Their strikes were tough affairs, such as the Colorado mine strike of 1903, and they were put down just as brutally.

They were a defiantly radical group, practically anarchists. Their idea was to ultimately sign up all the workers of the world into one big union, and then call a general strike to decide who was going to run the world, the workers or the bosses. They demanded open class warfare, and became a national force when they won a hard fought strike in 1912 in the textile mills of Lawrence, Massachusetts. However, they went too far by trying to shut down factories engaged in war production during World War I, and this gave the government the excuse to put them out of business.

 With every union card, the Wobblies handed out a little red songbook, whose cover carried the motto: "To Fan the Flames of Discontent." Inside were the words to about 50 parodies, like those today performed by Weird Al Yankovic. The songs were roared out by Wobblies at meetings, on picket lines, and in the jails where Wobblies were often found.

THE REFORMERS AND DO-GOODERS

The problems of labor and the farmers, the excesses of nineteenth-century capitalism, and political corruption led to the rise of a reform movement called "Progressivism." These reformers affected American politics from 1890 until the American entry into World War I in 1917.

The Progressives crusaded against the abuses of urban political bosses and corrupt robber barons. They wanted the federal government to become involved in the regulation of business. Almost all the notable figures of the period, whether in politics, philosophy, scholarship, or literature, considered themselves to be Progressives.

Writers and journalists used the power of the pen to expose practices and principles that were proving inadequate for a modern twentieth-century urban state. Articles dealing with the evils of trusts, high finance, impure foods, and abusive railroad practices began to appear in both the daily newspapers and in magazines as *McClure's* and *Collier's*. These authors, such as the journalist Ida May Tarbell, who crusaded against the Standard Oil Trust, became known as *muckrakers*.

STRICTLY DEFINED

Muckrakers is the name applied to American journalists, novelists, and critics who in the first decade of the twentieth century attempted to expose the abuses of business and corruption in politics. The term derives from the word *muckrake* used by President Theodore Roosevelt in a speech in 1906, in which he agreed with many of the charges of the muckrakers but asserted that some of their methods were sensational and irresponsible. He compared them to a character from John Bunyan's book *Pilgrim's Progress* who could look no way but downward with a muckrake in his hands and was interested only in raking the filth.

The muckrakers uncovered the evil in every type of industry. Upton Sinclair, in his novel *The Jungle*, exposed the horrible and unsanitary conditions in the Chicago meat-packing houses. Theodore Dreiser in *The Financier* and *The Titan* laid bare the unsavory machinations of big business. Frank Norris's *The Pit* revealed how behind-the-scenes manipulations affected the grain market in Chicago. Lincoln Steffens's *The Shame of the Cities* uncovered political corruption. Such "literature of exposure" had a significant effect in rousing the people to action, and they demanded that their political leaders do something. In reaction, states enacted laws to improve the conditions under which people lived and worked. Legislatures passed child labor laws, raised the age limits for working in the factories, shortened the work day, restricted night work, and required children to attend school.

THE NEW CENTURY

In September 1901, while attending an exposition in Buffalo, New York, President McKinley was shot and killed by an assassin. (He was the third president to be assassinated.) The bombastic Theodore Roosevelt, the hero of San Juan Hill, and McKinley's vice president, became president, something the party had never envisioned.

FYI Robert Todd Lincoln, the son of Abraham Lincoln, was present when his father died from an assassin's bullet. He was secretary of war under Garfield and went to the train station to speak to the president, arriving just as Garfield was shot. He was also at the exhibition at which McKinley was assassinated. And in a strange twist of fate, although he had died many years before John F. Kennedy was shot, they are both buried in the same cemetery!

HOUR'S UP!

1. The Boxers were all of the following except:

   A. The Boxers attacked the foreign embassies in Peking.

   B. The Boxers wanted an end to foreign control of China.

   C. The Boxers were trying to obtain control of the opium trade.

   D. The Boxers were Chinese in revolt against their Empress.

2. The Granger or Grange movement took its name from:

   A. Popular movie star Stewart Granger

   B. The popular song "Home, Home, on the Grange"

   C. The Lone Granger

   D. The Latin word for grain

3. The Populists were:

   A. The origin of the word "pop" star

   B. The original name of the "Up with People" singers

   C. Worried about being crucified on a "cross of gold"

   D. Not very popular

4. Robert Todd Lincoln was involved in the assassination of every U.S. president except:

   A. Abraham Lincoln

   B. James A. Garfield

QUIZ

C. William McKinley

D. John F. Kennedy

5. Muckrakers were all of the following except:

    A. Christened in a speech by Teddy Roosevelt

    B. A character in the book *Pilgrim's Progress*

    C. Novelists who were reformers and do-gooders

    D. Sanitation workers in New York City

HOUR 15
World War I

CHAPTER SUMMARY

LESSON PLAN:

In this hour, you will learn about the Square Deal, the income tax, the Federal Trade Commission, immigration, the First World War, and the Russian Revolution.

You will also learn ...

- That Teddy Roosevelt wasn't playing poker when he dealt the Square Deal.
- Why the Supreme Court held the income tax to be unconstitutional, but that didn't help the poor taxpayer.
- That a doughboy who was going "over there" had nothing to do with the Pillsbury Doughboy.
- That the League of Nations is not a club for superfriends.

The march of the United States onto the world stage took a giant leap forward with its entry into World War I. For the first time in its history, American soldiers left the Western Hemisphere to fight overseas in a major war. This was a different kind of war, it was not being fought for independence, or to preserve the union, or to repel foreign invaders. Instead, the United States was fighting to change the course of world history, to take its concept of liberty, freedom, and democracy, which was born and nurtured in the New World, back to the Old World from which their ancestors had originated. Victory by the allies did indeed topple kings, and the last vestiges of the old feudal system were swept away to make way for new European democracies.

THE SQUARE DEAL

President Theodore Roosevelt and Progressive leaders in Congress were convinced that reform could only be effective if it was accomplished on a national scale. Roosevelt, who wanted to give the people what he called a "Square Deal," started with increased government enforcement of the antitrust laws, and soon he was being called the "Trust-Buster." This was followed by the extension of government regulatory control over the railroads. One of the first bills to be passed to deal with railroad abuses was a requirement that they publish their rates, to ensure that everyone paid the same amounts for hauling freight.

FYI Teddy Roosevelt called his domestic policy the "Square Deal." When his cousin Frank Roosevelt became president, he cashed in on the enormous popularity of his famous cousin by calling his domestic policy the "New Deal."

Teddy Roosevelt's progressive measures cut across party lines. His immense popularity, coupled with a new prosperity, assured his victory in the 1904 election. With a clear mandate from the electorate, he renewed his reforms with new vigor. He demanded more drastic railroad regulation, and in 1906 Congress passed the Hepburn Act. This new law vested real authority in the Interstate Commerce Commission, who now had the power to regulate rates, and to force the railroads to surrender their interests in steamship lines and coal companies, which had operated to restrain free trade.

Roosevelt had made a significant Constitutional move, one that had met with hardly any resistance. He had established the right of the federal government to regulate, in areas that had previously been thought to be the exclusive province of the states. Emboldened, he carried the principle of federal control even further. He pushed through the Pure Food and Drug Law of 1906, which prohibited the use of any harmful "drug, chemical or preservative" in either food or medicine. To back up this law, it was followed by an act requiring federal inspection of all meat.

The constitutional hook on which this all rested was the concept of interstate commerce. From almost the beginning of the country, the Supreme Court had held that laws which were necessary to enforce the powers of the federal government could be implied from specific, enumerated powers. Because the federal government had the power to control interstate commerce, by inference, they could make laws in any area that affected that commerce. Roosevelt and his administration took this to the limit—in his estimation, if there was any chance that a good or service could end up in interstate commerce, then the federal government had the right to regulate that industry.

His next progressive step was to create a Department of Commerce and Labor, with powerful enforcement powers. Their investigations revealed that the American Sugar Refining Company had defrauded the government on import duties. The government took them to court, recovered more than $4 million in lost revenue, and sent a number of company officers to jail. They then went after the Standard Oil Company of Indiana, who had been receiving secret rebates on shipments over the Chicago and Alton Railroad. Once again, the government won, and the fine imposed on the company was more than $29 million.

FYI They named the Teddy Bear after Teddy Roosevelt, and he was also the namesake for a real life little bear cub rescued by forest rangers after a terrible forest fire, that they called "Hot-Foot Teddy," because his bear claws were badly burned. However, it wasn't long before they changed his name, and he became Smokey the Bear, the National Park Service's symbol for preventing forest fires. After a nationwide contest among school children, his motto became "Only You Can Prevent Forest Fires."

Another facet of Roosevelt's progressive agenda was conservation of the country's natural resources, and the establishment of national parks. As a young man with medical problems, he had gone west to toughen up, and had been exposed to the majestic forests, lakes, and mountains of the Rockies. He called for a sweeping program of conservation, reclamation, and irrigation. During his time in office, Roosevelt nearly tripled the acreage in the national parks, and instituted reforms designed both to prevent forest fires, and to replant timber in those areas that had already been destroyed by the lumber companies.

THE INCOME TAXMAN COMETH

Roosevelt was followed as president by his hand-picked successor, William Howard Taft, who continued Teddy's policies, including his reforms. Perhaps the most drastic measure to be passed during his term of office was the 16th Amendment, which authorized a personal income tax. This amendment was required because the Supreme Court had struck down the income tax that had been passed previously as unconstitutional, stating that the federal government did not have the authority, under the Constitution, to tax the people directly. In light of the Supreme Court decision, the only way they could institute the personal income tax was with a constitutional amendment.

JUST A MINUTE

Teddy Roosevelt was at the height of his popularity in 1908, and could have easily been reelected president, but he respected the tradition established by Washington, that two terms were enough. Ironically, the only one to ever violate that tradition was his cousin, Frank Roosevelt, who was elected to four terms. After the second Roosevelt, they made the Washington tradition official, with a constitutional amendment, so that no one would ever violate it again.

Another change to the Constitution ratified during Taft's tenure was the 17th Amendment, which changed the way that senators were selected.

Under the original constitution, senators were selected by the state legislatures. The people did not like this, as it gave them too little control over the Senate, and in 1913, for the first time, with the passage of the 17th Amendment, the people gained the right to directly elect their senators, a system which has remained in place since then.

Despite the fact that he was Teddy Roosevelt's hand-picked successor, Taft was never as popular. In addition, some of his measures alienated even members of his own party, such as his support of high protective tariffs, and his opposition to the entry of Arizona into the Union, because their Constitution contained a clause permitting the recall of judges. Roosevelt was not pleased with the actions taken by his successor, and tried to garner the Republican nomination for himself for the next election. When his own party failed to nominate him, but again nominated Taft, Teddy formed his own party, the Progressives, in an attempt to get back into power. However, all that he managed to do with this maneuver was split the vote of the Republican Party, and the Democratic candidate, Woodrow Wilson, was swept into office.

Woodrow Wilson instituted a number of reforms. The first was a revision of the tariff laws, lowering the tariff on imported raw materials, food, cotton, wool, iron, steel, and many other items. Wilson was convinced that he could protect domestic industry, and at the same time, reduce the cost of living for the average American.

 Woodrow Wilson was our most academic president. Prior to taking office, he was president of Princeton University, and he had spent his entire life as a professor in academia. He is also the only president to hold a Ph.D., which he received from Johns Hopkins University.

Wilson's next reform was a reorganization of the banking and currency system with the passage of the Federal Reserve Act. Since the end of the Bank of the United States, the entire banking and currency system of the country had been under the control of the states and private banks. The act created a Federal Reserve Board, and divided the country into twelve districts, in each of which was a Federal Reserve Bank. These district banks were to hold the cash reserves of those banks that joined the system. Before the Federal Reserve Act, control of the money supply was in the hands of unregulated private banks, who were constantly making loans in excess of their cash reserves. When a bank panic occurred, and depositors tried to turn their bank paper into gold coin, the bank quickly ran out of money, and went bankrupt, leaving the remaining depositors without any recourse. By requiring all national banks to join the Federal Reserve System, to invest 3 percent of their holdings in the system, and to hold another three percent subject to call, the "Fed" curtailed the money and credit flow problems characteristic of the late 1800s and early 1900s. The federal reserve note now became a medium of exchange on which the business community could rely. Although the system had to be retooled after the Great Depression, and also after the financial crisis in the 1970s, it is still the system that remains in place today.

The next great reform was the creation of the Federal Trade Commission, an extension of Teddy Roosevelt's "trust-busting." This new agency had real teeth: They could issue orders prohibiting a business from engaging in "unfair methods of competition." This was followed by the Clayton Antitrust Act, which made illegal a number of specific corporate practices that had previously been completely legal, but which had encouraged the formation of large, powerful trusts. Practices that were made illegal by the new law included interlocking directorates, price discrimination, the use of the injunction against organized labor, and controlling stock in corporations in similar enterprises.

Other laws were passed to provide specific relief to various segments of workers in society. Debt-ridden farmers found some relief in the Federal Loan Act, which made low interest loans available. The Seamen's Act of 1915 was designed to improve living and working conditions on board American flag ships. The Federal Workingman's Compensation Act in 1916 created a system for civil service employees to obtain compensation for disabilities that arose as a result of their work environment. For railroad workers, the Adamson Act created an eight-hour work day.

GIVE ME YOUR HUDDLED MASSES

The United States has always considered itself a nation of immigrants. The early settlers were primarily white Protestant Europeans, and African slaves. Before the Revolution, approximately half of the emigrants were from England, the remainder were primarily Scots-Irish, German, Dutch, French, Swedish, Welsh, and Finnish. A fifth of the population was African slaves.

In the early years, the country had no clear immigration policy. There was little support for stopping immigration when the country was in need of an increasing supply of workers. In addition, Americans always viewed immigrants as a cheap source of labor. As a result, in the early years of the country, very few official restrictions were placed upon immigration into the United States.

JUST A MINUTE

At the first census, in 1790, the population was 3.9 million. By 1850, this was 23 million, and in 1900 it had risen to 74.6 million. In 1950, it was 149.9 million, and in 2000, the total population of the United States was more than 281 million.

Immigration was slow in the late eighteenth and early nineteenth centuries. Europe was ravaged by the Napoleonic Wars, and European governments wanted to keep all their young men of military age. However, by the 1840s immigration began to increase. This was spurred by the potato blight in Ireland, and by continual unrest in Germany, especially the Revolution of 1848. The building of the transcontinental railroad led to the wholesale importation of Chinese *coolies*. Immigration was actively encouraged during the Civil War, as recruiters from the Union Army scoured Europe for volunteers, who would receive free passage to America as part of their enlistment contract. The South was enraged by a Union army made up increasingly of liberated slaves and European immigrants, many of whom did not even speak English.

STRICTLY DEFINED

Coolies were unskilled laborers from the Far East who worked for low or subsistence wages. A large portion of present-day Asian Americans descended from the coolies who were brought to America to build the railroads.

After the Civil War, immigration turned from a trickle into a torrent, as Germans, Italians, and other Europeans arrived in large numbers. At the turn of the century, Jewish immigration soared, as they fled increasing persecution from the Czar in Russia. Between 1890 and 1921, another 19 million people arrived, including immigrants from Italy, Russia, Poland, Greece, and the Balkans, as well as non-Europeans from Japan, Canada, and Mexico.

In the face of such a flood of immigration, the percentage of nonnative born Americans soared, and the American people became alarmed. Organized labor was concerned that continued immigration would force down wages. Other groups, such as the Immigration Restriction League, wanted to restrict immigration on racial or religious grounds, afraid that the entire American culture would be subverted by unrestricted immigration from around the world. The Johnson-Reed Immigration Act of 1924 created the quota system, and immigration was regulated on the basis of national origin.

The Great Depression of the 1930s slowed down immigration to a standstill. With no jobs available for anyone, it was hard to justify allowing new people into the country. With public opinion violently opposed to any sort of immigration, even persecuted European minorities were not allowed to enter the United States in the years before World War II.

In 1965, Congress changed the immigration law again. Rather than by country, the quotas were regulated by hemisphere. Immigration preference was given to relatives of U.S. citizens, and preference was also given to those with critical job skills needed by the United States. Another change to the immigration laws in 1978 did away with the geographical quotas completely, and created a single restriction of 290,000 immigrants per year. This number was reduced to 270,000 by the Refugee Act of 1980.

QUOTABLE QUOTES

 The inscription on the Statute of Liberty says: "Give me your tired, your poor, your huddled masses, yearning to breathe free, the wretched refuse of your teeming shore. Send these, the homeless, tempest tossed, to me: I lift my lamp beside the golden door."

These immigration restrictions, however, did little to restrict the illegal immigration, which dwarfed legal immigration by at least two to one. This illegal entry was especially acute from Mexico and other Latin American countries, who daily crossed the southern U.S. border to find work, higher wages, and improved education and health care for their families. In addition, there was substantial illegal migration from countries such as Ireland, as well as from China and other Asian nations.

THE WORLD AT WAR

In 1914, an Austrian Archduke in the Balkans was assassinated by a Serb revolutionary. This act, because of entangling alliances, almost immediately threw all of Europe into war. At first the war had little effect on the United States, but since the "business of America is business," industries were soon hard at work turning out munitions for foreign sale.

Initially, Americans tended to be on both sides of the controversy. At the outbreak of the war, one third of all Americans were either foreign born, or had a foreign born parent, a large proportion of whom were German, and these immigrant groups often favored their country of origin. Both sides used propaganda to swing public opinion. Unlike World War II, where there was obviously a good side and an evil side, in World War I, there were just two sides, slugging it out, with catastrophic casualties, for reasons that were not entirely clear to Americans.

That was all to change in February 1915, when Germany announced that it would attack and sink any merchant ships found in British territorial waters. German military leaders were realists, and saw that the Allied war effort was being supported by imports. They reasoned that the war could be brought to an end by putting a stranglehold, by use of their submarine fleet, on all shipping headed for England.

The United States was neutral, and interpreted that to mean that they could trade with both sides in the conflict, without intervention. This was not the commonly held view of neutrality, however, and even Great Britain believed that supplying munitions to a belligerent constituted a violation of neutrality. Nevertheless, President Wilson issued a statement, in which he warned Germany that he would hold them "strictly accountable" for sinking any American flagship vessel. When the British liner *Lusitania* was sunk by a Germany submarine, with more than 1,200 people on board, of which 128 were Americans, public reaction in America against Germany was almost universal.

FYI MYTH: The *Lusitania* was actually carrying war munitions, and that is why she blew up. This is based on the fact that only one torpedo was fired, but eye-witnesses saw and heard two explosions. FACT: Not only was she not carrying munitions, but even her own magazine didn't blow up. Recently divers on the wreck discovered a massive hole aligned with her coal bunkers. The torpedo ignited the coal dust, which caused the second explosion.

However, while Americans were outraged, they were not ready to enter a war in Europe. The words of George Washington, echoing across the centuries, and warning about foreign entanglements and foreign wars, still reverberated in the nation's capital. Nor was Germany anxious to add another country to those allied against them—they were already taxed to the utmost by the grinding land war.

To placate the United States, Germany issued orders to all of its submarine commanders to give fair warning to all ocean-going vessels, even if they were obviously enemy merchant ships, before sinking them. This was of course a great show of good faith, because it was very dangerous for a submarine to surface, and to make any kind of signal, because of the risk of becoming a target for a nearby warship, or even having the deck guns of the merchantman take a pot shot at them. When, in March 1916, the Germans torpedoed the French ship *Sussex*, injuring several Americans, President Wilson issued an ultimatum. He told the Germans that they would have to abandon submarine warfare, or the United States would be forced to go to war. Germany backed down, realizing that they had to keep America out of the war at any cost. This action made Wilson a great hero, and he won reelection on the slogan: "He kept us out of war."

OVER THERE, OVER THERE ...

In 1917, the Germans changed their mind, and announced that they would resume unrestricted submarine warfare. This time, it wasn't just Americans dying on foreign ships, by April, five U.S. vessels had been sent to the bottom. Wilson, the man who had kept us out of war, immediately asked Congress for a declaration of war.

The New York National Guard was mobilized, including their regiment in Harlem. Sent to France, they were immortalized by their German enemies, who dubbed them the "Hellfighters" because of their ferocity in battle.

A new draft law was passed, the National Guard was mobilized, and ultimately 1.7 million men would go into uniform. When they arrived in France, the French wanted to use them as replacements in their divisions, but General John J. Pershing insisted that the entire American army get their own sector of the front, and fight as a unit. In 1918, fresh American troops played a decisive role in the summer offensive. In November, American forces took an important part in the vast Meuse-Argonne campaign, which cracked Germany's vaunted Hindenburg Line.

With the American entry into the war, with more troops getting off the boat every day, and with munitions flowing to the allies, the Germans realized that it was only a matter of time before they would be defeated. However, if they were going to end the war before total annihilation, it would have to be on honorable terms, and with a mutual armistice.

President Wilson, realizing that the war could be stopped, started by declaring the war aims of the Allies. He listed these aims in his "Fourteen Points," which he submitted to the Senate in January 1918. They included the end of secret treaties, freedom of the seas, the removal of tariffs, mutual reductions in national armaments, the reduction of colonial empires, and self-rule and unhampered economic development for European nationalities. The last and fourteenth point he considered the most important: the creation of a League of Nations to afford "mutual guarantees of political independence and territorial integrity to great and small states alike."

JUST A MINUTE

World War I ended at 11 A.M., November 11, 1918 (the eleventh hour of the eleventh day of the eleventh month). The day became known as "Armistice Day," and became a national holiday 12 years later by Congressional action. If the idealistic hope had been realized that World War I was "the War to end all Wars," November 11 might still be called Armistice Day. However, more wars followed, including World War II and Korea, so that in 1954 Congress changed the name of the holiday to Veterans Day.

The German army was exhausted, and they realized that peace with honor was better than peace with total defeat. Now that they had seen Wilson's position, they appealed for peace on the basis of his Fourteen Points. The Allies agreed to negotiate on that basis, and an armistice went into effect on November 11.

THE LEAGUE OF NATIONS

Germany came to the peace table, ready to negotiate a peace in accordance with Wilson's Fourteen Points, but what they faced were Allies determined to extract revenge. What finally emerged from the peace process was to set the stage for another war 20 years later. Among the most onerous of the demands was a requirement that the defeated nations pay for the cost of the war, "reparations" that were never repaid because the defeated nations were in worse shape than the victors and unable to afford such payments.

One after the other, Wilson's Fourteen Points were discarded, until the only point remaining was the League of Nations. That, at least, he was able to keep in the final Treaty of Versailles. However, when he brought the treaty back for ratification by the Senate, which was controlled by the Republicans, they refused to ratify it. Wilson, an amateur in politics, had made a critical miscalculation when he refused to send any Republicans to Paris to be on the Peace Commission. Then, he refused to make any sort of minor changes in the treaty, changes that would have ensured passage through the Senate. He then tried to travel around the country to rally support for the treaty, but was stopped by a stroke. Without the United States as a member of the League of Nations, it was doomed from the start, and it never became an effective instrument of international relations.

JUST A MINUTE

The end of the war was eclipsed by the greatest influenza epidemic ever to hit the United States. It had already ravaged Europe, and when it reached America, the flu killed more than half a million people in less than a year.

REDS

Americans were soon concerned with a greater threat than wars or epidemics, and that was a new type of government: communism. Ever since the American Revolution, the world had been convinced that American democracy was the natural evolution for government, that the demise of a monarchy would always mean a democratic form of government. Therefore, the Bolshevik Revolution of 1917 in Russia came as a great shock. The monarchy was overthrown, and replaced with a Marxist administration. Here was a new form of government, and it wasn't democracy.

Americans were worried that not only could communism rise in other countries, and gradually take over the world, but that it could also take hold in the United States. Such was the beginning of the "Red Scare," which would plague the planet from its takeover in Russia in 1917, until the fall of the Berlin wall in 1989. This fear of communist takeover became reality when, in April 1919, the post office intercepted more than 40 bombs addressed to prominent citizens.

In response, the Attorney General created a new organization within the Justice Department, the Federal Bureau of Investigation (FBI), and appointed J. Edgar Hoover to head it. Hoover began collecting files on known radicals, and soon raids by the FBI led to the deportation of scores of people.

QUIZ

HOUR'S UP!

1. Teddy Roosevelt called his ideas for domestic policy the:
    A. Good Deal
    B. Square Deal
    C. Raw Deal
    D. New Deal

2. Teddy Roosevelt summed up his foreign policy with the words "Speak softly and always":
    A. Wear a big smile
    B. Do a big shtick
    C. Carry a big stick
    D. Have a really big air force

3. The Russian Revolution was fought by all of the following except:
    A. Bolsheviks
    B. Reds
    C. Whites
    D. Blues

4. The anniversary of the day that ended World War I has become a national holiday and is called:
    A. Mother's Day
    B. Memorial Day
    C. Groundhog Day
    D. Veterans' Day

5. The organization formed after World War I to solve the world's problems was the:
    A. United Nations
    B. League of Nations
    C. Justice League of America
    D. League of Their Own

HOUR 16
The Great Depression

CHAPTER SUMMARY

LESSON PLAN:

In this hour, you will learn about the Roaring Twenties, Prohibition, the Great Depression, the Scopes Trial, the Ku Klux Klan, the Works Progress Administration, bread lines, and the Dust Bowl.

You will also learn ...

- How Clarence Darrow made a monkey out of William Jennings Bryan.
- That the Dust Bowl isn't a championship football game.
- That the KKK isn't a Southern grocery store chain called "Triple K."
- That speakeasy wasn't a new type of universal language.

The end of the First World War ushered in a period of unprecedented prosperity in the United States. Throughout the Roaring Twenties, fortunes were made on Wall Street as the value of stocks spiraled upward. However, the stock market crash in 1929, followed by an unprecedented period of drought that struck the Midwest, combined to throw the country into the worst depression in history. As the people struggled through the 1930s, the federal government, under what FDR termed the "New Deal," became involved to a greater degree in the national economy than ever before. Through a vast array of new government agencies, the federal government tried one solution after another in an attempt to bring the country out of the depression.

THE ROARING TWENTIES

In 1919, the states ratified the 19th Amendment to the Constitution, allowing female suffrage, making the 1920 presidential election the first one in which women would cast their vote. The victor was the Republican candidate, Warren G. Harding, whose campaign rejected Wilson's idealism, showing that at this point in history, the American people were primarily interested in prosperity.

FYI Warren G. Harding died in office under mysterious circumstances, and it has been rumored that he was poisoned by his wife because of his marital infidelities. It doesn't help her case that she refused to allow an autopsy. An alternate theory is that she poisoned him because the Teapot Dome scandal was about to be exposed, and she wanted to save his reputation. She shouldn't have bothered; few Americans today even know he was president.

Governmental policy in the 1920s was based on the belief that if government fostered and encouraged private business, prosperity would eventually encompass the rest of the population. Therefore, the Republicans were interested in creating the most favorable conditions for U.S. industry. New, higher tariffs guaranteed domestic manufacturers a monopoly. One of them, the Smoot-Hawley Act of 1930, had rates so high that economists petitioned President Hoover to veto it, fearful that other nations would respond with high tariffs of their own. There were also cuts in income taxes, excess profit taxes, and corporate taxes, in the belief that high taxes prevented the rich from investing in new industrial enterprises.

TEAPOT DOME

Teapot Dome was an oil reserve scandal with its origins in the administration of President Harding. In 1921, by executive order of the President, control of naval oil reserves at Teapot Dome, Wyoming and Elk Hills, California, were transferred from the Navy to the Department of the Interior. The oil reserves had been set aside for the navy by President Wilson. In 1922, Albert B. Fall, U.S. Secretary of the Interior, leased, without competitive bidding, the Teapot Dome, Wyoming, fields to Harry F. Sinclair, an oil operator, and the field at Elk Hills, California, to Edward L. Doheny.

These transactions became the subject of a Senate investigation conducted by Senator Thomas J. Walsh. It was found that in 1921, Doheny had lent Fall $100,000, interest-free, and that upon Fall's retirement as Secretary of the Interior, Sinclair also "loaned" him a large amount of money. The investigation led to criminal prosecutions. Fall was indicted for conspiracy and for accepting bribes. Convicted of the latter charge, he was sentenced to a year in prison and fined $100,000. Sinclair was subsequently sentenced to prison for contempt of the Senate and for employing detectives to shadow members of the jury in his case. The oil fields were restored to the U.S. government through a Supreme Court decision in 1927.

SILENT CAL

Vice President Calvin Coolidge, nicknamed "Silent Cal," became president after Harding's death in 1923, and then was elected in his own right in 1924. Coolidge continued the conservative economic policies of the Republican Party, which focused on encouraging private business as a way to bring prosperity to all Americans. The government provided businesses with construction loans, profitable mail-carrying contracts, and other indirect subsidies. Railroads, which had been put under government control during World War I, were restored to private management by the Transportation Act of 1920. Similarly, the Merchant Marine, which had been operated by the government during the war, was sold to private interests.

QUOTABLE QUOTES

 Calvin Coolidge said, "The chief business of the American people is business."

World War I had been a time of increased prosperity for farmers, as the demand for foodstuffs, both domestically and overseas, had lead to increasing prices. With the additional income, farmers had opened up new lands, and had purchased machinery to further increase production. However, with the end of the war, prices began falling, especially for wheat and corn. The high tariff policy of the Republican administration was partly to blame, because this effectively shut down foreign markets. As other countries raised their tariffs in response, American exports of foodstuffs gradually declined, and when the Great Depression occurred, the agricultural sector was already in dire straits.

DON'T GIVE ME YOUR HUDDLED MASSES

By the 1920s, Americans were worried about immigration: One third of the population was either of foreign birth, or at least one of their parents had been born in another country. Between 1900 and 1915, more than 13 million people arrived. And the ethnic mix of immigrants had changed. Rather than being Protestants from northern Europe, they were Jews and Catholics from southern and eastern Europe. The newcomers were resented because they took away low-paying jobs, maintained their Old World customs, and lived in urban ethnic neighborhoods. Most important, unlike earlier ethnic groups, who had tried to become as "American" as they could as quickly as they could, many of the new immigrants resisted assimilation into the larger American culture.

JUST A MINUTE

Ironically, in 1997, a study titled "Sons of Immigrants: Are They at an Earnings Disadvantage?" Barry Chiswick discovered that men in America with foreign-born parents have higher earnings on average than those with native-born parents. The earnings advantage is approximately 8 percent for those with a foreign-born father, 4 percent for those with a foreign-born mother, and 6 percent for those with two foreign-born parents.

New organizations arose to meet this perceived immigrant threat. An all-new Ku Klux Klan (the name was derived from the Greek word *kyklos*, which means "circle"), distinct from that which had existed after the Civil War, emerged calling for "100-percent Americanism." Unlike the Klan of Reconstruction, which had only campaigned against African Americans, the new Klan restricted its membership to native-born white Protestants, and campaigned against Catholics, Jews, immigrants, and African Americans. With a larger list of enemies, the Klan was able to appeal to people in the North and Midwest as well as the South, and membership took off to new heights.

This antiimmigrant hysteria resulted in the Immigration Quota Laws of 1924 and 1929. Under the new laws, the annual number of new arrivals was limited to 150,000. This immigration was to be allocated to different ethnic groups according to their percentage of national representation in the population of the United States according to the 1920 Census. This statute was so eminently equitable a solution that it undercut the nativist organizations, whose reason for existence was virtually extinguished by the law. Ironically, it was almost immediately rendered moot by the onset of the Great Depression, when virtually all immigration ground to a standstill.

CULTURE CLASH

During the Roaring Twenties, many people were shocked by the changes in manners, morals, and fashion. These changes were especially prominent in the usual harbingers of new ideas: young people, and those on college campuses.

F. Scott Fitzgerald captured the energy and turbulence of the times in works such as *The Great Gatsby*. He was part of an influential movement of writers and intellectuals dubbed the "Lost Generation." Many of them, like Ernest Hemingway, had seen action in World War I and returned dissatisfied with the materialism and spiritual emptiness of life in the United States.

As an increasingly modern, urban, secular society came into conflict with the older, rural, conservative, and traditionally religious segment of society, many Americans rejected the new morality and retreated back into the traditional values. Typical of the time was fundamentalist preacher Billy Sunday, a professional baseball player turned evangelist.

Part of the religious right's reaction to technological change had been the passage of laws to prohibit the teaching of evolution. They had been most successful in the Bible Belt, primarily in the South and Midwest. Leading this crusade was the elderly politician William Jennings Bryan, who generations before had been famous for his "cross of gold" speech, but who now was the acknowledged leader of the religious right.

The culture clash came to a head with the "Monkey Trial," which pitted the Bible's interpretation of creation against that of Charles Darwin and his theory of biological evolution. The great state of Tennessee had been one of those to pass a law against the teaching of evolution. When a high school teacher, John Scopes, purposefully violated the law by teaching evolution to his biology class, he was put on trial, and the American Civil Liberties Union (ACLU) stepped in to defend him. William Jennings Bryan volunteered his services as public prosecutor, and Clarence Darrow, the leading lawyer of his time, defended Scopes. The high point of the trial was when Darrow called Bryan to the stand, as an "expert" on the Bible, and then proceeded to publicly humiliate him by revealing his gross ignorance of the real world. Although Scopes was convicted, and had to pay a small fine, the trial was really a victory for modern technology over fundamentalist religion, and only served to reinforce the paranoia of those who perceived the disappearance of traditional values from American life.

QUOTABLE QUOTES

William Jennings Bryan, at the Scopes Monkey Trial, said: "I am more interested in the rock of ages than in the age of rocks."

Another example of culture clash is often called the "Noble Experiment." After a century of lobbying, in 1919 those opposed to any sort of alcohol consumption pushed through the 18th Amendment, and ushered in the era of Prohibition. This amendment prohibited the manufacture or sale of any kind of alcoholic beverage. Drinking was indeed a social evil: The worker who would drink up his entire paycheck was not just a cliché, he was a reality. Saloons full of men who should have been with their families, and public drunkards staggering through the streets, were a public problem. Unfortunately, the solution bred its own sort of evil. Like modern drug lords, it fostered organized crime in America, because it was a large industry, and it required a complex organization to produce, bottle, warehouse, wholesale, distribute, and retail the goods, something that could not be accomplished by a single individual, or by a small gang of criminals. Once established, organized crime became part of the social fabric of America. Another permanent side effect was that it decreased, across all segments of society, respect for the law, a problem that did not go away with the repeal of prohibition. Everyone was breaking the law, even the police were "winking" at violations, or actually on the payroll of the gangsters. Illegal bars, called "speakeasies," were everywhere. By 1933, Americans realized that Prohibition was a very good idea in theory and a very bad idea in practice, and it was repealed.

JUST A MINUTE

The Twenties, prohibition, and gangsters added more words to the English language, such as pep, addict, fetish, Freudian slip, fixation, sundae, tank, and clip joint. There were new terms to refer to people: *beaut, Joe College, Joe Zilch* (loser), *gold-digger, two-timer, playboy, sugar daddy, big cheese,* and *dumbell* (stupid girl, an abbreviation of dumb-belle). There were new dating terms, such as *heavy petting, hickie, park* (make out), *carry a torch, blind date, necking, whoopee,* and *stuck on.* There were new drinking terms, such as *gin mill, fried, crocked, ossified, juiced, moonshine, sauce, hooch, hair of the dog,* and *upchuck.* There were also new slang terms, such as *copasetic, bunk, baloney, banana oil, nifty, swell, ritzy, swank, peppy, goofy,* and *hard-boiled.*

BLACK EXODUS

Black Americans, most of whom had stayed in the South after the Civil War, were increasingly moving north. This accelerated into a wave of migration between 1910 and 1930, peaking during 1915 and 1916. Although they were coming from an agricultural background, most were moving toward cities such as Detroit, Chicago, and New York. Even though they were still subjected to discrimination, the northern cities provided better jobs, and more opportunity for personal freedom, than was possible in the rural South.

In an attempt to help enfranchise these migrants, W.E.B. DuBois and other African American intellectuals founded the National Association for the Advancement of Colored People (NAACP). In New York, there arose an African American literary and artistic movement, which has been called the "Harlem Renaissance." Like the "Lost Generation" of white writers, many of these were black soldiers who had seen action in France with the Harlem Hellfighters and other black units, had been exposed to European culture and society while in France, and had returned home, where they rejected traditional black conceptions of themselves, and their place in society.

THE GREAT DEPRESSION

On Black Friday in October 1929, the stock market crashed. Overnight, stocks lost 40 percent of their value. Americans kept hoping for a recovery, but by 1933, their stock was worth less than a fifth of what it had been on that black day. Banks went bankrupt, people lost their life savings, businesses and factories closed their doors. As more and more people were thrown out of work, jobs became impossible to find. A familiar sight on the street was men trying to sell apples to feed their families. Bread lines were common in most cities. Thrown out of their homes, hundreds of thousands roamed the country in search of food, work, and shelter. By 1932, one fourth of all Americans were unemployed, and the depression was showing absolutely no signs of abating.

One of the problems, ironically, was the increased capacity of the country to produce manufactured goods. Factories, with their increased mechanization, were turning out products faster than the people were able to purchase it. Most people had little discretionary income with which to purchase goods, especially farmers and minimum wage earners. The surplus capital that was available in the country, in the hands of the upper and middle class, had been siphoned off into investments in a stock market that was spiraling up at a frenetic pace. When the stock market crashed, even this money was no longer available in the economy.

QUOTABLE QUOTES

In October 1932, Bing Crosby recorded what became the anthem of the Great Depression, "Brother, Can You Spare a Dime?" The song was originally written for a Broadway musical "New Americana." At the time it was recorded, one out of every four Americans was out of work. Bing Crosby and Rudy Vallee each recorded the song shortly before President Roosevelt's election, and both versions were at one time or the other number one in the charts. However, it was Bing's interpretation, with its ominous baritone drone, that proved to be the one that would stand the test of time.

Herbert Hoover had just come into office when the crash occurred. The depression was a worldwide phenomena, and the Republicans were convinced that the United States had been dragged down by the rest of the world. They believed that eventually, the industriousness of the American people would correct the problem, and that the country would gradually regain its prosperity. The Democrats, on the other hand, weren't willing to wait for a miracle, and they promised to put all of the resources of the federal government behind solutions to fix the economy. If one solution didn't work, they argued, they would try another.

Given such a desperate national crisis, and the fact that the Republicans had struggled for more than three years and had found no solution, it was a foregone conclusion that the country was going to opt for different leadership. This was exacerbated by the positions of the political parties: The incumbents were intent on doing nothing, the challengers were promising to try everything. Put in such terms, it is a wonder that the outcome was not more uneven. Roosevelt won a resounding victory, taking close to 60 percent of the popular vote. His mandate was clear: He was willing to try any kind of political or economic solution. In many ways, this election was a victory for the democratic process. In other countries around the world, governments were toppling and control was being seized by dictators who promised to solve the people's problems. The transition was going to be radical in America as well, but at least it was done within the structure of the legitimate government. The Great Depression was probably the greatest test of the American system since the Civil War.

THE NEW DEAL

The inauguration of Franklin Delano Roosevelt (FDR) as president immediately engendered a feeling of optimism in the country. He called his program to fix the country the "New Deal," and it was basically an abandonment of the "laissez-faire" capitalism that had been the bulwark of the American economic system up until that time. Whereas in Europe and elsewhere in the world, the national government had exerted various controls over business and commerce for over a generation, the booming prosperity of America had withstood any serious efforts by lawmakers to rein it in. The regulation and control of the economy which had begun under Progressives such as Teddy Roosevelt was now being implemented in earnest, as the full ramifications were realized of allowing virtually unfettered capitalism in a modern industrial country.

FDR, in his inaugural address, stated: "The only thing we have to fear is fear itself."

The New Deal was put into place with great speed. The people were suffering, and there was no time to be wasted, no time to see which solution might work, and which one might not. The result was mishmash; some programs were badly run and some programs contradicted other programs. During the entire time, the Republicans were constantly complaining and criticizing. In retrospect, it is hard to tell if any part of the New Deal actually made a difference, as many have argued that the real end to the Great Depression only came when the war industries cranked up production for World War II. Whatever the verdict on the New Deal, however, at the time, the people at least had a feeling that the government was doing something, and that was in the final analysis the most successful facet of the entire New Deal.

One of the first actions FDR took was in the banking industry, because the nation's credit system was on the verge of collapse. The Federal Deposit Insurance Corporation (FDIC) was created to insure savings-bank deposits up to $5,000. The banks were closed, the bank examiners went over the books, and the banks were allowed to open again only if they were solvent.

New governmental agencies were created to generate credit for both industry and agriculture. The administration tried to encourage moderate inflation (the Great Depression had actually created *deflation*). It was hoped that this inflation would provide relief to debtors, who could pay off their debts with cheaper dollars, and that it would also cause an upward movement in commodity prices. To control the stock market, new and more stringent regulations were imposed upon the sale of securities on the stock exchange.

STRICTLY DEFINED

Deflation, the opposition of inflation, is a contraction in the volume of available money that results in a general decline in wages and prices. During the Great Depression, deflation resulted in wages falling 30 percent in the United States from 1929 to 1933. Persons were not able to pay their debts, which were now greater, with their wages, which were now lower, and bankruptcies resulted.

The large number of unemployed created a serious problem. The payment of welfare, outright gifts to the unemployed poor, was not the American way. All of these unemployed workers were a valuable work force, and in addition, people needed work to heighten their self-esteem. Many of the men who were now out of work had worked all of their lives. To suddenly be placed in a position where they did not work was to many physically debilitating. The government's solution to this was to hire millions of people to work for the government. The agency created to accomplish this was called the Civil Works Administration (CWA). Although criticized as "make work," it created jobs as diverse as highway repair and school teaching.

Another program to put people to work was the Civilian Conservation Corps (CCC). The government was afraid that if young people did not enter the workforce, they would never develop the job discipline they would need in later life. In order to capture these young people, and in addition to get them off the city streets where they would only cause trouble, Congress created this force, limited to young men between 18 and 25 years of age. They were taken to large camps in the country, which were run in a military style, and the men even wore surplus army uniforms. They were put to work in the open, in the fresh air of the countryside, undertaking conservation projects important to the country. They planted trees to fight soil erosion and to maintain national forests, they eliminated stream pollution, they created fish, game and bird sanctuaries, and they undertook projects to conserve coal, petroleum, shale, gas, sodium, and helium deposits.

JUST A MINUTE

Each of the New Deal agencies had a multiple letter abbreviation, and they were soon dubbed the "Alphabet Agencies." Examples were the CCC (Civilian Conservation Corps), PWA (Public Works Administration), AAA (Agricultural Adjustment Act), TVA (Tennessee Valley Authority), NRA (National Recovery Administration), FERA (Federal Emergency Relief Administration), WPA (Works Progress Administration), and the FSA (Farm Security Administration).

The Agricultural Adjustment Act (AAA) was designed to provide economic relief to farmers. This was the beginning of the subsidy system, in which the government would pay farmers not to grow crops. It was hoped that this would make certain farm products scarce, and push up prices. The money to pay the subsidies came from taxes on the industries that processed and packaged the food. However, by the time that the plan was in place, the growing season had already begun, and many farmers had to plow under crops that were already growing. The Secretary of Agriculture called this destruction "a shocking commentary on our civilization." However, it accomplished its goal, and farm production dropped.

Unfortunately, although the AAA was successful, the tax on the industries that processed and packaged the food was ruled unconstitutional in 1936. Congress therefore passed a new law for the relief of the farmers, and paid those who reduced their acreage of soil-depleting crops (such as corn, wheat, cotton, tobacco, and rice), achieving virtually the same goal, but in a more environmentally friendly way. The total amount of crops was reduced, and the land was less ravaged by the crops that were planted. By 1940, this new program had enrolled almost six million farms, and prices on agricultural commodities began to rise.

THE GRAPES OF WRATH

As if the Great Depression were not enough, the weather was also conspiring to make life miserable in the United States. Throughout the 1930s, but especially from 1935 until 1938, a horrible drought hit the Great Plains, followed by great wind and dust storms, which blew away the topsoil. This final plague on America became known as the "Dust Bowl." The wind and dirt destroyed crops, cars, and machinery, and injured people and livestock.

Life on the plains soon became intolerable for many people, and they were forced to abandon their farms. During the 1930s, almost a million people left Oklahoma, Arkansas, Texas, and Missouri, driving west toward California and the hope of a better life. Because so many were from Oklahoma, they were known as "Okies." As the farmers left, other people in these states, such as professionals and store owners, bereft of customers, were forced to also take up the road to the west. Once they arrived in California in their hundreds of thousands, there was little if any work for them, and what little work there was, such as competing with the migrant workers to pick crops, was extremely low paid because of the fierce competition for jobs.

FYI   The plight of the Okies is very vividly and accurately told in John Steinbeck's book *The Grapes of Wrath*, for which he received a Pulitzer Prize.

The Soil Conservation Service, established in 1935, was the New Deal response to the Dust Bowl. The wind and drought was not totally responsible for the terrible damage. Had the land still been covered in prairie grass, the soil would have been held in place. Methods of farming that were perfectly suitable for Europe, with its high rainfall, were disastrous when practiced on the plains. The Soil Conservation Service trained the farmers in methods to reduce erosion, such as planting rows of trees around fields as a wind break.

THIS NRA DOES NOT HAVE CHARLTON HESTON

Another set of "alphabet agencies" created by the New Deal were the National Recovery Administration (NRA) and the National Industrial Recovery Act (NIRA), both created in 1933. The target of these agencies was industry. The law attempted to end destructive competition by establishing fair competitive practices. The goal was to create more jobs. With these new workers bringing home a paycheck, there would be more consumers in the marketplace. With more money available to purchase goods, there would be increased production, which would in turn result in more workers being hired. Although the business community found the NRA to be helpful in jump-starting recovery, once the economic upswing began, business leaders changed their tune, and began to complain about regulation. In 1935, the Supreme Court held that the NRA was unconstitutional.

In 1935, as industry began to recover, Congress turned their attention to the problems of labor with the passage of the National Labor Relations Act. This law defined unfair labor practices, protected the right of employees to establish unions, established collective bargaining, and placed restrictions on the ability of companies to interfere with unions. The act also established the National Labor Relations Board to supervise collective bargaining, to administer employee elections, and to ensure that workers were protected when they tried to start a union.

One of the most productive of the "make work" programs was the Works Progress Administration (WPA). Men were employed to construct buildings, roads, airports, and schools, many of which are still standing today.

Nor were the arts neglected. Congress established the Federal Theater Project, the Federal Art Project and the Federal Writers Project, which employed actors, painters, musicians, and writers. In addition, the National Youth Administration provided employment for students, and established training programs for the unemployed youth.

SOCIAL SECURITY

The jewel in the crown of the New Deal, and one of the programs that is still in existence, is the Social Security Administration (SSA). Every citizen in the United States still has a Social Security number, and expects a Social Security check when they reach retirement age.

Conservatives complained that the Social Security system was un-American, that it ran contrary to precepts of self-reliance, and that it was an unwarranted incursion by the federal government into a field which should have remained the exclusive province of private industry and the states. However, while it appeared on the surface to be a radical federal program, it was actually quite conservative. Social Security was funded by payroll taxes on the earnings of workers, with a single fixed rate for all, regardless of income. It still remains one of the few government programs that is entirely self-supporting, with revenues from the taxes of current workers being used to pay the benefits of current recipients. While it occasionally runs a large surplus, which Congress tries to raid, or a deficit which has to be paid from the Treasury, it is by and large a self-supporting and autonomous government agency. Today, Social Security is one of the largest domestic programs administered by the U.S. government.

Hour's Up!

1. The President in office when the stock market crashed was:

    A. Warren Harding

    B. Herbert Hoover

    C. Woodrow Wilson

    D. William Howard Taft

2. The attempt to ban the sale and drinking of liquor with a constitutional amendment was called:

    A. Inhibition

    B. Apparition

    C. Prohibition

    D. Transition

3. Franklin Roosevelt called his ideas for domestic policy the:

    A. Good Deal

    B. Square Deal

    C. Raw Deal

    D. New Deal

QUIZ

4. The Great Depression was caused by:

   A. Underground atomic testing

   B. Reds, Greens, and Pinks called Downers

   C. The San Andreas Fault

   D. Black Friday

5. The "Monkey Trial" was all of the following except:

   A. A public humiliation for national figure William Jennings Bryan, who volunteered to prosecute the case for the government

   B. Instigated by those who wanted the version of the creation of man found in the Bible to be the only one taught in public school

   C. A great victory for those who believed in Darwin's theory of evolution

   D. Defendant Scopes was acquitted of all charges

HOUR 17
World War II

CHAPTER SUMMARY

LESSON PLAN:

In this hour, you will learn about the Japanese invasion of Manchuria, the Desert Fox, the campaign to take the Philippines, the invasion of Europe, and the dropping of the atomic bomb.

You will also learn ...

- That Tojo was not the little dog in *The Wizard of Oz*.
- That the Nisei isn't a new model being introduced by Toyota.
- That the Desert Fox is not an endangered species.
- That an atomic bomb is not country music slang for a record that really bombs big.

The Great Depression was a global event, which devastated the economy of not only the United States, but countries around the world. But while in America, the people never abandoned their faith in democracy as the solution to their economic woes; in other countries, dictators arose who offered a different solution to the problems of the people. In three such countries, Japan, Germany, and Italy, these leaders also made the people another promise, that of world domination. It took another devastating war, a world war of unprecedented proportions, to put an end to their madness. Before it was over, the United States, England, Russia, and their allies had fought a global war against evil, and more than 55 million people were dead.

ROOSEVELT WINS A SECOND TERM

Despite Republican complaints about the New Deal, Roosevelt won a landslide victory for reelection over Republican Alfred M. Landon in 1936, receiving 60 percent of the popular vote and winning the electoral votes of every state except Maine and Vermont.

Support for Roosevelt's Democratic Party came from organized labor, farmers, immigrants, African Americans, the South, and urban ethnic groups from Eastern and Southern Europe. The Republican Party was primarily businessmen, and the middle class from small towns and the suburbs. This political alignment was to remain virtually unchanged for more than 30 years.

The overwhelming mandate that Roosevelt received in the 1936 election made it clear that the people wanted the New Deal, and more importantly, they wanted the federal government to take a much more active, some would say intrusive, part in the economic life of the nation. They also clearly wanted many elements of the welfare state, which had already arisen in many European countries.

The stage was set for the classic tug of war between the two parties (which continues even today). The Democrats, like the early Federalists, advocate a strong central government, which closely controls the economy of the nation, regulates business, and provides a massive welfare system for the populace. The Republicans, ironically, whose origins were in a civil war in which they stood firmly against states rights, have now become the party that favors a weaker central government and less governmental control. They advocate a greater role for the states, and rely on private enterprise, and the natural efficiencies of capitalism, to ensure a prosperous nation. Because the two parties are fairly evenly balanced, and because the House, the Senate, and the presidency regularly changes from one party to the other, the country never swings too far to the left or the right, but seems to keep on a steady keel.

QUOTABLE QUOTES

In a radio address in 1938, Roosevelt reminded the American people that: "Democracy has disappeared in several other great nations, not because the people of those nations disliked democracy, but because they had grown tired of unemployment and insecurity, of seeing their children hungry while they sat helpless in the face of government confusion and government weakness through lack of leadership. ... Finally, in desperation, they chose to sacrifice liberty in the hope of getting something to eat. We in America know that our democratic institutions can be preserved and made to work. But in order to preserve them we need ... to prove that the practical operation of democratic government is equal to the task of protecting the security of the people. ... The people of America are in agreement in defending their liberties at any cost, and the first line of the defense lies in the protection of economic security."

WHILE AMERICA SLEPT

The Great Depression was a great problem in the United States, but a much more serious threat was developing overseas while Americans were focused on trying to shake off their domestic economic problems. In Japan,

Italy, and Germany, the depression had spawned dictators with imperialistic and expansionist aspirations. As early as 1931, Japan occupied the Chinese province of Manchuria, and set up a puppet state they named Manchukuo. Italy, under the control of fascist dictator Benito Mussolini, invaded Libya and Ethiopia. Germany, having been taken over by Adolph Hitler and the National Socialist (Nazi) Party, seized the Rhineland from France.

FYI Haile Selassie, Emperor of Ethiopia, was cheered during 1935 in almost every movie house in the world when he appeared in a newsreel. He became famous when he went to the League of Nations, and pleaded with them to help his country after they were invaded by Italy. He was so well known, he became *Time* Man of the Year. His name entered the U.S. vocabulary with the expression, "Well! If that's so, then I'm Haile Selassie!"

The aggression of the Axis Powers (Japan, Germany, and Italy) did not push America to mobilize; quite the contrary, the country seemed determined to remain neutral and isolated. The example of the First World War, rather than encouraging a call to arms, operated to discourage those who had been fooled into thinking that the previous World War was going to "make the world safe for democracy." They had been taken for a sucker before, they weren't going to fall for the same line a second time.

However, Americans had reason to be concerned. In 1938, the Nazis rolled over the border, and in one swift action incorporated all of Austria into the Third Reich. Hitler declared that he was going to unite all of the German peoples under one flag, and his next annexation demand was the Sudetenland area of Czechoslovakia, which was populated heavily by German speaking peoples. England and France were alarmed by this new demand from a megalomaniac whose demands seemed to have no bounds, and the outbreak of war in Europe seemed possible at any moment.

The United States announced that if Europe went to war, neither side in the conflict could look to America for aid or assistance. Congress scrambled to pass legislation that would ensure the neutrality of the country. Remembering how the sinking of American shipping had dragged the country into the First World War, these statutes prohibited trade with any of the warring nations. It was hoped that this strategy would prevent the United States from becoming embroiled in the approaching conflict.

Neville Chamberlain, the prime minister of England, was convinced that one last appeasement of Hitler would put an end to his demands. He turned over Czecho-slovakia to the Führer, and then returned to England, waving the treaty over his head as he got off the plane, announcing "peace in our time." He couldn't have been more wrong.

The Nazis swallowed up Czechoslovakia, but they had no intention of stopping there. In 1939, using a manufactured incident on the border as an excuse, the "blitzkrieg," or lightening war of the Nazi war machine, overran Poland in a manner of days. The Polish cavalry made a gallant attempt to defend the country, but they were no match for the highly mechanized storm troopers of the German Wehrmarcht, or the deadly Stukas that rained down death from the sky. With the Nazi invasion of Poland, England and France declared war.

Even though America as a country was officially isolationist, the people were far from neutral. Public feeling was clearly on the side of the Allies: The people were shocked by the aggression perpetrated by Hitler, Mussolini, and Japan against other countries. Many in America, including Roosevelt, felt that America entering the war was inevitable, and that the longer the United States stayed on the sidelines, the harder it was going to be to defeat the Axis powers in the end.

FYI Ironically, in 1938 *Time* magazine chose Adolf Hitler as the Man of the Year. Using that sort of standard, it is surprising that in 2001 they didn't choose Osama bin Laden.

The war was going increasingly bad for the Allies. The entire country of France surrendered, and the British army was barely able to escape from the Continent through a valiant evacuation across the channel at Dunkirk. However, they were forced to leave behind all of their equipment, and for the moment, Britain was unable to do more than defend itself from invasion. The Luftwaffe immediately began an air war against England, termed the Battle of Britain, to gain air superiority preparatory to a German invasion of the country.

As the world's democracies crumbled before the Axis onslaught, debate raged in the United States over whether to enter the war, or at the very least, to aid the Allies with food, munitions, and other war supplies. The vocal wing of the isolationists were the America First Committee, who included Midwestern conservatives and left-leaning pacifists. The other side of the debate was upheld by the Committee to Defend America by Aiding the Allies.

Faced with the increasingly likely possibility that with their rate of advance, the Axis powers would soon be entering the Western Hemisphere, the United States slowly started to take defensive measures. First, they joined with Canada in a bilateral defense treaty, the Mutual Board of Defense. Then they extended collective protection to the Latin American republics in the Western Hemisphere. Realizing that the army and navy that were in place were completely inadequate to protect America from invasion, Congress began voting increasingly larger amounts for the defense budget. Then, in September of 1940, they enacted, by the slim margin of one vote, the first peacetime draft law ever passed in the history of the United States.

All of those measures were defensive in nature, but in 1941, Congress finally came off the fence and decided to officially take sides in the conflict. They enacted the Lend-Lease Program, authorizing the president to send arms, munitions, and equipment to any country that he considered vital to the defense of the United States. While it was couched in terms of defense, its implementation was clearly partisan. The president used this law to begin sending supplies to Great Britain, the Soviet Union, and China, all of which were allied against the Axis powers.

JUST A MINUTE

By the end of World War II, the United States had supplied their allies with more than $50 billion worth of equipment under the Lend-Lease program.

In 1940, Roosevelt was challenged for the presidency by Wendell Wilkie, and set a precedent in American politics when he broke with George Washington's tradition, and ran for a third term. It was difficult for the Republicans to contest the election, since they agreed with the administration on foreign policy, and had no viable alternative to the New Deal on the domestic front. Because the country was slowly coming out of the depression, and also appeared to be on the road to war, the electorate saw no reason to change horses in the middle of the stream.

PEARL HARBOR

Although Americans were fixated on the war in Europe, Japan was just as aggressively moving forward in its conquest of Asia, which it called the "new order." They forced Britain, which was battling for its very survival, to withdraw from Shanghai in China, and from the Burma Road. France, which was already defeated, was forced to turn over Indochina.

The United States, as a major Pacific power, became increasingly alarmed. Japan had few natural resources, and relied heavily on imports for its war industry, including scrap iron from the United States. As a way to slow down the Japanese military machine, the United States imposed an embargo on the export of scrap iron and oil to Japan. This was followed by a freeze on Japanese commercial assets in the United States.

QUOTABLE QUOTES

 Because so much American scrap iron was sold to the Japanese before World War II, including old junk cars, a standard comment in the Pacific when a pilot would knock down a Japanese fighter was, "I just shot down another Ford."

The Japanese were alarmed by the actions of the United States. General Tojo, the new prime minister of Japan, sent a special envoy to demand that the United States release the frozen Japanese assets. The United States agreed to release the money, if Japan would withdraw from China and Indochina. Although the Japanese asked for two weeks to study the proposal, they had no intention of agreeing, and immediately implemented a war plan that they had drawn up many years previously. The plan called for a preemptory strike against the United States, to knock out the Pacific fleet.

QUOTABLE QUOTES

 Imperial Admiral Yamamoto, who conceived and planned the Pearl Harbor attack, had tried to talk his superiors out of it repeatedly. He knew well the industrial strength of the United States, and the temperament of its people. After the attack, he said "We have awakened a sleeping giant and have instilled in him a terrible resolve."

On Sunday morning, December 7, 1941, Japanese carrier-based planes attacked the U.S. Pacific fleet at Pearl Harbor, Hawaii. In the surprise attack, they sank 19 ships, including 5 battleships, destroyed more than 150 planes, and killed more than 2,300 soldiers, sailors, and civilians. However, the Japanese failed to accomplish their goal, because they missed the most vital part of the American fleet, the aircraft carriers, which were at sea. Ironically, their attack helped those in the United States who had been advocating naval superiority by air power, in a sea service that had been dominated by a "battleship mentality." Without their battleships, the navy was forced to fight a carrier war.

Americans were incensed by the Japanese raid on Pearl Harbor on December 7, 1941, in the same way that they would later be outraged by the attacks on America on September 11, 2001, at the World Trade Center and the Pentagon. President Roosevelt termed Pearl Harbor "a date which will live in infamy."

THE WORLD AT WAR

Overnight, the isolationists were ignored. The day after Pearl Harbor, Congress declared war on Japan, and three days later Germany and Italy, who had mutual defense treaties with Japan, declared war on the United States. World War II would prove to be the greatest war in which the nation would ever fight.

JUST A MINUTE

 On January 6, 1942, President Roosevelt announced staggering goals for war production that year: delivery of 60,000 planes, 45,000 tanks, 20,000 antiaircraft guns, and 18 million deadweight tons of merchant shipping.

Although some preparations for war had occurred during the preceding year, the country was in reality mobilizing from ground zero. Virtually overnight, the entire industrial capacity of the country had to be retooled, factories went from making Fords to tanks. Populations moved, as workers clustered in communities around the defense plants. The government instituted rationing of the civilian population to ensure that sufficient goods and foodstuffs were available for the war effort. By the end of 1943, approximately 50 million men and women were in war-related occupations. The draft went into high gear, as the country set about conscripting armed forces in excess of 15 million men.

THE NISEI

Because of the sneak attack on Pearl Harbor, Americans were paranoid about the Japanese. Even native born Americans of Japanese ancestry were suspected of being fifth columnists, saboteurs, and spies. In Hawaii, where a large percentage of the National Guard was of Japanese descent, the army immediately took away their weapons. But the most radical step was the internment camps. Normally, during wartime, belligerents intern any enemy nationals who are unlucky enough to be caught in their country on the outbreak of war. But the internment of Japanese Americans went far beyond those who were still Japanese citizens; it included not only naturalized Americans, but also those who were natural born citizens of the United States, second generation Japanese known as "Nisei."

These internment camps, or "relocation centers," were spread over the southwest United States. Life in these centers was as American as apple pie, they even had Boy Scout troops. And even more ironically, these camps had military recruiting centers. The Nisei, anxious to prove their loyalty to America, enlisted and fought for the United States, while their parents remained in the concentration camps, proudly displaying the star in the window, which indicated that they had a son overseas. One distinguished unit, the 442nd Regimental Combat Team, was one of the most decorated combat units in Europe during World War II.

JUST A MINUTE

The Nisei during World War II sustained 9,486 wounded and more than 600 killed, the highest casualty rate of any American unit during the war. For their heroism, the men won 52 Distinguished Service Crosses, 560 Silver Stars, and even 1 Medal of Honor. On June 21, 2000, President Clinton awarded the Medal of Honor to 20 additional Nisei for their actions during World War II.

"EUROPE FIRST" POLICY

The Allies decided that while they would fight the war on both fronts simultaneously, the priority was "Europe First," so the majority of assets would be allocated to the war in Europe. Then, when Germany and Italy were defeated, the full attention of the allies would be concentrated on the defeat of Japan in the Pacific theater.

Although defeated on the Continent, the British had held in North Africa. German General Erwin Rommel, the "Desert Fox," had tried to take Egypt and the Suez Canal, to cut England off from its colonies, but the British were able to stop their advance.

Meanwhile, the United States had accomplished a miracle in mobilizing for the war effort. Less than a year after Pearl Harbor, on November 7, 1942, an American army was landed in French North Africa. The infusion of fresh American troops, well supplied and well armed, was able to turn around the stalemate in North Africa. The German juggernaut was also stopped on the Eastern Front, where the Soviet Union, by incurring immense losses, had brought the Nazi advance to a grinding halt at Leningrad and Moscow, and had then defeated the Germans at Stalingrad.

With the German advance stopped on all fronts, the Allies were now faced with the daunting task of driving the Nazis back to Germany. By July 1943, using North Africa as their staging ground, a combined allied force of British and American forces had stormed ashore in Sicily, and then pushed forward onto the Italian mainland. Italy surrendered, and although this removed one of the Axis powers from the war, it did not remove the German divisions from Italy. It was a bloody and costly war of attrition against crack Nazi troops, and Rome was not finally liberated until June 4, 1944, just two days before the allied invasion of the continent at Normandy.

Although the Italian campaign was steadily driving the Nazis back towards Germany from the south, and the Russians were driving west towards Berlin, it was decided to open a third front in northern France by driving straight across the channel from England. General Dwight D. Eisenhower was appointed Supreme Commander of Allied Forces in Europe. On D-Day—June 6, 1944—U.S., British, and Canadian divisions dropped from the sky and splashed ashore on the beaches of Normandy in northern France. After horrendous fighting, the beachhead was established, and the invasion force began their drive toward Germany. On August 25, Paris was liberated. That Christmas, the Germans launched a successful massive counteroffensive in Belgium, known as the Battle of the Bulge, but this only caused a temporary stall in the Allied advance. By March 1945, Allied troops had advanced into Germany from the west, and the Russians had entered from the east. On April 30, Hitler committed suicide as Berlin fell. On May 8, the remainder of the Third Reich surrendered, and the war in Europe was over.

THE WAR IN THE PACIFIC

The war in the Pacific had started badly for the United States. Almost immediately after Pearl Harbor, the Japanese had invaded the Philippines, and the defeat of the forces there resulted in the largest single surrender in the history of the United States.

However, the entry of the Americans into the war soon brought the Japanese advance to a halt. They had planned on striking at Australia, but in the Battle of the Coral Sea, the Japanese navy was damaged so badly that they had to give up the idea of any further expansion to the south. This engagement was unique in world history, because it was the first naval battle in which the entire fight was conducted by carrier-based planes. This was followed by the second such engagement, the Battle of Midway, in which once again the enemy fleets never sighted each other; the entire engagement was determined by aircraft launched from the carrier decks. Midway was a great defeat for the Japanese navy: They lost four carriers, but perhaps most important, after that battle they had to abandon all hope of advancing east across the central Pacific. For the remainder of the war, the Japanese would be fighting a defensive action, as the United States advanced steadily toward their home islands.

FYI Lieutenant Colonel "Jimmy" Doolittle had submitted a crazy plan to the army. He proposed putting U.S. Army bombers on Navy aircraft carriers, steaming across the Pacific, and then bombing Japan. Amazingly, his plan was approved, and his "Tokyo Raid" was a great success. Coming only a few months after Pearl Harbor, it gave Americans an immense psychological boost, and in addition it shocked the Japanese, who had previously been convinced that their homeland was invincible.

The Allied strategy in the Pacific was called "island hopping." Each major engagement would bring them closer to Japan, until finally, they would be within striking distance of the home islands. And every island didn't need to be taken, early on in the war, because they had also developed the "bypass" strategy, in which islands would be skipped and allowed to wither on the vine, cut off from their lines of supply. Once a new island was taken, the airfield would be repaired, fighters and bombers landed, and control of the Pacific within range of that airfield would be secured. This island hopping campaign resulted in Allied amphibious assaults at Guadalcanal, the Solomons, the Gilberts, the Marshalls, and the Marianas, as the U.S. Marines took island after island.

By June 1944, as the army was landing in Europe at Normandy, the U.S. Navy was defeating the Japanese navy in the Battle of the Philippine Sea, and paving the way for General Douglas MacArthur's invasion of the Philippines. The Battle of Leyte Gulf, another decisive defeat of the Japanese navy, restored control of the seas around the Philippines to the Allies. By February 1945, U.S. land forces had taken Manila, and the Japanese were retreating back toward their home islands.

QUOTABLE QUOTES

 When General Douglas MacArthur was forced to leave the Philippines when the Japanese invaded, his immortal words to the people of the Philippines were, "I shall return."

The raising of the American Flag on Mount Suribachi, on the island of Iwo Jima, was captured by a combat cameraman, became a cover of Life magazine, and has now been enshrined in stone as the Marine Corps monument in Washington, D.C.

The Allies next target would give them an airfield within striking distance of Japan, and as a result, the Japanese resistance on the island of Iwo Jima, in the Bonin Islands, was incredibly fierce. They dug in, making excellent use of the natural caves and rocky terrain of the volcanic island. The Japanese navy threw itself against the American navy in continual suicidal kamikaze attacks from the sky, as Japanese pilots flew bombs laden with explosives straight into the carriers. It was a bloody fight, perhaps the most famous in Marine Corps history, but finally, with more than 6,000 Marines lying dead, the island was secured. The Japanese fought to the death, with no thought of surrender, and virtually the entire Japanese garrison on the island was wiped out. With the airfield secure, the 20th U.S. Air Force could begin their mission of launching air attack after air attack against the Japanese homeland.

THE ATOMIC AGE BEGINS ...

President Truman had watched in horror as Germany had continued to fight long after it was defeated, and his counselors told him that the battle to conquer Japan would be even worse. Even Japanese children were being trained for suicidal Banzai attacks. He was then briefed on an alternative, a new superweapon: the atomic bomb, which had been developed by the top secret Manhattan Project. After much discussion, he ordered the bomb to be used if the Japanese did not surrender by August 3. To make the surrender palatable, the Allies issued the Potsdam Declaration on July 26, guaranteeing that the Japanese would not be enslaved if they surrendered. However, it warned, if they did not give up, they would be subjected to "utter destruction."

JUST A MINUTE

The U.S. Army had calculated that it would incur a million casualties in the invasion of Japan, and with typical military efficiency, contracted for the manufacture of one million Purple Hearts, the military decoration for those killed or wounded in action. When Truman dropped the atomic bomb, those medals went into a warehouse. However, neither Korea, Vietnam, Granada, the Gulf War, Kosovo, Bosnia, not even the War in Afghanistan have made any significant dent in the supply of medals, which will probably last the army forever.

The Japanese refused to surrender, so a committee of U.S. military officers, political officials, and scientists were given the task of deciding where to drop the new weapon. The guidance from Truman was clear, only areas with clear military value would be targeted. As a result, cities such as Kyoto, which had been Japan's ancient capital, and which was a repository of many national and religious treasures, were to be considered immune from any attack. After much debate, the industrial city of Hiroshima, which also had a significant number of military installations, was chosen.

On August 6, 1945, a U.S. bomber, the *Enola Gay*, dropped an atomic bomb on the city of Hiroshima, killing approximately 85,000 persons. In the face of such a horrific demonstration, President Truman had expected an immediate surrender from Japan, and when none was forthcoming, he realized that his advisors were correct in their assessment of the determination of the Japanese to resist. He therefore reluctantly authorized another attack.

On August 8, 1945, a second atomic bomb was dropped, this time on the industrial city of Nagasaki, killing approximately 70,000 persons. The mood of the American people at that time was such that they wanted a quick end to the war, and in addition they had little sympathy for the Japanese, after learning of the horrible atrocities that they had inflicted on American prisoners of war. In addition, the Americans realized that the Japanese had been extremely cruel to their fellow Asians. For example, during the Japanese invasion of Nanking, more than a million Chinese had been systematically raped and murdered. This second atomic bomb convinced the Japanese that the United States had more than one of these terrible weapons, and they finally surrendered.

FYI The final death toll for World War II exceeded 55 million persons.

HOUR'S UP!

1. Haile Selassie was all of the following except:

   A. *Time* Man of the Year

   B. Emperor of Ethiopia

   C. Speaker before the League of Nations

   D. The expression Nazis used before they changed to "Haile Hitler"

2. Adolf Hitler's father's real name was:

   A. Max Bialystock

   B. Leo Blum

   C. Alois Schickelgruber

   D. Melvin Kaminsky

3. Mussolini was known for all of the following except:

   A. Making the trains run on time

   B. Invading Ethiopia

   C. Fascist dictator of Italy during World War II

   D. First Italian astronaut

4. During World War II, the horrific prime minister of Japan was:

   A. Toto

   B. Mojo

   C. Tojo

   D. Bozo

QUIZ

5. The only government to deliberately kill thousands of civilians by exploding an atomic bomb without warning in an unsuspecting city is the:

    A. Taliban of Afghanistan

    B. Communists of Russia

    C. Nazis of Germany

    D. United States of America

HOUR 18
The Cold War

CHAPTER SUMMARY

LESSON PLAN:

In this hour, you will learn about the Berlin Airlift, the Cold War, the Marshall Plan, the Korean War, and the Containment Policy.

You will also learn ...

- Where the buck stopped.
- Why the spy came in from the Cold War.
- Why there is a Union Label, but not a Confederate one.
- What happens to old soldiers.

The end of World War II, and the total defeat of the Axis powers, left an international power vacuum. Germany, Italy, and Japan were devastated, England and France, although technically the victors, were hardly in better shape. The two superpowers who emerged from the conflict were the United States and Russia. Although allies during the war, it had always been an uneasy alliance, with a serious underlying ideological difference. The United States was the champion of democracy, and the USSR was the cradle of worldwide communism. With their mutual enemies destroyed, an uneasy peace almost turned into another world war over the city of Berlin. However, after teetering on the brink of war, their disagreements turned into a Cold War. While there was never an outbreak of outright hostilities between the two countries, the tension between the two superpowers cast its shadow over the entire world for nearly half a century.

THE POLITICS OF WAR AND PEACE

Even before the United States entered World War II, planning was underway for the structure of the postwar world. The first meeting took place months before Pearl Harbor, when President Roosevelt met with Winston Churchill in Newfoundland, Canada. The document that they created, the Atlantic Charter, bore many similarities to Wilson's Fourteen Points, which he had created in the hopes of forging a better world after the end of World War I. The grandiose objectives of the Atlantic Charter included: no territorial gains by the victors, no border changes without the consent of the indigenous peoples, the inalienable right of all people to choose their own structure of government, the restoration of self-government to those who were deprived of it, economic cooperation between all nations, freedom from war, freedom from fear, freedom from want, freedom of religion, no restrictions upon the use of international waters, and the abandonment of the use of force as an instrument of international policy.

QUOTABLE QUOTES

 In the Atlantic Charter, Roosevelt incorporated "The Four Freedoms" that he had outlined in a speech that he delivered on January 6, 1941: "we look forward to a world founded upon four essential human freedoms. The first is freedom of speech and expression—everywhere in the world. The second is freedom of every person to worship God in his own way—everywhere in the world. The third is freedom from want, which, translated into world terms, means economic understandings which will secure to every nation a healthy peacetime life for its inhabitants—everywhere in the world. The fourth is freedom from fear, which, translated into world terms, means a world-wide reduction of armaments to such a point and in such a thorough fashion that no nation will be in a position to commit an act of physical aggression against any neighbor—anywhere in the world."

The next meeting between the United States and England was the Casablanca Conference, held in Casablanca, Morocco, in January 1943. At that meeting, Roosevelt insisted that the only terms upon which the Allies would end the war with the Axis powers would be "unconditional surrender." There were a number of reasons for this policy. First, he did not want a repeat of the "armistice" after World War I, in which the defeated peoples, especially Germany, had held to the fiction that they had not really been defeated. Roosevelt wanted each of the military régimes to admit, in no uncertain terms, that their countries had been completely vanquished. In addition, he wanted the leaders in these countries, in Germany, Italy, and Japan, removed from office, and the people free to choose their own leaders, free of any despotic dictatorship or military junta.

At the next meeting, in Cairo, Egypt, in November 1943, the Anglo-American conference was expanded to include Chiang Kai-shek, the leader of the Nationalist forces in China who were fighting the Japanese. At this conference, the primary focus was on Japan, and the postwar status of that country. It was agreed that Japan would be stripped of every territorial conquest which it had made in the past, including the peninsula of Korea, which it had acquired as early as 1911.

Later that month, the conference was expanded to include Joseph Stalin, the leader of the Soviet Union, at a meeting in Tehran, Iran. The most significant achievement of this meeting was the agreement to create a new international organization that would replace the League of Nations, to be called the United Nations.

THE YALTA CONFERENCE

By February 1945, the Allies knew that victory was certain. Italy had surrendered, Allied troops were pouring into Germany, and the Japanese were falling back onto their home islands. In February 1945, another meeting was held, this time at Yalta. The Soviet Union did not want to enter the war against Japan, as long as there was any possibility of a threat from Germany, but they agreed that as soon as Germany surrendered, they would attack Japan. The Soviet Union also agreed on the boundaries for Poland, which would be roughly the same as those at the end of World War I, known as the Curzon line. It was further agreed that in the newly formed United Nations, the United States, England, and the Soviet Union would comprise a Security Council, with the right to veto any action of the United Nations that might compromise their national security. In addition, the Allies agreed to divide Germany into occupation zones after the war, and to establish a tribunal to try war criminals.

There was one point on which the Soviets would not agree at Yalta, however, and that was reparations to be paid by Germany. Roosevelt and Churchill knew that reparations were a recipe for disaster—this had been amply proved after World War I. The Soviet Union insisted that Germany must pay for the damage they inflicted on the USSR. Unable to agree, they could only defer discussion until a later meeting.

THE POTSDAM CONFERENCE

After the defeat of Germany, the heads of the U.S., British, and Soviet governments met again at Potsdam, Germany, a suburb outside Berlin, from July 17, to August 2, 1945, to decide on the future of Germany. They agreed that it was critical that they immediately begin to "de-educate" the children of Germany, the infamous "Hitler Youth." They also outlined the principles that would control the democratic political structure of the country. Provision was also made to put on trial the Nazi leaders, for what was defined as "crimes against humanity."

Once again, the Soviet Union raised its demand that it receive reparations from Germany. As a concession, it was permitted to remove industrial machinery and factories and relocate them in Russia. However, none of the powers would agree to the $10 billion in reparations demanded by the Soviet Union.

JUDGMENT AT NUREMBERG

The trial of Nazi war criminals began in November 1945 at Nuremberg, Germany, for "crimes against humanity." The four major countries of the Allied cause—Britain, France, the Soviet Union, and the United States—conducted the trials. The crimes for which the Nazi war leaders were charged included plotting and waging aggressive war, violating the laws of war, and violating the laws of humanity. Perhaps the most important charge, and the one which most shocked the world, was genocide, especially of Jews, gypsies, homosexuals, Slavs, and other ethnic groups that the Nazis found objectionable. The trials lasted for more than 10 months, and resulted in the conviction of all but 3 of the 22 accused.

FYI The International Military Tribunal that was established to conduct the Nuremberg Trials was supposed to continue for many years. However, by the end of the first round of trials, the Cold War had set in, and the United States needed Germany as an ally against the USSR and its threat of global communist domination. The International Military Tribunal never convened again, despite the fact that there were many war criminals left to try.

UNITED NATIONS

The Allies wasted no time in establishing the United Nations. Even before the fall of Germany on April 25, 1945, delegates from 50 nations met in San Francisco, California, to begin the work of establishing the United Nations.

The purpose of this new organization, designed to replace the League of Nations, was to create a forum wherein international differences could be discussed peacefully, and resolutions obtained for disputes between countries. Also important were goals that were established to find cures for the diseases of the world, and to bring an end to famine and hunger.

The United States, which had envisioned the League of Nations, and then rejected it, did not make the same mistake with the United Nations. The charter for the United Nations was approved by the Senate with only two negatives votes. The new headquarters for this worldwide organization was established at New York City.

The ratification of the UN charter signaled the end of American isolationism. It was finally acknowledged that the United States was one of the world's great superpowers, and that it was impossible for this country to exist in isolation from the rest of the globe. Only by taking a firm leadership role in this new world order was it going to be possible to avoid the pitfalls which had lead to a conflict such as World War II.

THE BUCK STOPS HERE

Right before the end of World War II, Franklin D. Roosevelt, by then in his fourth term, and in declining health, suddenly died. He was succeeded by Harry S Truman, who had been an artillery officer in World War I, and then a Democratic senator for Missouri, before becoming vice president.

QUOTABLE QUOTES

Harry Truman had a sign on his White House desk, since famous in American politics, which read "The Buck Stops Here."

Truman had not been well prepared to assume the top spot, and he knew it. Roosevelt had not kept him in the loop on important matters, and as a result his knowledge of what had been negotiated at the various conferences was less than what he needed to handle his new position. In addition, he had little prior experience in international affairs. "I'm not big enough for this job," he told a former colleague. However, despite his lack of experience, he had two strengths: He was a quick learner, and he was not only decisive, but he could make decisions quickly. He was going to need these qualities, because the world was almost immediately in crisis again.

THE WAR TURNS COLD

The United States and the Soviet Union had been uneasy allies during World War II. Thrown together because of their common enemy, Nazi Germany, distrust had existed ever since the First World War, when the United States had sent troops to fight in the Russian Revolution on the side of the White Russians against the Reds. Even after Lenin's victory, the United States did not recognize the Communist government in Russia until 1933.

FYI The "hot" war between the United States and Russia is long forgotten in the United States, but not in Russia. President Wilson started with a naval blockade of Communist Russia, and then sent troops to Murmansk, Archangelsk, and Vladivostok to help overthrow the Russian Revolution, a move that was supported by both Britain and France. The U.S. soldiers, who ironically were in a joint command, allied with the Japanese, fought in Russia for two years. The Sino-American forces fought from Vladivostok westward all the way to Lake Baikal, where they supported Czech and White Russian troops that had declared an anti-Communist government at Omsk. They briefly maintained front lines as far west as the Volga. However, when the White Russian army disintegrated, the American troops were pulled out.

The United States and Russia had quite different aims at the end of World War II. The United States wanted to create a world in which every country was modeled after the United States, with the same precepts of liberty, equality, and democracy. However, the world was in chaos, the imperial European empires were crumbling, and in their wake came unstable new countries ravaged by civil wars, poverty, crime, ethnic divisions, and internal dissension. The United States, which firmly believed in the ability of capitalism to solve the worlds troubles, wanted to stimulate world trade, both to create markets for American products, and to help revitalize the economies of the European countries that were devastated by the carnage of World War II.

The Soviet Union, on the other hand, had its own agenda. First and foremost were the ideological differences; the Communist theories of Marx and Lenin were vastly different from American democracy. In addition, when the Czar had been deposed, the new Communist government had adopted, almost verbatim, the same centralized, autocratic style of government, which had characterized the old régime. In addition, while World War II had barely touched the continental United States, it had devastated Russia. Twenty million Soviet citizens had died—some of the larger battles, such as Stalingrad and Leningrad, had accounted for over a million casualties alone. The Russians were justifiably paranoid about another invasion from the west: Their experiences with the French under Napoleon and two world wars in which Germany had come close to occupying the entire country, had made them determined to create what they defined as "defensible" borders.

THE CONFLICT BEGINS

The first serious disagreement between the two superpowers arose over Poland. Historically a war-torn country with few natural borders, the Soviets looked upon Poland as a buffer state against western aggression. As such, they wanted it totally and completely under their influence. The Yalta Conference had contained a provision calling for "free and unfettered" elections in Poland, thus, the United States demanded complete self-determination for the Poles. Truman had been completely briefed on the provisions of the Yalta conference, and he was determined to make sure that the Soviets lived up to their side of the agreement. His inflexibility on this matter, and the Russians equally stubborn refusal to countenance anything but complete control, was the beginning of the Cold War.

QUOTABLE QUOTES

"From Stettin in the Baltic to Trieste in the Adriatic," Churchill said, "an Iron Curtain has descended across the Continent."

The Soviets were well positioned to enforce their will on the countries of Eastern Europe. At the end of World War II, the massive Soviet Army, which had fought its way to Berlin and defeated the powerful Nazi juggernaut, was still in position. There were occupation forces in garrisons all over Central and Eastern Europe. Soon, in every country, the democratic party was crushed, and the Communist Party was in control. The last country to succumb was Czechoslovakia in 1948.

CONTAINMENT

The United States was alarmed by the Soviet takeover of Eastern Europe, and was afraid that left unchecked, they would soon take over the entire subcontinent, and ultimately, the world. In response to this growing threat, they developed the policy of "containment." Simply put, the United States realized it could not oust the Soviets from those countries in which it had already established control, but it could "contain" the problem by preventing any other countries from being taken over. Although they were convinced that communism was wrong, and would one day fall of its own volition, in the interim, they had to preserve democracy in the rest of the world.

The first test of the containment policy came in Greece, which ironically was the birthplace of democracy. Communist forces had plunged the country into civil war. Great Britain had been supplying aid to Greece to fight these Communist insurgents, and also to Turkey, to keep them from giving the Soviet Union the right to build naval bases in the Bosporus. However, in the postwar years, England was having severe financial problems of her own, and could not continue the aid.

In a statement that came to be known as the "Truman Doctrine," he declared, "I believe that it must be the policy of the United States to support free peoples who are resisting subjugation by armed minorities or by outside pressures."

The United States realized that they were going to have to find the money to fund both Greece and Turkey, or run the risk of communism spreading to these two countries. Truman went to Congress, and asked for $400 million for economic aid for Greece and Turkey. He got the money, but in order to do so, he had to "scare the hell out of the country." Truman did a good job, in fact, many people think he did too good a job. He hipped up such a hysteria about communism, that he set the stage for Senator McCarthy and the investigations of the House of Representatives and their attempts to find Communists behind every door in America.

MARSHALL PLAN

Another facet of containment was ensuring that the countries of Western Europe, those that were not occupied by the Russian army, would not turn to communism. All of Europe had been devastated by the war, factories were destroyed, homes were gone, people were starving. In those countries, the Communists were reminding the people of their wartime record of resistance to the Nazis. Moscow was funneling money into these Communist parties in these countries, and U.S. operatives were sending this information back to Washington.

 George C. Marshall had been the Army Chief of Staff during World War II, prior to becoming the Secretary of State. He was awarded the Nobel Peace Prize in 1953 for his plan for the reconstruction of Europe.

George Marshall was the Secretary of State. He realized that what was needed was a second mobilization, this time not of soldiers and munitions, but of weapons to fight "hunger, poverty, desperation, and chaos." In cooperation with the countries who desperately needed the help, a plan for revitalization of Europe was devised, with a price tag of $17 billion. While this seemed incredibly expensive, it was only a fraction of what it had cost the United States to fight World War II. Congress appropriated the money for what was to become one of the most successful foreign aid programs in history. Because of his initiative, it was called the "Marshall Plan."

BERLIN AIRLIFT

When the guns stopped firing in Germany at the end of World War II, the county was full of Allied soldiers, who at first were the conquerors, but who quickly became the policemen, and then the backbone of the recovery effort. Germany was divided into four zones, one each for the United States, Soviet Union, Britain, and France. The capital, Berlin, was also divided into the same four zones.

The four zones were supposed to be a temporary expedient; they were never envisioned as a permanent division of the country. It was quite clear to everyone, except the Soviets, that Germany was not about to rise again and try to conquer Europe. Their paranoia, no matter how justified by past events, led them to veto every proposed plan to reunite the country. Finally, the United States, Britain, and France decided to go ahead and unite their three zones into one, independent country, which became known as West Germany. The Russian Zone became known as East Germany.

The reunification of the three zones caused an immediate reaction in Moscow. Convinced of the threat of a reunited Germany, they immediately reacted by closing all Allied access to the city of Berlin. Because Berlin was geographically located deep in the Soviet zone, closing the land access to Berlin effectively cut off the city from all sources of supply. Effective June 23, 1948, Berlin was under siege.

FYI One air crew had a unique idea, which they dubbed "Operation Little Vittles." On each flight into Berlin, they would tie candy to little parachutes made out of hand-kerchiefs, and drop them to the children of the city.

Political leaders in the United States were convinced that the loss of Berlin would be just the beginning, that it was the precursor to the fall of all of Europe. As a result, they were determined to keep Berlin supplied, no matter what the cost, no matter how long the siege would last. Supplies were flown into Berlin until Stalin finally called off the blockade.

The Berlin Airlift lasted 231 days. During that time, U.S., French, and British planes delivered nearly 2,250,000 tons of goods. They flew a total of 277,264 flights.

The Berlin Airlift, combined with the Soviet domination of the countries of Eastern Europe, convinced the United States and its Allies that the Soviet Union was a real and serious threat to their security. In 1949, in conjunction with 11 other countries, the United States organized NATO (North Atlantic Treaty Organization). It was a true mutual defense treaty, which the United States had not entered into since their alliance with France during the American Revolution. The basic precept of the charter was clear: An attack on one country would be considered an attack on each and every one, and they would all be allied until the threat was defeated. In response, the USSR created the Warsaw Pact, an "alliance" of those countries under its Communist domination.

FYI When NATO was formed, it was always envisioned that the charter would be invoked by a Russian attack on Germany, followed by a rallying of all of the NATO countries around Germany in an effort to defeat the Russians. No one ever envisioned that it would be over half a century later that the clause would be triggered, by an attack on the United States by Afghanistan. All of the nations of NATO are allied with the United States in the war on terrorism.

Alarmed by the threat of Soviet aggression, the National Security Council instigated a comprehensive review of American foreign policy, as well as the defensive capabilities of the United States. Their conclusion was that the Soviet Union was determined to institute Communist governments wherever they could in the world. The recommendation of their report was that the United States must stand ready to assist any nation, wherever located, that appeared to be in danger of being taken over by a Communist government. This report immediately resulted in increased defense spending, and also increased foreign aid by the United States to counter perceived threats to democracy around the world.

THE KOREAN WAR

American concern about the spread of communism was further intensified by events in China. Nationalist China had been an ally during World War II, and they had been instrumental in the defeat of the Japanese in the Pacific theater. However, China had actually been two countries during the war, the Nationalist government under Chiang Kai-shek, and the Communist forces under Mao Tse-tung. With the end of the Japanese threat, these two forces had plunged into civil war, and in 1949 the Communists finally established conclusive control over the entire country, except the island of Taiwan, which split and became a separate country under the control of the democratic forces. China is a massive country, and Americans saw this as a significant spread of communism. These fears were reinforced when Mao announced that they were going to ally with the Soviet Union in their ideological struggle with the United States.

While communism might have been contained in Europe, it certainly was not under control in Asia. The United States was determined that no other Asian countries fall under Communist control, and this fear of the spread of communism would ultimately involve the United States in wars with two of China's neighbors, Korea and Vietnam.

Korea, like Germany, had been divided at the end of World War II. The entire Korean Peninsula had been conquered by Japan in 1911, and now that they were defeated, they were divested of all their conquests. The dividing line for the two zones of influence was the 38th parallel: The land to the north was occupied by the Soviet Union, which resulted in a Communist government, while the land to the south was occupied by American forces, and adopted a democratic government. Unlike in Germany, where the troops remained, in Korea the soldiers, both Soviet and U.S., were soon pulled out, and the countries left to their own devices.

Although this shot looks like an outtake from the TV series M*A*S*H, it is actually a combat camera shot of an actual M.A.S.H. medical unit in action during the Korean War.

The army of North Korea, in June 1950, crossed their southern boundary, and invaded South Korea, with the goal of bringing the entire peninsula under the control of the Communist-dominated government in the north. The United States, in fact the entire world, was alarmed. The United States saw the entire invasion as part of the international Communist conspiracy to take over the world. In one of its first major initiatives, the newly formed

United Nations condemned the action, and when the North refused to withdraw, resolved to send United Nations troops to force the North Koreans to leave.

FYI The Soviet Union could have used its veto power in the Security Council to scuttle the entire Korean War before it even started. However, ironically, at that point in history, it was boycotting the United Nations to protest its decision not to admit China. During this moment of opportunity, before the Soviet Union returned to take its normal position on the Security Council, the United States was able to push through a resolution branding North Korea as an aggressor and authorizing the use of force to expel them from South Korea. The Soviet Union would never be absent again.

President Truman ordered General Douglas MacArthur, the hero of the war in the Pacific during World War II, to Korea. The UN forces had been pushed as far south as Pusan, and MacArthur wanted to avoid having to fight his way back up the Korean peninsula. Utilizing the old "island-hopping" strategy from World War II, and making maximum use of his naval superiority, MacArthur executed a daring landing at Inchon, a port city north of Seoul. Such a landing would force the North Koreans to retreat, for fear of being cut off in the south.

MacArthur was too successful. The North Koreans not only retreated, but he chased them all the way to the Chinese border. This turned out to be a great strategic blunder. China, alarmed at what they perceived to be a threat to both their country, and to communism, entered the war on the side of North Korea. They poured across the Yalu River, all of the gains evaporated, and the UN forces were driven back to the 38th Parallel.

MacArthur advocated bombing mainland China, while at the same time supporting a landing by the Nationalist Chinese, who were in exile in Taiwan. Their aim would be to topple the Communist government. This would bring both China and all of Korea into the democratic fold. When Truman rejected his plan, MacArthur tried to go over his head, and go straight to the American people. However, the president is the commander in chief, and therefore Truman, enraged at such insolence, fired MacArthur on the spot.

QUOTABLE QUOTES

 General MacArthur, after being fired, made a speech in which he said, "Old soldiers never die, they just fade away."

The average American was fervently against communism, and could not understand Truman's restraint in fighting a limited war. His popularity plummeted after he fired MacArthur, and he received the lowest approval rating of any president up to that time. With the war at a stalemate, and both sides virtually back to the pre-war borders, a truce was finally negotiated, and the war ended.

HOUR'S UP!

1. From 1946 to 1989, the United States and Russia were engaged in the:
    A. Great War
    B. World War
    C. Hot War
    D. Cold War

2. The United States was trying, with the "Containment Policy," to prevent the spread of:
    A. Sex
    B. Drugs
    C. Rock and roll
    D. Communism

3. The leader who referred to the dividing line between democratic and Communist Europe as the Iron Curtain was:
    A. Stalin
    B. Franklin Delano Roosevelt
    C. Winston Churchill
    D. Harry S Truman

4. General MacArthur made a speech in which he said: "Old soldiers never die, they just …"
    A. Go away
    B. Get blown away
    C. Run away
    D. Fade away

QUIZ

5. The president who had a sign on his desk that said "The Buck Stops Here" was:

A. Franklin Delano Roosevelt

B. Richard Nixon

C. Harry Truman

D. Warren G. Harding

PART IV

America Leads the World

HOUR 19

Civil Rights

CHAPTER SUMMARY

LESSON PLAN:

In this hour, you will learn about the Fair Deal, the Eisenhower administration, Joseph McCarthy and the House Un-American Committee, the rise of network television, the evils of rock and roll, and the beginnings of the Civil Rights movement.

You will also learn ...

- There was an Ike before Tina Turner.
- That Senator Joseph McCarthy wasn't a puppet belonging to Edgar Bergen.
- That Massive Retaliation is not a Bruce Willis film.

The worldwide Cold War, in which the United States was aligned as the leader of the free world against the forces of the international communist conspiracy, was reflected on the domestic front. In the struggle against communism, the average American was concerned with fifth columnists, those living in the United States whose allegiance was not to democracy and their own country, but to the international communist conspiracy and the enemy. The person who capitalized on this national fear was a United States Senator, Joseph McCarthy, who used the power of Congress to search out and expose those whose allegiance was suspect.

THE FAIR DEAL

With the end of World War II, those in the service, many of whom had been overseas for years, wanted to come home, and get their lives back to normal. Truman's first priority was to retool the wartime economy, which was geared up to make tanks and bombs, and get it back onto a peacetime footing, turning out Fords and Chevrolets. However, as the GIs returned, there was a serious housing shortage, and in addition they faced competition for employment with those who had not served, women who were still working, and their fellow returning veterans, who numbered more than 13 million. In response to this crisis, Congress passed the GI bill, which helped their transition back to civilian life by providing guaranteed home loans, and financial aid to attend college or to obtain industrial training. By putting a large majority of the returning soldiers into school, rather than into competition for jobs, they accomplished two goals: They educated the returning veterans, and they reduced the unemployment rate by removing them from the workforce.

Harry Truman called his domestic program the Fair Deal, and he patterned it after Roosevelt's New Deal. Truman wanted to use the federal government to ensure economic opportunity and social stability, and he struggled to use it for that purpose in the face of powerful political opposition from conservative legislators determined to reduce the role of government. They argued that now that the country had come out of the Great Depression, there was no longer any need for big government.

FYI Ironically, Harry S Truman became *Time* Man of the Year because of his decision to kill hundreds of thousands of people with the atomic bomb. However, it did bring to an end World War II, and probably saved the lives of a million American soldiers, as well as several million Japanese civilians, including women and children, who were being trained to defend their "home island" with human waves of banzai attacks against the "invaders."

The end of the war resulted in massive unemployment, as the war industries came offline. In addition, because wages had been stagnant during the war, those with jobs felt that they were entitled to pay raises, and almost five million workers went on strike in 1946. The first industries to be hit by these strikes were the automobile, steel, and electrical industries. When the strikes spread to the railroads and to the coal miners, Truman realized that the country was in danger of becoming paralyzed by big labor, and took action against the strikers. However, this alienated millions of working-class Americans, who felt that the federal government should be on the side of the workers, not management.

In response to these concerns, Truman submitted to Congress a 21-point program, which called for government protection against unfair employment practices, a higher minimum wage, increased unemployment compensation, housing assistance, a proposal for health insurance, and legislation on atomic energy.

Such a diverse legislative agenda made it unclear which programs were a priority for Truman. In response to what they alleged was indecisive leadership by Truman, in the 1946 congressional elections the Republicans ran on a platform of "Had enough?" and voters responded by turning the Democrats out of both houses in record numbers. This was the first time that the

Republicans had controlled both the House and the Senate since the onset of the New Deal, and they were determined to reverse the liberal big government direction of Roosevelt's four administrations.

With a hostile legislative branch, Truman could only watch helplessly as they cut spending and reduced taxes. Few thought that he had any chance in the 1948 presidential elections, and the polls only seemed to confirm that his Republican opponent, New York governor Thomas Dewey, was going to win by a landslide. In fact, on election night, many newspapers declared "Dewey wins!" and there is even a famous photograph of Truman holding up one of these newspapers. However, the supporters of the New Deal were solid: They included organized labor, farmers, and African Americans, and Truman accomplished one of the great upsets in American politics when he won the election, and returned to the White House for another term.

QUOTABLE QUOTES

 Harry S Truman told newspapermen that the period should be omitted in his middle initial. He explained that the "S" did not stand for any specific name, but was a compromise between the names of his two grandfathers, Anderson "Shipp" Truman and "Solomon" Young.

During Truman's second term, he had mixed success with his Fair Deal. He made two significant moves forward on the Civil Rights front: He banned racial discrimination in the federal civil service, which had been notoriously unfair in its hiring practices, and he signed an executive order putting an end to segregation in the armed forces. Overnight, the federal government became the place in government where African Americans had the best chance for upward mobility. Truman was also able to raise the minimum wage, and to expand Social Security. However, he failed to push through his national health insurance program, or any of his measures to aid education.

MASSIVE RETALIATION

Dwight D. Eisenhower, immensely popular as the commander in chief of the Allied forces in Europe during World War II, swept into the presidency in 1953. Not only was he a war hero, but he had a natural, father-figure persona that made him incredibly popular. People were not voting for a political platform, they were voting for the man, and his campaign slogan reflected that. It was simply "I like Ike," perhaps the most simplistic and apolitical campaign slogan of all time.

FYI Dwight D. Eisenhower, who became a five star general before leaving the military, is the highest-ranking military president in history. Washington was a two star general during the Revolution (which was the highest rank at that time), and he subsequently received, in 1798, one year before his death, a third star, making him the first lieutenant general.

Eisenhower's greatest concern was communism, and its goal of world domination. After the war, he had served first as the army chief of staff, and then as the commander of the newly formed NATO, and he was well prepared to tackle this issue. He realized that Moscow envisioned a worldwide revolution, in which each country in turn would be taken over by the Communist Party. In his first inaugural address, he declared, "Forces of good and evil are massed and armed and opposed as rarely before in history. Freedom is pitted against slavery, lightness against dark." In his mind, and that of most Americans, the Communists were dedicated to world conquest.

When it is deto-nated, the explosion of an atomic bomb creates a distinctive mushroom cloud.

Eisenhower, as a military man, was committed to preventing any outright Communist attack on America. He developed a new policy, that of "massive retaliation." Under this new doctrine, the United States proposed to build such an immense arsenal of nuclear weapons, with the capability to deliver them against their targets in the USSR, that they would never contemplate attacking the United States. To back up this threat, new and more powerful nuclear weapons were being developed. Not only did the military have the original type of atomic device developed by the Manhattan Project during World War II, but they had since created the more powerful and devastating hydrogen bomb. Any attack on the United States would be discouraged by the knowledge that the response would be such a massive retaliation of nuclear weapons that it would virtually annihilate the attacker.

The concept of massive retaliation, however, was only meant to be implemented in the event of an actual attack upon the United States itself. Eisenhower was not about to use nuclear weapons in other theaters of operations. Thus, he refused to use them in Indochina in 1954, and as a result the Communist forces were successful in forcing the French to withdraw from the country. In the Middle East, Eisenhower declined to use force when British and French troops occupied the Suez Canal and Israel invaded the Sinai in 1956, following Egypt's nationalization of the canal. The United States used diplomatic pressure to force British, French, and Israeli troops to withdraw from Egypt, which retained control of the canal.

THE RED MENACE

Americans had long feared radical subversion, and anti-Communist hysteria was fueled by postwar events. In 1949, the Soviet Union exploded their first atomic device, and shocked Americans were immediately ready to believe that the United States was in imminent danger of a Soviet attack. In 1948 Alger Hiss, a former assistant secretary of state and an adviser to Roosevelt at Yalta, was accused of being a Communist spy by Whitaker Chambers, a former Soviet agent. Hiss denied the accusation, but was convicted of perjury. In 1950, a British-American spy network was uncovered that had transferred to the Soviet Union information about the development of the atomic bomb. The capture and trial of Ethel and Julius Rosenberg for divulging atomic secrets increased paranoia about a domestic Communist danger. Attorney General J. Howard McGrath declared there were many American Communists, each bearing "the germ of death for society."

In 1947, the House Committee on Un-American Activities had investigated the motion-picture industry to determine whether Communist sentiments were being given positive treatment in popular films. When some writers invoked their 5th Amendment right not to testify, they were cited for contempt of Congress and imprisoned. Hollywood took the hint, and began a vigorous campaign of self-regulation, fearful that if they did not clean up their own house, that Congress would do it for them. It soon became impossible for any creative person to obtain work if there was anything in their background that could be interpreted as demonstrating Communist leanings or affiliation.

However, that was only the beginning of the hysteria, which has been likened to the Salem witch trials in their ferocity, and the inability by many of those accused to refute the accusations that were thrown against them. The person who came forward to lead this crusade against communism was Senator Joseph R. McCarthy, a Republican from Wisconsin. In 1950, he stepped upon the national stage when he announced that he had compiled a list of 205 Communists that were known to him in the State Department. His allegations struck a responsive chord with a public that was highly concerned about Communist infiltration in American government.

FYI Senator Joseph McCarthy was an extremist, and an opportunist, but he was no coward. Even though his position as a judge exempted him from military service, McCarthy enlisted in the Marines, and risked his life by volunteering to fly tail-gunner on many combat missions. Some of his detractors quibbled about the number of combat missions he flew, but they missed the point—he didn't have to fly any.

When the Republican Party gained control of the Senate in 1952, Senator McCarthy became committee chairman. He was now firmly in control, and in addition, he had a public forum for his anti-Communist crusade. With the ability to mobilize extensive press and television coverage for his senate hearings, he charged many top-level officials with treachery. Playing up his tough-guy reputation, he would use vulgar expressions to characterize the "vile and scurrilous" objects of his attack.

McCarthy exerted enormous power. He offered the public scapegoats, feeding off public concern about the situation in Korea and the worldwide spread of communism. He heightened the fears that had initially been stirred up by Truman's own anti-Communist efforts. However, as is usual with demi-gods, they eventually go too far, and so did McCarthy. Even though television was in its infancy, it was already reaching millions of homes, and the hearings were widely viewed. As Americans watched McCarthy's savage tactics on the tube, public support turned to revulsion. When he overstepped himself by challenging the United States Army when one of his personal assistants was drafted, it was the beginning of the end, and ultimately the Senate condemned him for his conduct.

THE ECONOMY TAKES OFF

The United States, in the aftermath of World War II, experienced a phenomenal period of prosperity. One reason for this was the complete devastation of European, Japanese, and other industrial centers by the war. During the war, the factories in the United States were completely untouched, and quickly switched back to the production of peacetime goods. As a result, in the immediate postwar period, the United States became the world's richest country.

JUST A MINUTE

The gross national product, a measure of all goods and services produced in the United States, was $200 billion in 1940, $300 billion in 1950, and by 1960 it had jumped to more than $500 billion.

No new cars had been produced during the war, and thus there was incredible pent-up demand, both from those who had stayed behind, as well as from returning servicemen eager to resume their civilian lifestyle. The automobile industry increased fourfold between 1946 and 1955. These same servicemen, who had started a baby boom almost from the very first night they returned home, needed homes for their growing families, and used their GI home loans to start a housing boom. In addition, the government was spending a lot of money on the defense budget to arm for the Cold War, and this money pumped up the economy.

The postwar period also saw a new wave of corporate mergers, similar to those that had occurred in the 1890s and the 1920s. However, these differed from the earlier mergers. Previously, corporations had sought vertical integration of a singular industry, to allow them to control all facets of production, or horizontal integration, in an attempt to monopolize the industry. However, the trend in the 1950s was toward a new type of merger, the conglomerate: corporations with holdings in a variety of unrelated industries. International Telephone and Telegraph, for example, bought Sheraton Hotels, Continental Banking, Hartford Fire Insurance, and Avis Rent-a-Car.

Another new corporate phenomenon was the rise of the franchise corporation, in which the right to use the corporate logo was licensed to thousands of local independent entrepreneurs. One of the most successful of these new start-up operations was McDonald's, which offered an easily recognizable logo, standardized buildings, a familiar menu, and common operational plan, in a consolidated fast-food restaurant chain. In an increasingly mobile society, patrons were assured that no matter which franchise they entered, it would look just like the one back home.

FYI A new McDonald's restaurant goes into business every six hours. At this rate of building, soon no person on the globe will be more than a short trip from the golden arches. This chain is the second largest owner of real estate in the world. The only larger holder of real property is the Catholic Church.

As corporations changed, so did the workers and the jobs. Previously, the majority of the workers had produced goods; now the pendulum was swinging toward service jobs. By the mid-1950s, the majority of workers held "white-collar jobs," working as corporate managers, teachers, salespersons, and other office positions. Corporations began to offer a guaranteed annual wage, long-term employment contracts, medical plans, and other fringe benefits. In addition, the trend toward service jobs began to erode traditional class distinctions.

Not every facet of society was prospering, however. For farmers, gains in productivity brought about by scientific farming and mechanization were leading to agricultural consolidation, as farming became big business. Family farms were unable to compete with the giant monoliths, and increasingly, they were selling their holdings to the large corporations. The small farmers left the land, and moved to find jobs in the city.

THE BURBS

Where Americans lived was changing. In the postwar period, people moved from the old industrial Northeast and the rural South to the West and the Southwest. Sun Belt cities like Houston, Miami, Albuquerque, Tucson, and Phoenix expanded rapidly. Los Angeles County, if it were a state, would have been the ninth largest state by population, outstripping 41 other states. By 1963, California had more people than the state of New York.

Perhaps the most radical creation of postwar America was a totally new concept in housing, the suburb. The idea of living in a single family dwelling in a totally residential community, and then traveling into the city to work during the day, was a concept that became commonplace in the 1950s, as the parents of baby boomers went in search of affordable homes for their expanding families. To create such cheap housing, builders like William J. Levitt built entirely new assembly line communities, which were essentially the housing equivalent of the Model T Ford. An entire tract of land would be razed, and then a large number of identical homes would be turned out in rapid succession, using mass production. Levitt's houses were prefabricated, partly assembled in a factory, and then assembled on the lot. Levitt's methods cut costs and allowed young couples to own their own home in these instant villages such as Levittown.

FYI William Levitt learned to build houses in the late 1920s when his father was stuck with 40 unfinished houses. Working with existing construction crews, William and his brother Alfred soon learned the building business on the job. In the midst of the Great Depression, Levitt & Sons had great success building housing in exclusive neighborhoods of northern Long Island, where the upscale market could still afford luxurious housing in spite of the Depression. During World War II, as an officer in a Navy Seabees construction unit, he learned everything there was to know about mass-producing housing. When the war was over, Levitt & Sons was well positioned for the new market of building low cost quality housing, financed by federal credit and GI loans.

As the families moved to the suburbs, they were followed by the retail businesses. But rather than locating in the neighborhoods, as had been traditional in the cities, large numbers of stores were clustered together in large shopping centers. The number of these shopping centers rose from 8 at the end of World War II to 3,840 in 1960. With easy parking and convenient evening hours, customers no longer went into the city for shopping.

Another innovation of the postwar era was television. Although it had been invented in the 1930s, the onset of World War II had stopped the manufacture of sets and the creation of networks. When industries were released from war production, television sets began to once again roll off the assembly line, and the public snapped them up as fast as they were made.

JUST A MINUTE

 In 1946, there were fewer than 17,000 television sets in the entire country. Three years later consumers were buying 250,000 sets a month, and by 1960 three quarters of all families in America owned at least one set.

By 1955, the average American family was watching television four to five hours a day. Children watched *Howdy Doody Time* and *The Mickey Mouse Club*, while the parents preferred situation comedies like *I Love Lucy* and *Father Knows Best*. For the first time in history, the average citizen was subjected to large amounts of televised advertising, which he could not ignore in the same way as print ads. The advertising industry went into high gear to create increasingly sophisticated advertisements for the average American.

THE BEATNIKS

For most Americans during the 1950s, conformity was the norm, and even young people adhered to traditional values. Though women such as "Rosie the Riveter" had gone into the workplace as part of the war effort, after victory, women quickly returned to their traditional role of mother and homemaker. Life was simple, men were expected to be the breadwinners, and women raised the babies. Sociologist David Riesman explained the importance of peer-group expectations in his book, *The Lonely Crowd*. He termed such a society "other-directed," and his thesis was that this created a stable society. The new technology of television helped to reinforce this shared social consciousness, through shows such as *Leave It to Beaver, Ozzie and Harriet, The Donna Reed Show,* and *Father Knows Best.* Everyone was comforted by the fact that their next door neighbors were the same as them, and the families they saw on television were also the same.

However, even in this homogenous cultural effluent, there were noncon-formists. A number of writers, the "beat generation," rebelled against these conventional and all-encompassing values. The "beats" went out of their way to challenge the accepted indicia of respectability, and to shock the rest of the culture.

FYI Jack Kerouac created the term "Beat Generation" in a 1948 conversation with novelist John Clellon Holmes, who then wrote an article in *The New York Times,* "This Is the Beat Generation." Kerouac's "beatness" was describing bright young Americans who'd come of age during the Second World War but couldn't fit in: They were "beat" because they didn't believe in straight jobs and had to struggle to survive, living in dirty apartments, selling drugs or committing crimes for food money, hitchhiking across the country because they couldn't stay still without getting bored. The phrase "Beat Generation" was meant to echo Ernest Hemingway's description of his own crowd (which came of age during the First World War) as the "Lost Generation." On April 2, 1958, after the "Beat Craze" had influenced a flood of alienated young men and women to converge on the North Beach neighborhood of San Francisco, columnist Herb Caen of the San Francisco *Chronicle* wrote a column in which he created the term "Beatnik." The "nik" suffix might have evoked Yiddish slang ("nudnik," etc.) but was actually borrowed from *Sputnik,* a satellite that had just been launched by the Soviet Union, striking fear into the hearts of many Communist-fearing Americans.

The literary works of the Beatniks reflected their sense of rebellion. Jack Kerouac typed his best-selling novel *On the Road* on a roll of paper, without grammatical punctuation and paragraph structure. The book advocated the advantages of a counterculture lifestyle. Poet Allen Ginsberg produced the poem "Howl," which criticized the modern, mechanized world. When it was attacked as obscene and all of the copies were seized by the police, Ginsberg went to court and won, in the process becoming a nationally known figure.

Not only writers, but musicians and artists were also creating new art forms which did not conform to the accepted norms. Down in Memphis, black music was being brought to young kids by singer Elvis Presley. They called it rock and roll, and staid Americans were shocked by Elvis's wild beat, duck-tail haircut, and shaking hips. Members of the establishment were concerned that rock and roll would lead teenagers to illicit sex, drugs, crime, and other delinquent behavior.

WE SHALL OVERCOME

Returning African American servicemen were not content to return to their prewar status as second-class citizens. More than one million had fought for their country during World War II, and they now expected better treatment on their return. For the first time in history, there was a sense of rising expectations among this ethnic group.

Jackie Robinson forced the issue of racial equality into the national lime-light in 1947 when he was brought into the major leagues, which had previously been all white, and effectively broke baseball's color barrier. As the first black man in the major leagues, he encountered hostility from not only his opponents, but also his fellow teammates on the Brooklyn Dodgers. However, his outstanding rookie year helped to ease his acceptance by players and public alike, and paved the way for other black players, not only in baseball, but in other sports as well. Unfortunately, with the exodus of the best players from the Negro leagues, these organizations soon went bankrupt.

The Cold War also aided the emerging civil rights movement. The United States's position in the Cold War was one of moral superiority. Unfortunately, communism drew no racial barriers—each person was a "comrade." In fact, the Soviet Union was more ethnically diverse than the United States, with large black, Asian, and Muslim minorities. In order to be competitive in the Cold War, especially against the USSR and the emerging countries of Africa and Asia, it was necessary for the United States to be as egalitarian as their nemesis. It was impossible to retain a position of leadership of the free world, and still maintain racial discrimination domestically.

Harry Truman had supported the civil rights movement during his tenure in office, and as a politician, he also recognized the increasing importance of the black urban vote. Concerned with lynching and other types of mob violence still occurring against blacks in the South, he appointed a committee on civil rights to investigate discrimination. The committee's report confirmed blacks' continuing second-class status in American life, and called on the federal government to take the lead in securing the rights guaranteed to all citizens for this minority group.

As a result of this report, Truman developed a 10-point civil rights program, which he sent to Congress. This enraged white Southern Democrats, who split from the Democratic Party in 1948. Realizing he was going to be unable to muster sufficient Congressional support, Truman used the power of the presidency to issue an executive order which barred discrimination in federal employment, ordered equal treatment for all members of the armed forces, regardless of race, and appointed a committee to phase out all military segregation. By the end of the Korean War, the newly created Department of Defense had removed the last remaining racial distinctions in the military.

FYI Charles Lynch (1736–1796) was born near Lynchburg, Virginia. When a Tory conspiracy was discovered in 1780 in Bedford County, where he was justice of the peace, Lynch, a zealous patriot, presided over an extralegal court that meted out summary punishment to the Loyalists. Lynch clearly exceeded his authority, but he was later exonerated by the state legislature. This was the origin of the term "Lynch Law," and it was later to be applied to any illegal hanging, which in the future were to be referred to as "lynching."

Despite these gains, during the 1950s, blacks in the deep South had few civil or political rights. Even returning servicemen were denied the right to vote. If they tried to register, they faced beatings, loss of their job, eviction from their land, or possibly even a lynching. Jim Crow laws were rampant, and segregation was strictly enforced in street cars, trains, hotels, restaurants, hospitals, recreational facilities, and employment. The stage was set for a revolution, and it wasn't going to be long in coming.

Hour's Up!

1. General Eisenhower ran for president on the slogan:

   A. Take a hike.

   B. Buy a bike.

   C. I like Ike.

   D. I like Ike and Tina Turner.

2. Joseph McCarthy was all of the following except:

   A. Determined to expose every Communist in America

   B. A tail gunner during World War II

   C. A Congressman

   D. A Senator

3. Harry Truman's domestic program was called the:

   A. Square Deal

   B. Raw Deal

   C. New Deal

   D. Fair Deal

4. *Howdy Doody* was:

   A. Something you didn't want to step in

   B. Better than regular doody

   C. A Communist

   D. Not as annoying as Barney

5. The color barrier in professional baseball was broken by:

   A. Mickey Mantle

   B. Lou Gehrig

   C. Jackie Robinson

   D. Babe Ruth

HOUR 20

The Great Society

CHAPTER SUMMARY

LESSON PLAN:

In this hour, you will learn about desegregation, the New Frontier, the Great Society, the Cuban Missile Crisis, the Space Program, and the Vietnam War.

You will also learn ...

- That under "separate but equal," one side always gets a smaller 50 percent.
- That the poll tax wasn't designed to keep Poles from voting.
- That the New Frontier didn't have anything to do with space, exploring strange new worlds, or the starship Enterprise.
- That American-made cars are unsafe at any speed.

The 1960s were a turbulent time in the history of the United States, as radical and sweeping change permeated all segments of society. African Americans, who had legally been shorn of their inferior legal status a century before, were finally able to attain real and practical equality through affirmative social protest and favorable court actions. President Johnson, determined to bring the benefits of American prosperity to all segments of the population, pushed through legislation he termed "The Great Society." But the most far-reaching change was brought about by the war in Vietnam. The country was divided, one segment of society wanted to stop the fighting at any cost, others felt that the war was critical to stop the spread of communism. It was a nation divided, and the discord cut across generational and party lines, causing conflict throughout all segments of society.

SEPARATE BUT EQUAL

African Americans wanted to bring to an end the "separate but equal" standard that had been created by the U.S. Supreme Court in 1896 in the case of *Plessy v. Ferguson*. That standard had been used for decades to support rigid segregation in the South. Blacks realized that such facilities were indeed separate, but never equal.

The end of *Plessy* came in 1954 when the Supreme Court, presided over by a Republican appointee, Chief Justice Earl Warren, reversed that case with their decision in *Brown v. Board of Education*. The Court declared, after examining 60 years of evidence of the state of affairs under *Plessy*, that "separate facilities are inherently unequal," and decreed that the "separate but equal" doctrine could no longer be used to justify separate public schools.

FYI *Animal Farm* was George Orwell's satirical shot at the foibles of society. By putting wisdom in the mouths of animals, Orwell uses an age-old artifice and proves again how the pen can be mightier than the sword. In his world, the pigs decide that they are more intelligent than any other barnyard animal, and thus they must rule the entire farm. Their motto becomes, "All Animals Are Created Equal, but Some Are More Equal Than Others."

It was one thing for the Supreme Court to order desegregation, it would be an entirely different matter to enforce it. President Eisenhower immediately ordered the desegregation of the schools in the District of Columbia, which were under federal control, as a model for the rest of the country to follow suit.

However, his example fell on deaf ears in the deep South. In Little Rock, Arkansas, the desegregation plan called for admitting nine black students into an all-white school. The governor, using the pretense that violence would erupt, mobilized the National Guard to deny the students access to the school. Eisenhower, a military man, employed a military solution. He federalized the National Guard, which instantly changed their commander in chief from the governor to the president. He then gave them orders to enforce, rather than block, the desegregation plan. For the first time since Reconstruction, federal troops were used to protect black rights in the South.

FYI In 1955, as part of the battle for desegregation, Rosa Parks fought for her space on the front of the bus. She had another fight in the year 2000, at the age of 87, battling for her space on the Internet at www.rosaparks.com. A man named Shaw had created it with the intent of selling it at auction. In achieving her victory over Shaw, she relied on the new federal law that bans "cyber-squatting," the pre-empting of Internet domain names with the aim of selling those names to the company or prominent person with ties to the name. She has donated the site to the Rosa and Raymond Parks Institute for Self Development in Detroit, which will use the website to educate visitors on Mrs. Parks historic refusal to yield her seat on a Montgomery, Alabama, bus, which was a turning point in the civil rights movement.

African Americans were emboldened to stretch the segregation laws until they broke. In Montgomery, Alabama, Rosa Parks, a 42-year-old black seamstress, sat down in the front of a bus, in the section that the law said was for white people only. She was arrested for violating the segregation statutes. Black leaders seized on the notoriety of the case to organize a boycott of the bus system. This thrust Martin Luther King Jr., a young minister of the Baptist church where the blacks met, into the national limelight as the spokesman for the protest. "There comes a time," he said, "when people get tired … of being kicked about by the brutal feet of oppression." King was himself arrested, but this didn't stop the boycott, which ultimately cut bus ticket sales by 65 percent. Ultimately, the Supreme Court ruled that bus segregation, like school segregation, was unconstitutional, and the civil rights movement chalked up another important victory.

African Americans were also out to establish their right to vote. The 15th Amendment to the U.S. Constitution had been passed right after the Civil War, with the express intention of guaranteeing that blacks would be able to vote. However, many states had implemented laws to frustrate this African American suffrage, especially the poll tax and the literacy test. Eisenhower, working with Senate majority leader Lyndon B. Johnson, pushed through the Civil Rights Act of 1957 as a way to correct these inequities. The first such civil rights legislation in 82 years, it authorized federal intervention in cases where blacks were denied the chance to vote. When this law did not have the desired effect, Congress passed the Civil Rights Act of 1960, which provided stiff penalties for anyone who interfered with the African Americans' right to vote.

STRICTLY DEFINED

A **poll tax** is a capital tax levied equally on every adult in the community, and they have long been attacked as being an unfair burden upon those less able to pay. Poll taxes enacted in Southern states between 1889 and 1910 had the effect of disenfranchising many blacks as well as poor whites, because payment of the tax was a prerequisite to voting. In 1964, the 24th Amendment to the U.S. Constitution outlawed the poll tax in federal elections. In 1966, this prohibition was extended to all state and local elections by the U.S. Supreme Court, which ruled that such a tax violated the equal protection clause of the 14th Amendment to the Constitution.

THE NEW FRONTIER

John F. Kennedy (JFK) entered the race for the presidency in 1960. He was the son of an Irish American bootlegger who had used his enormous wealth to send his sons to Harvard, purchase the position of ambassador to the Court of St. James, and then launch his sons into politics. He was up against a difficult challenger. His opponent was Richard Nixon, who had been in the public eye for two terms as the vice president. His strategy to overcome Nixon's inherent advantage as an incumbent was to get before the American people in a series of debates, to be watched by the entire country on television. During these debates, Nixon sweated profusely and appeared nervous, and at times uncertain. Kennedy, on the other hand, came across as able, articulate, and energetic, and spoke about moving aggressively into the new decade, for "the New Frontier is here whether we seek it or not."

QUOTABLE QUOTES

 In his inaugural address, John F. Kennedy said: "Ask not what your country can do for you—ask what you can do for your country."

Kennedy won the election, but by such a narrow margin that he did not have a clear mandate. In addition, even though his own Democratic party was in control in both houses of Congress, he was opposed in many of his initiatives by the conservative Southern branch of his own party. They blocked his programs for federal aid to education, for health insurance for the elderly, and for a new Department of Urban Affairs.

Kennedy also failed in his attempts to stimulate the economy. He had alienated many business leaders early in his administration, when he rolled back what he considered an excessive price increase in steel. When he tried to push through a tax cut to provide capital and stimulate the economy, these same business leaders pressured conservative leaders in Congress to block the measure.

 FYI The similarity between the "New Frontier" of John F. Kennedy and the "Final Frontier" of Capt. James T. Kirk of the USS *Enterprise* in the television series *Star Trek* is no coincidence. When the series was pitched to the network by Gene Roddenberry in 1964, it was less than a year after the presidential assassination. Kirk explored "strange new worlds" and saw fit to change or fix them when they needed it, despite the "prime directive" telling him not to upset the status quo. Similarly, Kennedy repeatedly violated the "social norms" of his planet, especially in areas such as Civil Rights, when he thought it was the right thing to do.

Kennedy did have some victories. He secured funding for the Space Program, whose goal was to put a man on the moon by the end of the decade, and he created the Peace Corps, whose purpose was to send men and women overseas to help developing countries. He was preparing a legislative agenda for the last year of his term, which would have moved aggressively on such issues as civil rights, when he was assassinated while riding in an open car in Dallas, Texas.

Kennedy's liberal reputation comes more from his style of leadership and his professed ideals than from the passage of any legislation. However, because the liberal agenda that he set out in the final year of his presidency was subsequently enacted by his vice president and presidential successor, Lyndon Johnson, he has gone down in history as a progressive force for change in American society.

THE CUBAN MISSILE CRISIS

In 1959, Communist insurgents, led by revolutionary leader Fidel Castro, had overthrown the government of Cuba, and then quickly gained the financial support of the Soviet Union. As the new Cuban government's ties with the Soviet Union became increasingly stronger, relations with Cuba became more and more strained, and ultimately the United States broke off diplomatic relations.

As a result of the revolution, a huge wave of Cuban exiles, primarily the intelligentsia, the professionals, and the ruling classes, migrated to the United States as political refugees. Their top military leaders advocated an invasion, to topple the Communist régime, and to reassert a democratic government in Cuba. They were supported in this dream by the U.S. Central Intelligence Agency (CIA), which provided the training, and the U.S. Air Force, which committed to provide air support to ensure that the landing force was not decimated on the beaches. In 1961, the brave band of Cuban soldiers stormed ashore at a beach in the Bay of Pigs. However, Kennedy decided to pull the air cover. Without that support, they didn't have a chance, and they were quickly defeated.

FYI If Fidel Castro had had a slightly better fastball, the history of Cuba might have been very different. While in high school in Cuba, Castro had been an outstanding athlete in not only baseball, but also in basketball and track. In September of 1947, the 20-year-old Fidel Castro was given a tryout by a major league team. Joe Cambria, the legendary scout for the old Washington Senators, saw Fidel pitch, but didn't offer him a contract. Cambria said that Castro, a right-handed pitcher, did not have enough of a fastball to pitch in the big leagues. The dejected Fidel, his dreams of fame and fortune as a professional baseball player crushed, attended law school, was sent to prison as a revolutionary, and then disappeared into the Cuban socialist underground.

A year after the infamous Bay of Pigs debacle, the administration learned that the Soviet Union was installing nuclear missiles in Cuba, missiles that had the capacity to reach any part of the United States. Kennedy realized that this time he would have to stand firm. After considering a number of different options, including another invasion scenario, he settled on a course of action: He demanded that the Soviet Union immediately remove all the weapons that had been installed to date, and he imposed a quarantine to prevent the importation of any further missiles. To enforce that embargo, he immediately employed the U.S. Navy to cordon off the island by sea, and the U.S. Air Force to fly a sky cap to interdict any movement by air.

The days following Kennedy's announcement were tense, as the world teetered on the brink of nuclear war. The Soviets did not want to back down, but in the final analysis, they only had two choices, withdraw their weapons, or launch a preemptive strike that would turn the world into a nuclear wasteland. Critics of Kennedy argued that they could have taken the second option, his supporters felt he had taken the only option under the circumstances. In any event, the Cuban Missile Crises marked a change in United States–Soviet relations: Both parties realized that they would have to deescalate the arms race, or risk a nuclear winter. The following year, both countries, along with Great Britain, signed the Limited Test Ban Treaty, prohibiting nuclear weapon tests above ground, the first step toward the limitation of nuclear weapons.

THE SPACE PROGRAM

The Soviet Union was not only a serious challenger to the United States in the field of nuclear weapons, but they were also winning the space race. In 1957 they placed into orbit an unmanned satellite named *Sputnik*. The American military realized that such a rocket could have just as easily carried a nuclear weapon for a payload. It was a year later before the United States could launch into orbit its own satellite, *Explorer I*. However, no sooner had America put up their satellite, then the Russians were once again ahead, when they put a man into orbit. Kennedy responded with a pledge to put a man on the moon, and bring him back, by the end of the decade.

The first series of flights were with the Mercury astronauts, and in 1962 John H. Glenn Jr. became the first one to orbit the earth. This was followed by the *Gemini* program, whose capsules carried two astronauts. The program was given the name because *Gemini* means "twins" in Latin and in the astro-logical charts. The *Gemini* project put man into space longer, and in more complicated maneuvers, than ever before, and included both the first manned linkup of two spacecraft in flight, as well as the first "space walks," in which the astronauts left the spacecraft, traveling in space protected only by their spacesuits.

FYI On February 20, 1962, U.S. Marine Corps pilot John Glenn was the first American to orbit the Earth. In October of 1998, John Glenn, then the Senator from Ohio and 77 years old, returned to the space program and traveled back into space, becoming the oldest astronaut to venture into outer space.

The next space program was *Apollo*, which carried three astronauts, and was the project specifically designed to achieve Kennedy's goal of reaching another world. In 1969, before the end of the decade, Neil A. Armstrong became the first man to walk on the moon.

Unfortunately, having reached the goal of putting a man on the moon, most Americans lost interest in the space program, or felt that the money could be better used back on earth for domestic programs. Future *Apollo* missions were cancelled, and only one of the two Skylabs that had been planned was ever built.

THE GREAT SOCIETY

Upon the assassination of President Kennedy, he was succeeded in office by his vice president, Lyndon Johnson, who immediately announced that he would both retain the key staff from Kennedy's administration, and continue the legislative programs that Kennedy had initiated. In addition, he was going to add his own legislative agenda, which was aimed at eliminating poverty, and spreading the benefits of prosperity to all citizens. He termed his program "The Great Society." Because the assassination had occurred at the end of Kennedy's first term, Johnson was soon up for reelection, and he won a landslide victory over conservative Republican candidate Barry Goldwater.

Lyndon Johnson had been majority leader in the Senate before becoming Kennedy's vice president, and was a masterful politician. He had a justly deserved reputation as a man who could get things done. When necessary to push through legislation, he could plead, cajole or threaten as necessary to achieve his ends. No card was unplayable in his estimation, including calling on the memory of the dead president to ramrod through his agenda. Using these tools, he was able to push through in 1964 the Civil Rights Act, which Kennedy had introduced. It was the most far-reaching piece of civil rights legislation enacted since the Reconstruction.

Having won on civil rights, Johnson then transferred his attention to another of Kennedy's programs, poverty. He announced, "This administration today, here and now, declares unconditional war on poverty in America." The

Office of Economic Opportunity provided training for the poor, and established various programs to give the underprivileged a voice in housing, health, and education programs.

FYI There have been only two presidents named Johnson, both were born in '08 (1808 and 1908), and both were vice presidents who succeeded to the top office when their president was shot (Lincoln-Johnson, Kennedy-Johnson). These were not the only coincidences. Presidents Lincoln and Kennedy were both elected to Congress in '46 (1846 and 1946), both were directly concerned with civil rights for blacks, and both were elected president in '60 (1860 and 1960). Both were shot from behind and in the head, on a Friday before a federal holiday, in the presence of their wives, while in a Ford (Lincoln—theater/Kennedy—car). Lincoln was shot in a theater and his assassin hid in a warehouse, Kennedy was shot from a warehouse and his assassin hid in a theater. Both assassins were from the South, both had three names (John Wilkes Booth, Lee Harvey Oswald), both had names totaling 15 letters, both were born in '39 (1839 and 1939), and both were killed before being brought to trial.

The next initiative of the Great Society was medical care. More than 20 years previously, President Truman had tried to implement national medical care, but did not have the political clout to push it through Congress. Johnson was able to get Congress to approve two programs. Medicare was a health insurance program for the elderly, paid for by payroll taxes. Medicaid was a type of welfare program that provided life-sustaining health-care assistance for the poor who could not afford any other type of health insurance.

Kennedy had failed in his efforts to provide aid for elementary and secondary schools. However, Johnson was able to push through Congress a program that gave money to the states based on the number of children enrolled from low-income families. Funds could be disbursed not only to those attending public schools, but also to those in parochial and other types of privately supported schools.

As part of his Great Society, Johnson pushed through a law creating HUD, the Department of Housing and Urban Development, and this act included provisions for rental assistance for the poor. Other measures passed as part of the Great Society include reform of the immigration laws, and financial assistance to artists and scholars.

The Johnson administration also addressed highway safety issues when it pushed through two transportation bills. The first law gave the states funds for the development of safety programs. The second created the first set of federal safety standards for automobiles, and created an agency to implement these new regulations. The impetus for these new standards was Ralph

Nader, a consumer rights advocate. In his book *Unsafe at Any Speed: The Designed-In Dangers of the American Automobile*, he argued that American cars were dangerous to the driver and passengers, even in low-speed accidents. Nader castigated the automobile manufacturers for sacrificing safety in favor of style. He named specific models, such as the Corvair, in which faulty engineering was the direct cause of highway fatalities.

FYI General Motors went ballistic when Ralph Nader came out with his book *Unsafe at Any Speed*. GM wanted to discredit him, so they had him followed, and sent prostitutes to trap him. Nader was outraged at their conduct, sued, and won a judgment against GM. As a result of his book, Congress created the National Highway Traffic Safety Administration (NHTSA). Ironically, this was the same federal agency that subsequently determined that the Corvair models Nader spent an entire book lambasting were in fact just as safe as other models of car made during the early 1960s. Nader's assertions that GM knew the Corvair was more prone to rollover accidents than other models was directly contradicted by NHTSA data that showed that the Corvair was no more likely to be involved in rollover accidents than comparable models.

Johnson's Great Society was the greatest passage of legislation since Roosevelt's New Deal. He was more successful early in his administration, when he still had the sympathy of the nation behind him as a result of the Kennedy assassination. Later, this momentum began to wane, and with it his ability to push through legislation. As was to be expected, some of the programs were great successes, and remain with us today; others did not live up to expectations. In the end, the Great Society reduced poverty. During the end of Johnson's administration, for example, black family income increased from 54 percent to 60 percent of white-family income.

GOOD MORNING, VIETNAM

Indochina was to be the next place where the forces of good and evil would face off in the Cold War. Vietnam had originally been a French colony, and then was overrun by the Japanese during World War II. With the defeat of the Axis powers in 1945, France returned to take control of the Indochina area. However, the Vietnamese, who had been fighting the Japanese for years, did not like the idea of one ruler being substituted for another. Almost immediately, the Vietnamese insurgents, Communists under the leadership of Ho Chi Minh, rebelled against the French. By 1954, the French had had enough of fighting the insurgents, and agreed to grant the Vietnamese their independence.

FYI Ho Chi Minh started out with the original name of Nguyen Sinh Cung, but was forced to abandon his real name after betraying patriot Phan Boi Chau to the French authorities for $10,000. His betrayal was especially infamous because Phan Boi Chau was the most well known of the Vietnamese activists who were struggling for the independence of Vietnam from the French. The real Ho Chi Minh, whose name he adopted, was an old Chinese beggar who died without any known relatives. Nguyen Sinh Cung, who could no longer use his real name, purchased his identification card from Chinese criminals. Buying the identification of the dead was a well-known practice among Chinese criminals at that time.

Vietnam was divided into two parts by an international convention in Geneva, Switzerland. In North Vietnam, Ho Chi Minh and his Communist supporters were in power. In South Vietnam, Ngo Dinh Diem, who was fervently anti-Communist, headed the government. The conference decreed that democratic elections would be held in two years to unify the country.

Ironically, it was not the North but the South that refused to honor the requirement to hold the elections. Eisenhower was convinced that if the election in Vietnam were to go Communist, this could in turn lead to the fall of Burma, Thailand, and Indonesia. Because of these concerns, Eisenhower backed Diem's refusal to hold the scheduled elections in 1956, and then increased economic and military aid to the South. When Kennedy came into office, he increased this assistance, and in addition sent military advisors, but the struggle between the North and South continued. In the end, Diem's unpopularity with his own people resulted in his overthrow and death in 1963.

Not only was the government in the South unpopular with the people, but there were civilian and military groups openly hostile to the established government. The National Liberation Front was a political party dedicated to establishing a Communist government in the South. Their military force, guerrillas known as the Viet Cong, were engaged in open revolution against the South Vietnamese government. They were openly assisted by North Vietnam, and were gradually gaining control, especially among the peasants in the countryside.

This was the situation in Vietnam that Johnson inherited when he assumed the presidency. Determined to halt Communist advances in South Vietnam, Johnson was looking for an excuse to escalate the war, and to bring in more American troops. This opportunity came when the North Vietnamese attacked two Americans in the Gulf of Tonkin, off the coast of Vietnam. On August 7, 1964, Congress passed the Gulf of Tonkin Resolution, which allowed the president to "take all necessary measures to repel any armed attack against the forces of the United States and to prevent further aggression." After his reelection in November 1964, he embarked on a policy of escalation. Starting with 25,000 troops in 1965, by 1968 the number of soldiers on the ground had increased to more than half a million. In addition, the Air Force initiated a massive bombing campaign that wrought havoc in both North and South Vietnam.

However, as the conflict escalated, with no discernable movement toward victory, Americans became increasingly disenchanted with the war. For the first time in history, people could watch the war on television, and it was a grisly and horrible sight. Most important, Americans did not see any cohesive U.S. strategy that would lead to an end of the war.

Protests against the war in Vietnam intensified. Resistance to the military draft was especially intense, and many young men were arrested for burning their draft cards. By 1968, public protests had become so intense, that Johnson decided not to run for another term. Many factors then came into play to undermine the Democratic Party in the 1968 election. One factor was the Democratic National Convention in Chicago, at which antiwar protesters were attacked by the police. Another factor was the assassination of Robert Kennedy, the brother of the slain president, who was running for president. Another factor was the third-party candidate, Alabama Governor George Wallace, who ran on a ticket of white resistance to civil rights, and who carried not only his home state of Mississippi, but also Arkansas, Louisiana and Georgia, all Democratic states. All of these factors worked together to elect Republican Richard Nixon, who told the American people that he had a plan to get the United States out of Vietnam.

Nixon's plan was straightforward. At the same time that he brought the ground troops home, he embarked on a massive bombing of North Vietnam, in an effort to force them to the peace table. He invaded Cambodia in 1970 to cut off North Vietnamese supply lines, which went through Cambodia to supply the Viet Cong in South Vietnam.

To many young Americans, this did not look like a plan to get out of Vietnam; in fact, it appeared to be an escalation of the war, even if the ground troops were leaving. Protests and antiwar demonstrations increased, especially among students. To make matters worse, at one such demonstration, at Kent State in Ohio, national guard troops who had been called up to keep order, most of whom were no older than the students, panicked and fired into the crowd, killing four of the students.

QUOTABLE QUOTES

Jane Fonda, daughter of Oscar-winning actor Henry Fonda, was a film actress, peace advocate, and outspoken critic of the war in Vietnam. She made a trip to North Vietnam, in which she abused American POWs, made statements hostile to the United States government, assured the North Vietnamese that the American people wanted their government to pull out of South Vietnam, and was photographed trying to shoot down a U.S. fighter with an antiaircraft gun. Vietnam veterans are convinced that her conduct inspired the North Vietnamese to keep fighting, and that she might have single-handedly lost the war for the United States. Veterans still sport bumper stickers that say "Vietnam Veterans are not Fonda Jane," and even today veterans stage demonstrations at any location where she is making a movie.

Nixon realized that there was never going to be "peace with honor," as the American people wanted their country out of the war, no matter what the cost. A cease-fire, negotiated by Nixon's national security adviser, Henry Kissinger, was signed in 1973, and the American troops went home. Without support from the United States, South Vietnam could not hold out, and in the spring of 1975, Saigon fell, leaving North Vietnam in control of the entire country, and leaving a savage scar on the collective memory of the American people.

HOUR'S UP!

QUIZ

1. The Supreme Court theory about race relations which was declared unconstitutional was:

   A. Identical but different

   B. Free but independent

   C. Separate but equal

   D. Some are more equal than others

2. President Kennedy's plan for domestic reform was called the:

   A. Final Frontier

   B. New Frontier

   C. Last Frontier

   D. Wild Frontier

3. Ralph Nader wanted to convince the public that American-made cars were:

   A. Badly made

   B. Extremely ugly

C. Unsafe

D. Too expensive

4. The goal of the space program was:

    A. To explore strange new worlds

    B. To seek out new life and new civilizations

    C. To boldly go where no man has gone before

    D. To put a man where no man had gone before

5. Ho Chi Minh was all of the following except:

    A. Lead his country in expelling the French from Vietnam

    B. Led his country in expelling the United States from Vietnam

    C. Determined to expel the Communists from his country and turn Vietnam into a democracy

    D. Ho Chi Minh was not his real name

HOUR 21

The Minorities Take Charge

CHAPTER SUMMARY

LESSON PLAN:

In this hour, you will learn about détente, Watergate, the Women's Movement, Martin Luther King, the Latino Movement, and the Native American movement.

You will also learn …

- That Tricky Dick isn't the name of a porno star.
- Why the pill made women roar.
- What Martin Luther King was dreaming about.
- That César Chávez might have had something to do with Cesar lettuce, but not with Cesar salad.

After a highly successful first term as president, which included such achievements as reestablishing relations with China, Richard Nixon began his second term in serious trouble. Faced with allegations that are today collectively known as Watergate, he was ultimately pressured to resign. His vice president, Spiro Agnew, also resigned, but as a result of charges unrelated to those brought against the president. For the first time in its history, a president, Gerald Ford, who had never been elected by the populace, ruled the country.

Emboldened by the progress made by African Americans in achieving equality, other disadvantaged groups were soon demanding their fair share of the American dream. Women were successful in having the Equal Rights Amendment passed by Congress, but it failed to be ratified by the states. Latinos also agitated for greater opportunities, and Indians, renaming themselves Native Americans, demanded a greater share of the wealth of a country that had once been theirs alone.

TRICKY DICK

Richard M. Nixon took office after a period of Democratic rule from 1960 to 1968. He had already been in the White House for eight years, from 1952 to 1960, as the vice president under Eisenhower, before his defeat by Kennedy in 1960 in his bid for the presidency. Although Nixon was a Republican, and advocated a balanced budget, he also recognized that the federal government had taken on a greater role in people's lives, including the "safety net" of the welfare system. He wanted to retain these federal programs, while seeing them run in a more efficient and fiscally responsible manner.

FYI In 1950, Richard M. Nixon ran for the U.S. Senate against three-term Congresswoman Helen Gahagan Douglas. He accused Douglas, who opposed the activities of the Communist-hunting House Un-American Activities Committee, of being "pink right down to her underwear," and gave her the nickname "The Pink Lady." He used numerous other tricks, including mailings to the voters that said she was a Communist, Jewish, and a friend of the Negroes. In retaliation, Douglas christened Nixon with his long-time nickname, "Tricky Dick."

The economy was in bad shape during his presidency, inflation was up, the Dow-Jones average of industrial stocks fell dramatically, and unemployment crept toward record levels. He tried price controls, but they were not effective in helping the economy. This period of recession combined with inflation was tagged "stagflation," and signaled an end to the unprecedented period of economic growth that America had enjoyed since the economy had recovered after World War II.

A major reason for the economic downturn was rising energy prices, occasioned by the 1973 war between Israel, Egypt, and Syria. Because the United States had allied with Israel during the war, Saudi Arabia had imposed an embargo on oil exports to the United States, and then the other members of the Organization of Petroleum Exporting Countries (OPEC) had dramatically raised their prices. The shortages occasioned by the embargo, combined with the higher prices, forced the price of oil even higher. Because the high cost of energy affected all facets of the economy, it was impossible for the United States to break free of the recession.

QUOTABLE QUOTES

 Nixon coined the term "Silent Majority" in his speech on November 3, 1969, to refer to the vast number of Americans who were not vocal about their position, but whom he knew supported the war in Vietnam. The administration, the day after the speech, defined these people as the "large and normally undemonstrative cross section of the country that until last night refrained from articulating its opinions on the war."

Another priority on Nixon's agenda was the restoration of "law and order." Crime was on the rise, political protests were rampant, drug use was at an epidemic level, and the perceived increase in promiscuous sex on college campuses all combined to convince the average conservative American that the country was out of control. Nixon promised to use the power of federal government to restore a measure of normalcy and traditional values to the country.

DÉTENTE

With the end of the Vietnam War, it was possible for Nixon to deal realistically with Communist China. During the entire Korean and Vietnam War, the United States had tried to maintain the fiction that Nationalist China, who only controlled the island of Taiwan, was the legal government of all China. However, it had been more than 20 years since Mao Tse-tung's victory on the mainland, and to continue to ignore the "two Chinas" was becoming increasingly unrealistic. As part of his plan to establish relations with Communist China, Nixon became the first president to visit Peking (Beijing).

Nixon was anxious to pursue détente with the Soviet Union, so he also went to Russia. In very productive conferences with Soviet leader Leonid Brezhnev, he reached agreement on missile stockpiles, cooperation in space, and the establishment of new trading relations. The Strategic Arms Limitation Talks (SALT) resulted in an agreement that limited the number of nuclear weapons, and restricted the development and deployment of antiballistic missile systems.

WATERGATE

During his first term, Nixon had been faced with both a House and a Senate that were controlled by the Democratic party, making it difficult for him to push through any legislation. Nixon not only wanted to win the 1972 election, he wanted to win it so big that those running for the Senate and Congress on the Republican ticket would ride his coattails into office, and provide him with legislative control. Nixon's Committee to Reelect the President launched a massive fund-raising campaign to collect money before contributions had to be reported under a new campaign financing law.

As part of his "big win" strategy, Nixon's men decided to tap the telephones of the Democratic National Committee in the Watergate apartment complex in Washington, D.C. The idea was that by listening into their conversations, they would know what they were planning to do in their political campaign, and thereby gain an advantage. However, the burglars/wiretappers were caught, carrying documents that could be traced back to the White House.

Nixon tried to cover up the involvement of his people in the break-in. Six days after the arrest, he ordered the CIA to tell the FBI to stop its investigation, on the grounds of national security. The break-in was the tip of the iceberg: It was just part of a campaign to neutralize those people that Nixon and his advisors considered threatening, whom they tacked onto their "enemies list." In the election, Nixon got the "big win" he was after, but the press had continued to investigate the Watergate break-in, particularly reporters Bob Woodward and Carl Bernstein at the *Washington Post*, and when they finally broke the full story of conspiracy and cover-up, the Democratic majority in the Congress started impeachment proceedings against Nixon. As the evidence began to mount, and the scandal grew, political pressure forced Nixon to resign on August 9, 1974.

FYI President Gerald Ford was the only president never elected to that office. After the death of President Kennedy, and the succession of Lyndon Johnson, they had passed the 25th Amendment to the Constitution, which authorized the President to appoint a new vice president if the office became vacant. No one could have envisioned that the provision would come into play so soon, and with such unexpected results. When vice president Agnew was forced to resign as a result of taking bribes, Nixon appointed Ford as the new vice president. When Nixon in turn was forced to resign by the Watergate scandal, Ford succeeded to the presidency, without being elected. Because Ford failed to be reelected as president, he holds the distinction of being the only person to hold the office who was never elected as either president or vice president.

Gerald Ford's first priority was to restore people's trust in government after the Watergate scandal. Despite the fact that Ford had been appointed by Nixon, he did enjoy public trust and confidence, until he pardoned his former president.

The Peanut Farmer

At the next election, Ford failed to defeat Democratic challenger Jimmy Carter, a former peanut farmer and governor of Georgia. He cultivated a persona as a political outsider to Washington politics, which unfortunately was all too accurate. His political naiveté made it difficult for him to accomplish his political goals, at a time when the country, reeling from the turbulence of the Watergate scandal, wanted a strong and steady hand in Washington.

FYI While a number of presidents have been naval officers, Jimmy Carter is the only president to have graduated from the Naval Academy at Annapolis. And while many presidents have been in the military, and even risen to the rank of general, only two presidents have graduated from West Point: Grant and Eisenhower.

The Helsinki Conference occurred during his term. This was the largest summit conference in European history, attended by representatives from 35 European countries, the United States, and Canada. The conference produced the historic Final Act, which incorporated significant points desired by both East and West. Moscow obtained its long-sought recognition of the European borders that had existed since the end of World War II. The West obtained declarations of individual rights and human liberties, to which the Eastern bloc governments subscribed. Subsequently, the Western nations used periodic "Helsinki review meetings" to focus attention on human rights violations by Communist régimes in the Eastern bloc.

President Jimmy Carter was the instigator and mediator in the peace conference between Egypt and Israel, in which these countries ended their 30-year war. President Carter met with Egyptian President Anwar al-Sadat and Israeli Prime Minister Menachem Begin at the presidential retreat at Camp David, Maryland, to negotiate the peace treaty, and it was ultimately signed at the White House.

FYI Anwar al-Sadat and Menachem Begin shared the Nobel Peace Price in 1978, for bringing about peace between their two countries. Despite the ensuing conflict in the Middle East, the border between Egypt and Israel has remained peaceful, a testament to the work of these two men.

After extensive opposition in Congress, Carter pushed through Senate ratification of a treaty giving to the country of Panama the Panama Canal Zone, which had been deeded in "perpetuity" to the United States, and which had always been treated virtually as United States property since its creation. The treaty called for the zone to be turned over to Panama in its entirety by the year 2000.

When Carter became president, détente with the Soviet Union was in high gear, and he declared that the United States had escaped its "inordinate fear of communism." However, his insistence that "our commitment to human rights must be absolute" repeatedly angered the Soviet government. In spite of his antagonism of the Soviets, they signed the SALT II agreement, which further limited nuclear stockpiles, but then he was unable to get it ratified by the U.S. Senate.

Carter's ineptitude in foreign affairs came to the forefront in the Iranian hostage situation. The Shah of Iran was deposed by a fundamentalist revolutionary and Shiite Muslim leader, the Ayatollah Khomeini. The Shah, although his régime was corrupt, was friendly to the United States. When

Jimmy Carter allowed the Shah into the U.S. for medical treatment, angry Iranian militants seized the American embassy in Teheran and held 53 Americans hostage for more than a year. None of his efforts to free the hostages were successful, and he repeatedly referred to the fact that "America was being held hostage." He made it such an important event, that when he could not obtain their release, it became a serious issue for voters, and helped to ensure his defeat at the polls at the next election.

Carter also had to face a problem with inflation, which was being fueled by deficit government spending. He directed the Federal Reserve Board, the government agency responsible for controlling monetary policy, to increase the money supply to cover the deficit. When inflation continued to increase, he tried cutting the budget to slow inflation. However, he could only cut government spending by gutting the very social programs that were the hallmarks of the Democratic Party. By the end of his term, inflation was still out of control, deficits in the budget had mushroomed, and big business was alienated by high interest rates and falling bond prices.

The Democrats were perfectly positioned, after the Watergate scandal and the ineffective Ford administration, to retain control of the presidency. Yet a mere four years later, Carter's disapproval rating had reached 77 percent, and the people were ready for a return to Republican leadership.

WE SHALL OVERCOME

Emboldened by the advances in civil rights which they had accomplished in the 1950s, African Americans became convinced that reform through peaceful and nonviolent confrontation would continue to bring results. They were lead by the black clergy, organized under the Southern Christian Leadership Conference (SCLC), and drew their activists from organizations such as the Student Nonviolent Coordinating Committee (SNCC).

In 1960, black college students organized a sit-in at a segregated lunch counter at a Woolworth's in North Carolina. They captured nationwide media attention with their protest, and inspired demonstrations throughout the South. Realizing the value of media exposure, they next organized "freedom rides." Large numbers of blacks and whites would board buses headed south toward a targeted segregated terminal. When they arrived, the group would refuse to go to the part of the terminal designated for their race, mixing black and white in both sections. When the police arrived, the media was there to capture the entire confrontation on film.

QUOTABLE QUOTES

In 1963, more than 200,000 African Americans gathered in the nation's capital to demonstrate their commitment to equality for all, in what has become known as the "March on Washington." Martin Luther King Jr., one of the speakers, said in his speech to the multitude: "I have a dream that one day on the red hills of Georgia, sons of former slaves and the sons of former slave owners will be able to sit down together at the table of brotherhood." Each time he used the refrain "I have a dream," the crowd cheered.

Despite the nationwide exposure gained by the civil rights movement, however, real change was slow in coming. President Kennedy had been slow to push the Southern branch of the Democratic Party for reform, because he needed their votes on other issues. However, when James Meredith, an African American student, was refused admission to the University of Mississippi because of his race, Kennedy was forced to take action. He dispatched federal troops to compel the integration of the university.

Kennedy realized the need for a new, stronger, civil rights bill, and submitted it to Congress. However, they stonewalled it in committee, and it was still there when he was assassinated. It fell to President Johnson, with his years of skill in Congress, to push it through. Shamelessly trading on the nationwide sorrow felt by the nation over the death of their president, he virtually made this bill seem like Kennedy's last wish. In 1963, he told Congress: "No memorial oration or eulogy could more eloquently honor President Kennedy's memory than the earliest possible passage of the civil rights bill." They passed the Civil Rights Act of 1964, which outlawed discrimination in all public accommodations. The next year, he pushed through the Voting Rights Act of 1965, which authorized the federal government to register black voters when local officials refused to do so. Immediately, more than 400,000 blacks were registered, and by 1968 the number had reached 1 million. With their new franchise, black candidates began to appear and seek election to local and state offices.

Despite all of their gains, some black leaders were not satisfied—they wanted faster and more far-reaching change. One such leader was Malcolm X, an articulate leader who advocated that the black race be separated from the white, a policy diametrically in opposition to the goals of the civil rights movement. Another leader was Stokely Carmichael, a student who advocated "Black Power," to be achieved by either violent or nonviolent means.

Violence was not long in coming. Riots occurred in a number of big cities during 1966 and 1967, followed by the assassinations of both Martin Luther King and Senator Robert Kennedy, an outspoken advocate of civil rights who had taken a number of actions in support of blacks as attorney general when his brother was president. This growing black militancy alarmed the country, and many who had been sympathetic to the civil rights movement backed away from active support. This conservative backlash only further enraged those trying to push for greater civil rights.

The backlash was particularly strong on the issue of busing, which local communities fought in the courts. When the Supreme Court ruled that busing children was a permissible means of desegregating schools, Nixon denounced the ruling on television and unsuccessfully tried to push though Congress a moratorium on busing. Local communities were still fighting the issue in the courts, however, and they gained a victory in 1974 in *Milliken* v. *Bradley*, in which the Supreme Court set limits on the geographical area over which students had to be bused, invalidating an effort to bus inner-city black students to suburban schools.

The backlash was also strong against "affirmative action," the policy of giving black students priority in admissions over white applicants. In 1978, Allan Bakke, a white applicant to medical school, went to the Supreme Court, complaining that he had been denied admission to make room for less qualified black applicants. The Supreme Court ordered his admission, and ruled that racial quotas could not be used by colleges in their admission procedures.

I AM WOMAN, HEAR ME ROAR

Women watched the civil rights movement with interest. While the Suffragettes had won the right to vote for women two generations previously, and large numbers of women had worked in factories during World War II, little had changed in the generation since then.

JUST A MINUTE

In 1963, the average working woman still only made a salary equal to 63 percent of her male counterpart.

In 1963, author Betty Friedan published *The Feminine Mystique*, a critique of middle-class attitudes toward women that codified the discontent of millions of women frustrated by their "homemaker" role. Friedan argued that women often had no other option in life than "finding a husband and bearing children." She advocated that women seek out new roles and responsibilities in life, to enable them to realize their own personal and professional identities, and not allow their life to be dictated to them by a society dominated by men.

The women's movement of the 1960s and 1970s was centered in the middle class, and was infected by the spirit of rebellion that swept through middle-class youth in the 1960s. The women's movement was also affected by the sexual revolution of the 1960s, which had been instigated by the invention of the "pill," an oral contraceptive that left women free to engage in sex without the previously feared side-effect of pregnancy. And even if they became pregnant, they could still have an abortion, because in 1973 the Supreme Court in *Roe* v. *Wade* legalized a woman's right to abort her fetus. Women were now free to have sex when and where and with whom they wanted, with no unwanted side effects.

Liberated women decided to ban together. In 1966, they established the National Organization for Women (NOW) "to take action to bring American women into full participation in the mainstream of American society now." Within a year, they had mustered a thousand women to their cause, and four years later membership had reached fifteen thousand. NOW helped make women increasingly aware of the limitations imposed on them.

QUOTABLE QUOTES

In 1972, popular singer Helen Ready hit the charts with her big hit, whose lyrics included: "I am woman, hear me roar, in numbers too big to ignore." This became the unofficial anthem of the women's movement.

Liberated women coined a term for their new freedom, "feminism." Journalist Gloria Steinem founded a new magazine, *Ms.*, dedicated to advocating and exploring this new freedom. Another publication that developed these themes was a handbook published by a women's health collective, entitled *Our Bodies, Ourselves*, which sold close to a million copies.

Even though activists had been successful in including wording in the 1964 Civil Rights Act that guaranteed equality to women, realists knew that only with the passage of an amendment to the Constitution would the rights of women really be secure. They were successful in having the Equal Rights Amendment (ERA) passed by Congress in 1972. The wording was simple, but effective and to the point: "Equality of rights under the law shall not be denied or abridged by the United States or by any State on account of sex."

Under the procedures for the ratification of a constitutional amendment, it was necessary for it to be adopted by 38 states.

However, the women's movement fell victim to the same backlash that had befallen the civil rights movement. Having moved too far, too fast, the ERA became a target for conservative opponents, such as Anita Bryant, who warned the country that passage of the law would require unisex bathrooms. The ERA reached its high water mark when it was passed by 35 states, but then some states tried to recant their ratification. When the seven year time limit for ratification expired, they had still not reached the goal of 38 states, and the constitutional amendment died stillborn. To this day, women are still not equal to men under the Constitution.

LATINOS

The next minority group to seek equality were the "Latinos," an overarching term that encompassed the Spanish-speaking immigrants from other parts of the Western Hemisphere, whose origins were primarily in Cuba, Puerto Rico, Mexico, and Central America. They had been disenfranchised by their inability to speak English, their low education level, and their often illegal status as immigrants.

QUOTABLE QUOTES

During the 1970s, the catchphrases of Freddie Prinze on his hit TV show *Chico and the Man* became part of the popular vocabulary, including "Loooking goood!" and "Eet's not my job!" For the first time in network history, a Latino was the star of a primetime series. However, in the same way that African Americans forced *Amos and Andy* off the air and set back black TV shows for decades, the Latino community attacked their own show. They picketed the network, complaining that Freddie Prinze was not really Chicano because he was Puerto Rican. His retort was "If I can't play a Chicano ... then God's really gonna be mad when he finds out Charlton Heston played Moses." Despite the hoopla, the show was on the cover of *TV Guide* three times, Jack Albertson won an Emmy, and Freddie Prinze received a Golden Globe nomination.

When it was passed in 1935, the National Labor Relations Act had specifically excluded agricultural workers from those who had the right to form a union. But César Chávez, founder of the overwhelmingly Hispanic United Farm Workers, took on the grape growers of California. Chávez called for a nationwide consumer boycott of grapes that finally resulted in a union for the pickers. He then moved on to lettuce and other crops. Although farmers continued to fight him, Chávez had laid the legal groundwork for unions among agricultural workers, and they gradually began to make inroads such as higher wages and improved working conditions.

The Voting Act, passed primarily to help blacks become registered voters, also helped Hispanics. In 1961, Henry B. Gonzalez won election to Congress from Texas. Three years later Elizo ("Kika") de la Garza, another Texan, followed him, and Joseph Montoya of New Mexico was elected to the Senate. Both Gonzalez and de la Garza rose to positions of power as committee chairmen in the House. When Clinton became president, two prominent Hispanics were named to his cabinet. Former mayor of San Antonio Henry Cisneros became the Secretary of Housing and Urban Development (HUD), and former mayor of Denver Frederico Pena was named Secretary of Transportation.

INDIANS TURN INTO NATIVE AMERICANS

Prior to the 1960s, the United States policy regarding Indians had been to try to assimilate them into the mainstream culture of the country by taking them off reservations and moving them into the cities. These Native Americans often had difficulty adjusting to their new surroundings, and in 1961 the government discontinued this policy. Life on the reservation, while it allowed Native Americans to preserve their tribal society, was commonly one of poverty and alcoholism.

As African Americans, Latinos, and women asserted their rights, Native Americans decided that it was their turn. They founded the American Indian Movement (AIM), to assert their privileges with the federal government, and they began a series of lawsuits, in which they challenged treaty violations, contested lost water rights, and sought to regain lost tribal lands.

QUOTABLE QUOTES

Ten days before the U.S. Cavalry attacked the Sioux at Wounded Knee, the editor of the Aberdeen Saturday Pioneer, L. Frank Baum, later to become famous as the author of *The Wizard of Oz,* urged the extermination of all Native Americans. He wrote, "The nobility of the Redskin is extinguished, and what few are left are a pack of whining curs who lick the hand that smites them. The Whites, by law of conquest, by justice of civilization, are masters of the American continent, and the best safety of the frontier settlements will be secured by the total annihilation of the few remaining Indians." A week and a half after the fight, Baum expressed his approval by saying, "We had better, in order to protect our civilization, follow it up ... and wipe these untamed and untamable creatures from the face of the earth." Pretty brutal stuff from the creator of the "Lollipop Guild."

Like other minority movements, they also had a militant arm. In 1969, a war party of Native Americans raided Alcatraz Island in San Francisco Bay, seized it in the name of all Native Americans, and held it for two years until they were removed by federal officials. In 1973, warriors from AIM took over the South Dakota village of Wounded Knee, where soldiers in the late nineteenth century had attacked a Sioux encampment. Indian militants hoped to dramatize miserable conditions in the reservation adjacent to the town, where half the Native American families were on welfare, and a majority of the men were alcoholics. After one Indian was killed and another wounded, the Indians surrendered on condition that the government reexamine their treaty rights.

The main victory of the Indian movement was making the average American aware of the plight of the Native American. The federal government began to respond, and conditions on the reservations improved. As more and more tribes sent their brighter prospects to law school, they realized that the unique status of the reservations as federal property gave them a unique status. Since they were subject to tribal law, and not state law, they were free to erect gambling casinos on their property, and with the casino money, the American Indian began to acquire a new prosperity.

HOUR'S UP!

QUIZ

1. All of the following died by assassination except:

   A. John F. Kennedy

   B. Robert F. Kennedy

   C. John F. Kennedy Jr.

   D. Martin Luther King

2. The SALT agreements:

   A. Decreased the tariff on salt imports

   B. Were an attempt to get Israel, Palestine, and Jordan to agree to decrease the salt content of the Dead Sea

   C. Were signed in Salt Lake City

   D. Limited nuclear weapons

3. The only person to become president who was never elected to be either president or vice president was:

   A. Lyndon Johnson

   B. Gerald Ford

   C. Andrew Johnson

   D. Teddy Roosevelt

4. All of the following are associated with *Peanuts* except:

   A. Charlie Brown

   B. Snoopy

   C. Jimmy Carter

   D. Donald Duck

5. "The pill," which was invented in the 1960s, was designed to prevent:

   A. Rabies

   B. Babies

   C. Herpes

   D. Slurpies

HOUR 22
Changing Culture

CHAPTER SUMMARY

LESSON PLAN:

In this hour, you will learn about the Counter Culture, the Environmental Movement, Ronald Reagan, AIDS, the Moral Majority, and the Sandinistas.

You will also learn ...

- That the Woodstock generation is not a fan club for a little bird in *Peanuts*.
- That the "baby boom" is not a really small boom.
- That a Macintosh isn't always red, but it can be a mighty tasty kind of Apple (computer).
- That the Moral Majority might just be a minority.

As the baby boomers, who were a large segment of the population, became adults, the country changed with them. Their tastes were reflected in their music, clothes, and lifestyles, their causes became the causes of the whole country, as conservation and recycling, for example, became the norm. As the boomers changed the world, their parents, the generation of the Great Depression and World War II, became alarmed, as they watched their entire value system being replaced, before they were even in retirement, much less the grave. Two obvious manifestations of their conservative backlash were the rise of religious fundamentalist groups, similar to those of the Great Awakenings of earlier generations, and a messiah who arose with a persona that encompassed these traditional values, President Ronald Reagan. For two terms, he comforted the aging generation, and in many ways the 1980s repeated the economic success, military security, and conservatism that had been so comfortable for Americans during the Eisenhower period of the 1950s.

TUNE IN, TURN ON, AND DROP OUT, MAN

By the end of the 1960s, the baby boomers were coming of age. These young people, who had witnessed the upheaval of the assassinations of JFK, RFK, and MLK, integration, busing, freedom rides, the March on Washington, a man landing on the moon, and the Vietnam War, were primed to reject the traditional middle-class life of their parents.

The peace symbol, which became the semiofficial insignia of the peace movement and the baby boom generation, was created by using the semaphore stick figures for the letters "N" and "D," which stood for "nuclear disarmament."

This new generation was drawn to radical politics, unconventional standards of dress, and unconstrained sexual behavior. Men sported beards, and their hair grew longer. Instead of slacks, jackets, and ties, men wore blue jeans and T-shirts. Illegal, mind-expanding drugs were rampant, and rock singers overdosing on drugs soon ceased to be news.

QUOTABLE QUOTES

The hippies took the philosophy of the beat poets—freedom from moral restraint (free love), the quest for altered states of consciousness (getting high), and the withdrawal from society (going on the road), and turned it into a movement. Timothy Leary summed up the philosophy with the phrase, "Tune in, turn on, and drop out."

Virtually overnight, the music scene changed; conventional singers like Frank Sinatra were out, rock and roll was in. The British invasion took over: The Beatles, the Rolling Stones, and other groups were king. Singers such as Bob Dylan, whose songs included political or social commentary, were also popular. The greatest rock concert of all time, Woodstock, brought together many of these bands in a three day concert in upstate New York, and gave the baby boomers a new name, the Woodstock Generation.

TREE HUGGERS

Another new cause was the environmental movement, initiated by the publication in 1962 of Rachel Carson's book *Silent Spring*, which dramatically demonstrated the problems attendant to the unrestricted use of chemical pesticides such as DDT. The more the public became educated about the environment, the more concerned they became. It was apparent that industrial pollutants, automobile exhaust, oil spills, aerosol spray, and a million other toxic substances were ruining the environment, not only for the present generation, but for generations to come. On April 22, 1970, the first Earth Day was celebrated, the official day dedicated to preserving the environment.

STRICTLY DEFINED

The environmental movement coined a new phrase, **tree hugger.** It was originally applied only to those trying to stop the clean-cut destruction of virgin forests, but is now a term applied to most environmentalists.

Although the people were enthusiastic about cleaning up the environment, business was not, for one simple reason: It cost money and cut into corporate profits. In 1967, Congress passed the Clean Air Act, and in 1970, it amended it to provide uniform national air quality standards. Congress also passed the Water Quality Improvement Act, which made an offshore polluter, such as the corporate owner of a ruptured oil tanker, responsible for paying for the cleanup. Congress created the Environmental Protection Agency (EPA), a federal agency with the teeth to enforce the environmental laws.

MEGABYTES AND MICRO-COMPUTERS

The increasing number of service sector jobs and the arrival of the information age were both ushered in by the arrival of the computer. The federal government had been the leader in the development of computer technology. Starting in the 1950s, there was a need for the more rapid processing of data, which was driven by both military requirements and the space program. In the military sphere, the requirements of antiballistic missiles, with their complex guidance systems, required computer technology, and that same technology was critical to the development of the manned rockets that NASA was sending into space. Building on the base of this government-developed technology, in the 1970s two California whiz kids, working out of their garage, put together the first home computer, christened it the "Apple," and started a revolution in home computers. By the 1980s, there were millions of personal computers in homes and offices.

QUOTABLE QUOTES

In 1982, *Time* magazine, which had previously always named a real human being, dubbed the computer its "Man of the Year." They said "Will the computer change the very nature of human thought? And if so, for better or worse? There has been much time wasted on the debate over whether computers can be made to think, as HAL seemed to be doing in the film *2001,* when it murdered the astronauts who might challenge its command of the space flight. That answer is simple: Computers do not think, but they do simulate many of the processes of the human brain: remembering, comparing, analyzing. And as people rely on the computer to do things that they used to do inside their heads, what happens to their heads?"

It seemed that as much as there was expansion in the service sector and computer-based companies, that there was decline in the "smokestack industries," such as automobiles, steel, and textiles. The U.S. auto industry staggered under competition from such highly efficient Japanese carmakers as Toyota, Honda and Nissan, all of which turned out a higher-quality, more trouble-free car, even in the factories which they operated in the United States. By 1980, Japanese-controlled automobile manufacturers had taken more than 25 percent of the American market. In response, U.S. manufacturers tried to match the cost efficiencies and engineering standards of their Japanese rivals, and start winning back the share of the domestic car market they had ceded to imports over the previous two decades.

JUST A MINUTE

By the 1980s, three fourths of all employees worked in the service sector, in positions such as retail clerks, office workers, teachers, physicians, health-care professionals, government employees, lawyers, and legal and financial specialists.

The face of America changed in many ways. The population grew older, after the end of the "baby boom," which ran from 1946 to 1964, the birth rate declined, and the average age of the population began to rise. Lifestyles changed, households were no longer predominantly family-oriented—now more than 25 percent of all households were classified as nonfamily households, in which two or more unrelated persons lived together. Another change in the face of America was immigration: The reform of the immigration act in 1965 had changed the priority for immigrants from Western Europe, and now immigrants from Asia and Latin America had equal priority. A significant immigrant group during this time period was the Vietnamese, the upper class of Vietnam, the lawyers, teachers, doctors, military officers, politicians, and other professionals who were forced to flee with the fall of Saigon, who became known as the "boat people." In 1980 alone, almost one million new Americans arrived from overseas.

HOMOSEXUALS TURN GAY

Another group which had watched the efforts of the minority groups in their struggle for civil rights were the homosexuals. Copying the tactics of the civil rights movement, they advocated the same freedom from discrimination. One of their early victories was with the U.S. Civil Service Commission. In 1975, they lifted their ban on the employment of homosexuals. On a state by state basis, especially in states with a high gay population, like California, they were successful in introducing and passing legislation to remove discriminatory laws. However, like with most equal rights programs, their successes came too fast, and they then had to suffer through a backlash.

The gay community found themselves faced with a much greater problem than employment discrimination: the appearance of the *AIDS* virus. Because of their sexual lifestyle, the disease spread quickly through the homosexual community, and by 1992 more than 150,000 Americans had died from the disease. Eventually, almost a million Americans would be infected. As the disease spread to the rest of the world, medical researchers were mustered to developed a test for AIDS, so that there would be a way to test the blood supply and ensure that those receiving blood transfusions were not infected. Further research would develop methods of controlling the virus, and gradually the length of time that a person infected with the disease could survive would increase dramatically.

STRICTLY DEFINED

In 1981, a new word entered the language, **AIDS** (Acquired Immune Deficiency Syndrome), the name for a disease that strikes the body's immune system. AIDS is transmitted sexually or through the blood and other bodily fluids, and also strikes intravenous drugs users.

THE MORAL MAJORITY

Conservatives were feeling increasingly disenfranchised and powerless in national politics, as minorities and other vocal political groups grabbed center stage and focused the country on their own agenda. Many Americans felt that it was time for a return to a simpler time, one of limited government and traditional values.

Several groups emerged who focused on the feeling of powerless felt by these conservatives. One of these groups called itself the Moral Majority. Led by Baptist minister Jerry Falwell, it was comprised mainly of fundamentalist Christians, spiritual descendants of those responsible in an earlier era for the

"Monkey Trial." They regarded the Bible as the direct and inerrant word of God, and they were particularly concerned about an increase in crime and sexual immorality. Another group was titled the Christian Coalition, and was led by Pat Robertson. By the 1990s, this organization had become a powerful force within the Republican Party, and pushed the policies and platform of the party to the far right. They wanted to return religion to a central place in American life. Both of these groups were savvy regarding the media, and used television to develop large followings of devoted followers.

FYI In November 1983, the Reverend Jerry Falwell sued *Hustler* publisher Larry Flynt for publishing a satirical cartoon, which implied Falwell had an incestuous affair with his mother. The televangelist filed a libel suit, and a jury awarded Falwell $200,000 in emotional damages. Flynt appealed the ruling, which was unanimously overturned by the U.S. Supreme Court in 1988. The verdict was a landmark decision because it extended constitutional protection to offensive speech aimed at public figures, as long as it did not claim to be fact. The incident was woven into the plot of a 1996 feature film, *The People vs. Larry Flynt,* starring Courtney Love and Woody Harrelson.

INFANTICIDE

There was probably not a single issue that galvanized the Moral Majority, the Christian Coalition, and other right wing conservatives to action more than abortion. The medical procedure was legalized in the 1973 decision of *Roe* v. *Wade*, which created for women the right to terminate a fetus in the first weeks of pregnancy. It was not only the religious fundamentalists that were against abortion—they were joined in their fight by the Catholic Church and many political conservatives, who considered abortion to be murder. Utilizing the phrase in the Declaration of Independence, which promised a "*right to life*, liberty, and the pursuit of happiness," they named their cause "Right to Life." Those in favor of abortion termed their side "Pro-Choice." The Right-to-Lifers routinely attacked abortion and family planning clinics, and the abortion battle became a fixture of the political landscape.

Abortion and other issues galvanized the political right within the Republican Party. Calling themselves the "New Right," they assumed power and pushed the moderate and liberal elements into the background. They advocated strict limits on federal intervention in the economy, as well as the use of the powers of the federal government to support family values, curb homosexual behavior, and censor pornography. The New Right was also tough on convicted criminals, in favor of a large defense budget, behind a constitutional amendment to allow religious prayer in public schools, and against the Equal Rights Amendment.

Mr. Bonzo Goes to Washington

The messiah of the New Right was former actor Ronald Reagan, who during his Hollywood career had made primarily B movies. In the most infamous of which, *Bedtime for Bonzo,* he co-starred with a chimpanzee. He first appeared on the political landscape when he made a speech in support of Republican presidential candidate Barry Goldwater. Later, when the voters in California became nervous over the student rebellion at Berkeley, they found comfort in electing conservative and staid Reagan as governor of California. Reagan failed to take the Republican nomination for president from Gerald Ford in 1976, but at the next election he not only got the nomination, but he was able to turn Carter out of office. He won reelection in 1984 by a landslide against Carter's former vice president, Walter Mondale. As a result, it was a conservative Republican party that held the presidency for eight years, from 1980 until 1988.

FYI When Ronald Reagan was elected governor of California, he was working as the host of TV's *Death Valley Days,* from which he had to resign in order to take office. In the episode titled "Raid on the San Francisco Mint," Reagan plays real-life banker William Chapman Ralston, who saved San Francisco from financial ruin by stealing gold from the U.S. Mint, using it to convince the depositors that there were gold reserves in the bank, and stop the run on the bank. Mr. Reagan was cleverly able to take the plot of this TV show (a true story), rename it "Reagonomics," and sell it to the entire country all over again on television in his role as president. Unfortunately, in real life he was not able to stop the run on the savings and loans during his presidency like he did in the episode. In real life, Ralston went to prison for defrauding the U.S. government, although he was later pardoned by President Grant for saving the city.

President Reagan was a figure of reassurance and stability for many conservative Americans. He was known as the "Great Communicator," because of his ability to use television to connect with the people, a skill that he had developed during his years as an actor.

Reagan was convinced that the federal government was too intrusive. He strived to stop "waste, fraud and abuse," and to eliminate regulations affecting the consumer, the workplace and the environment that he believed were inefficient, expensive and impeded economic growth.

Supply-Side Economics

President Reagan believed that the nation would prosper if the power of the private economic sector was unfettered. He was an advocate of "supply-side" economics, an economic theory that holds that a greater supply of goods and services is the best road to economic growth. In order to increase the supply of goods and services, Reagan sought large tax cuts, because supply-side economists believed that a tax cut would lead to increased business investment, greater earnings, and through taxes on these earnings, increased government revenues.

Despite a narrow Republican majority in the Senate and a House of Representatives controlled by the other party, President Reagan succeeded during his first year in pushing through his economic program, including a 25 percent tax cut for individuals. The Reagan administration also persuaded Congress to vote significant increases in defense spending to counter a continual and growing threat from the Soviet Union.

Despite his attempts to jump-start the economy, the beginning of Reagan's administration was hit by a recession. The gross national product fell, unemployment went up, and many of America's industries ground to a halt. Large corporations were forced to layoff their workers, and during the downturn, other industrial countries such as Germany and Japan stepped into the gap, and took market share away from the United States. With reduced domestic production, American imports rose, resulting in an unfavorable balance of trade. Farmers were also hit hard. The rise in oil prices had increased farm costs, at the same time that the economic slump reduced the demand for farm products, leaving farmers in an economic pinch.

However, the recession had one benefit, and that was that it stopped the inflation that his administration had inherited from the Carter presidency. With the end of inflation, the economy began to recover. When the United States threatened to cut off Japanese imports, they voluntarily cut down their sales in the United States. The federal tax cut finally had its intended effect: First consumer spending began to increase, and then the stock market began to rise.

JUST A MINUTE

 During the 5 years of the Reagan economic recovery, GNP grew at an annual rate of 4.2 percent. The annual inflation rate remained between 3 and 5 percent from 1983 to 1987, except in 1986 when it fell to just under 2 percent, the lowest level in 20 years. From 1982 to 1987, the U.S. economy created more than 13 million new jobs.

However, a large part of this economic growth was based on deficit spending by the federal government. Reagan nearly tripled the national debt. This was exacerbated by the fact that Reagan cut taxes even more during his second term. His tax reduction plan not only lowered income tax rates, but simplified tax brackets, and closed loopholes to make the tax system more equitable.

JUST A MINUTE

From $74 billion in 1980, the budget deficit soared to $221 billion in 1986 before falling back to $150 billion in 1987.

One of the biggest contributors to the budget deficit, besides the cut in taxes, was the massive increase in the military budget, in response to the perceived increased threat from the Soviet Union. As history would subsequently show, the threat from the Soviet Union was actually decreasing, but at that time, it appeared to be increasing. However, the military buildup was not in vain, for Reagan had inadvertently built up the military just in time for the Gulf War, providing the Pentagon, for the first time in the history of the United States, the perfect weapon in place at the *beginning* of the war. In the past, the United States had always entered conflicts totally unprepared, with an antiquated and inadequate military force.

The increased military budget, massive tax cuts, and the growth in government health spending resulted in large federal deficits, as government spending far outstripped the reduced revenues that it was collecting. Some Reagan detractors alleged that the deficits were part of a deliberate strategy to curtail any further increase in domestic spending by the Democrats.

LATIN AMERICA

President Reagan wanted the United States to be more aggressive in its foreign policy, and the first place that he was put to the test was in Central America. El Salvador was endangered by guerilla activity that threatened the stability of its government, and Reagan responded with a program of military and economic aid. Reagan also tried to persuade them to put into place a democratically elected government, but they continued to employ right-wing death squads. Although the efforts of the United States were instrumental in keeping the government in power, they did not stop the violence, and the level of conflict actually increased. It was not until 1992 that a peace agreement was finally reached.

Reagan also involved the U.S. in Nicaragua. In 1979, Nicaraguan Communist revolutionaries, who called themselves the "Sandinistas," overthrew the dictatorial right-wing Somoza régime. The government of the Sandinistas had strong military ties to Cuba and the Soviet Union, and they refused to sever these Communist ties. In addition, they refused to reform their political system to accommodate democracy.

As it became increasingly obvious that the Sandinistas were going to remain a militaristic dictatorship with strong ties to the Communist bloc, diplomatic efforts were abandoned in favor of supporting the rebels, who were known as the Contras. However, this support was not favored in Congress, and in 1984 Congress voted to end all military aid to the Contras, although they continued humanitarian aid. Reagan was convinced that he should not abandon the Contras, and two years later he was able to convince Congress to appropriate another hundred million dollars for military aid to the rebels.

Unfortunately for the Reagan administration, a scandal broke, in which it was revealed that Oliver North and other White House staffers, in direct contravention of the Congressional prohibition against sending arms to the Contras, had conducted secret arms sales to Iran, and then used the money to secretly fund the Contras in their fight. Although Oliver North became a right wing hero from the affair, Congress was extremely displeased that their monetary constrictions had been circumscribed.

Unfortunately for the Contras, neither the money appropriated by Congress, nor the money funneled by Ollie North and his secret arms deals, was sufficient to turn the tide for the revolution, and ultimately the Contras ceased to be either an effective military or civil force in Nicaragua. Ironically, it was ultimately another political group, a political coalition led by Violetta Chamorro, that was able to win an election in the country and oust the Sandinistas from office.

The elections in Nicaragua were indicative of a democratic sweep across Latin America, as countries from Argentina to Guatemala increasingly ended their dictatorships, and placed into power democratically elected governments. Not only in Latin America, but in other countries around the world in which the United States had a historical interest, democracy was taking hold. In the Philippines, the "people power" of Corazon Aquino brought down the autocratic rule of dictator Ferdinand Marcos, and ended his wife's shoe collection, and in South Korea, the military junta was finally replaced by a democratically elected government.

GRENADA

Reagan utilized his growing military power, and made good on his anti-Communist rhetoric, when he authorized the direct use of military force for an invasion of the island country of Grenada. On October 25, 1983, U.S. forces landed on the Caribbean island as a result of an appeal for intervention by nearby countries. The invasion was sparked by the assassination of Grenada's leftist prime minister by members of his own Marxist-oriented party, and received approval from Reagan after it was learned that almost a thousand Americans were studying medicine on the island. After a short period of fighting, in which the U.S. troops overran not only the indigenous soldiers, but also their numerous Cuban "advisors," they captured significant numbers of Cuban military and construction personnel and seized caches of Soviet-supplied arms. After keeping the island under military rule for a month, the American troops pulled out of Grenada. A year later, the people were able to hold democratic elections.

JUST A MINUTE

Reagan's credibility for ordering the invasion was bolstered by what the Americans invading Grenada found on the island: a cache of weapons that could arm 10,000 men, including automatic rifles, machine guns, rocket launchers, antiaircraft guns, howitzers, cannon, armored vehicles, and coastal patrol boats. Of 800 Cubans, 59 were killed and 25 wounded. Forty-five Grenadians died, and 337 were wounded. America also suffered casualties: 19 dead and 119 wounded. The medical students came home unharmed and without a single casualty.

SOUTH AFRICA

In South Africa, the racist government refused to end their policy of apartheid, a policy designed to separate the races that was much more egregious than the United States' old "separate but equal." In 1986, the U.S. Congress, frustrated at the lack of progress toward integration, imposed a set of economic sanctions on South Africa, and when Reagan vetoed the measure, they overrode his veto. In December of 1988, in the last weeks of the Reagan administration, the many years of U.S. mediation resulted in a historic peace settlement, authorizing the independence of the territory of Namibia in southern Africa, and laid the foundation for the final triumph of Nelson Mandela and the end of apartheid in South Africa.

LEBANON

Reagan tried to help the moderate, pro-Western government in Lebanon by sending in the U.S. Marines to lend support to the weakening régime. However, this effort ended badly when terrorists attacked a Marine compound with a bomb, and the resulting explosion killed 241 Marines. In line with the U.S. modern aversion to casualties, Reagan ordered an immediate withdrawal of all American troops from the country.

In 1986, terrorists from Libya instigated terrorist attacks on U.S. military personnel in Europe. To demonstrate to those countries who were supporting terrorism that it would not be tolerated, and that such terrorism carried with it repercussions, U.S. Naval and Air Force aircraft attacked targets in Tripoli and Benghazi, Libya.

HOUR'S UP!

1. The large number of children who were born nine months after the soldiers returned from World War II were called:

   A. Boxers

   B. Bloomers

   C. Boomers

   D. Boobies

2. Fundamentalists who regarded the Bible as the direct word of God, and who were particularly concerned about an increase in crime and sexual immorality, were called:

   A. The Moonies

   B. Silent Majority

   C. Silent Spring

   D. Moral Majority

3. Ronald Reagan is all of the following except:

    A. Co-starred with a chimp in *Bedtime for Bonzo*

    B. His secret service code name was "Rawhide"

    C. Original choice to play Rick in *Casablanca*

    D. Gay rights advocate and activist

4. The personal computer that launched the hi-tech revolution was called a:

    A. Brainiac

    B. Univac

    C. Maniac

    D. Apple

5. The hippies' philosophy was all of the following except:

    A. Tune in

    B. Turn on

    C. Drop out

    D. Drop dead

Hour 23
Century's End

LESSON PLAN:

In this hour, you will learn about the Evil Empire, Star Wars, the Space Shuttle, Black Monday, budget deficits, the fall of the Berlin Wall, the invasion of Panama, NAFTA, the end of the Cold War, and the Gulf War.

You will also learn ...

- That even Ronald Reagan went to see *Star Wars.*
- That acid rain isn't a punk band.
- That Berlin Wall didn't fall all by itself.
- That neither George Bailey nor Jimmy Stewart were behind the Savings and Loan scandal.

During the 1980s, the defense budget was increased dramatically, with two completely unforeseen results. Ever since World War II, the United States had been the "arsenal of democracy." As the immense wealth of the United States was funneled into the defense buildup, the USSR, as was to be expected, tried to match the U.S. dollar for ruble. What even the intelligence analysts did not suspect, however, was how close the evil empire was to total collapse. Unable to keep up with the immense resources the United States was channeling into the defense buildup, the USSR was driven to total collapse.

Even as the USSR crumbled, and the Berlin Wall was torn down, another crisis was building in the Middle East. Iraq, confident that there would be no repercussions, had invaded Kuwait, their oil rich but militarily impotent neighbor to the south. The Iraqi's couldn't have planned their invasion at a worse time. The United States had built up their military forces to the highest state of readiness since World War II, and the enemy they were designed to deter had disappeared overnight. With such a mighty force at his disposal, the United States response to the Iraqi invasion was an easy decision for President Bush to make. Rather than demobilizing his great military force, Bush sent it to the Iraq desert, where they proved their worth by quickly destroying an army that many observers had thought was one of the greatest military organizations in the world.

REAGAN'S DEATH STAR

There were three events during Reagan's administration that increased Cold War tensions. The first was the brutal suppression by the Soviets of the Solidarity labor movement in Poland. The second was the shooting down of an off-course civilian airliner, Korean Airlines Flight 007, by the Russian air force. The third was the Soviet occupation of Afghanistan.

FYI Ronald Reagan was the first to create a new euphemism for the USSR; he called it the "Evil Empire."

President Reagan's concept for dealing with the Cold War threat of the Soviet Union was "peace through strength." To facilitate that policy, his administration spent unprecedented sums for a massive defense buildup, which included the deployment of intermediate-range nuclear missiles in Europe.

In 1983, Reagan announced his Strategic Defense Initiative (SDI). The purpose of this research program was to explore advanced technologies, such as lasers and high-energy projectiles, to defend the United States against Russian intercontinental ballistic missiles. Although scientists were leery of the technological feasibility of SDI, and others questioned the huge cost, the administration was determined to move forward with the project.

FYI In his address to the nation on March 23, 1983, President Ronald Reagan first announced his intention to develop a new system to reduce the threat of nuclear attack and end the strategy of mutual deterrence. He named the system "Star Wars," after the popular movie, so named because the system was designed to destroy missiles from space. The Soviets feared that the system would increase the risk of the United States launching a first attack, because U.S. officials would not fear retaliation.

Moscow was amenable to arms control, primarily because the Soviet economy was showing signs of strain under the level of spending necessary to compete with the massive U.S. defense buildup. In 1985, President Reagan and the new Soviet leader, General Secretary Mikhail Gorbachev, met in Geneva. They agreed to seek a 50 percent reduction in strategic offensive nuclear arms, and to limit intermediate-range nuclear forces. Then, at another summit meeting two years later, Reagan and Gorbachev signed the Intermediate-Range Nuclear Forces (INF) Treaty providing for the destruction of this entire category of nuclear weapons.

THE SPACE SHUTTLE

In 1981, the United States revitalized its space program with the launch of the space shuttle *Columbia,* the first reusable manned spacecraft. During the next four years, the shuttle demonstrated extraordinary versatility in the types of missions it could undertake. Astronauts conducted experiments in space, and launched, retrieved, and repaired other satellites while in orbit.

FYI The first Space Shuttle was originally to be named *Constitution,* in honor of the bicentennial of the U.S. Constitution. However, viewers of the popular TV show *Star Trek* started a write-in campaign urging the White House to select the name *Enterprise.* The *Enterprise,* designated OV-101, was rolled out of Rockwell's Air Force Plant 42, Site 1 Palmdale California assembly facility on September 17, 1976.

The new space program suffered a severe setback in 1986, when the space shuttle *Challenger* exploded as it was accelerating through the atmosphere, in full view of those who had come to witness the takeoff. All six of the astronauts, and a civilian schoolteacher who was to have been the first ordinary citizen in space, were all killed instantly. A moratorium was immediately placed on all shuttle launches, while NASA investigated the explosion and tried to determine the reason for the failure. By 1988, NASA was ready for another launch, this time of the shuttle *Discovery.* To prevent a reoccurrence of the *Challenger* disaster, they had made more than 300 design changes in the launch systems and computer software.

BLACK MONDAY

On October 19, 1987, which was later called "Black Monday," the stock market fell 22 percent. In everyone's mind, this was a repeat of the 1929 stock market crash, and everyone remembered that that crash had been followed by the Great Depression. While there were numerous causes for the fall, which were based in consumer anxiety, it was the computer revolution that really lay at the bottom of the crash. Utilizing the new computer technology, stock brokers had created "program trading," in which computers were programmed to automatically buy or sell shares when certain triggers were tripped in the computer program. As a result, as the stock market started to fall, the computers were automatically triggered to sell even more, and, thus, the stock market plummeted even further.

George Bush—the First Generation

President Reagan was at the height of his popularity at the end of his second term in office, but because of the Constitutional amendment passed after FDR'S four terms, limiting presidents to two terms, he was prohibited from running again. Therefore, Reagan's vice president, George Bush, rode his coattails, first to the nomination, and then into office as the next president.

Dukakis, the Democratic nominee who ran against Bush, tried to carry his message to the American people. He believed that poor Americans were hurting economically and needed help, that defense spending need to be curbed, and that the federal deficit had to be reduced. However, the public preferred Bush's message, "Read my lips. No new taxes." Bush won with an 8 percent lead in the popular vote. Unfortunately, during his presidential term of office, the realities of the budget deficit required him to eat his words, and ask for a tax increase to balance the budget.

 Millie, the First Dog, was a spaniel who earned more than four times as much as her master President Bush in 1991. Millie wrote *Millie's Book,* a look at the White House through her canine eyes, and it became a best-seller. Millie had puppies at the White House, one of which was adopted by George W. Bush, and named Spot. He now resides at his mom's former home, 1600 Pennsylvania Avenue, with his new dad. However, he has no plans to publish.

As was to be expected, Bush followed a conservative economic program that closely followed that of his former president and mentor, Ronald Reagan. In reality, he had little choice, because of a deficit reduction law that required spending cuts, and permitted little opportunity to add new budget line items. Therefore, any changes that Bush wanted to make would have to be in areas where someone other than the federal government was paying the bills.

Environmental protection and education were two areas where private industry and local and state government absorbed most of the cost, and provided an opportunity for Bush to change policy without affecting the federal budget. In 1990, Bush signed radical new legislation to reduce urban smog, automobile exhaust, toxic air pollution and acid rain, and passed most of the cost on to the actual industrial polluters. He also initiated and signed legislation ensuring physical access for the disabled, placing the costs for compliance on business. In addition, Bush launched a campaign to encourage volunteers to help with social problems, which he termed, in a memorable phrase, "a thousand points of light."

THE SAVINGS AND LOAN SCANDAL

One great difficulty for Bush in trying to deal with the budget deficit was the savings and loan crisis, which could not have come at a worse time. The savings and loans were federally insured, so that when they failed, the depositors' money was reimbursed by the FDIC, a federal insurance agency. The only problem is that the savings and loans were not properly regulated, at least not at the same level as they were insured. An economic downturn created difficulties, and suddenly, savings and loans were failing at a prodigious rate. The depositors' money had to be repaid by the federal government who insured them, and it was a massive payout that only served to balloon the deficit.

JUST A MINUTE

Of the more than 3,100 savings and loans that existed in the late 1970s, only 2,453 remained on June 30, 1990. By 1993, the total cost of reimbursing the depositors from failed thrifts, whose deposits were guaranteed by the government, was estimated at close to $500 billion.

PANAMA

During the administration of President Bush, crack cocaine and other addictions reached epidemic proportions, and Bush made one of the primary goals of his domestic agenda the "war on drugs." The United States had compelling evidence that Panama was one of the primary conduits by which Latin American drugs funneled into the United States, and that their dictator, General Manuel Antonia Noriega, was the kingpin of this Panamanian drug cartel. Just before Christmas in 1989, Bush asked for bipartisan support to invade Panama, arrest Noriega, and shut down his drug operation.

FYI Ironically, it was only 12 years earlier that President Jimmy Carter had signed a treaty with Panama, giving up the United States' perpetual right to the Panama Canal Zone, the 10 mile wide swath of land through which the canal runs. Just a decade later, the United States had to invade the same country it had just given away.

The invasion of Panama was an overwhelming success. Noriega was captured and taken to Miami, where he was convicted in federal district court of drug trafficking and racketeering. With Noriega removed, they were able to accomplish another goal: the restoration of democracy. Noriega had annulled the presidential election that had elected Guillermo Endara. The invasion of Panama restored democracy to the country, safeguarded the lives of American citizens living in Panama, and ensured that the Panama Canal would continue to operate.

NAFTA

One of the goals of the Bush administration had been to ratify the North America Free Trade Agreement (NAFTA) with Mexico and Canada, which became bogged down in endless debate during the Clinton administration. Those opposed to ratification included labor unions, who believed that NAFTA would encourage the export of U.S. jobs. Environmentalists were also against the act, believing that moving factories south of the border would place them into a country without the same federal controls on industrial pollution as the United States, and result in greater pollution of the planet.

FYI NAFTA provides for powerful international tribunals to enforce its provisions, and already they are flexing their muscle. United Parcel Service, the package-delivery company, filed a complaint contending that the very existence of the publicly financed Canadian postal system represents unfair competition that conflicts with Canada's obligations for free trade under NAFTA. If the tribunal upholds the UPS claim, government participation in any service that competes with the private sector will be threatened.

The Clinton administration, who negotiated the final agreement, argued that NAFTA would result in a greater flow of goods and services at a lower cost, and ultimately would make industry in all three countries more competitive in the global marketplace. The Republicans subscribed to the same theory, and with bipartisan support, NAFTA was finally ratified by Congress in 1993. Its supporters hoped that it would become the template for other trade agreements, eventually leading to a free trade agreement throughout the entire Western Hemisphere.

END TO THE COLD WAR

In the late 1980s, activist groups in many Eastern bloc countries were advocating an end to communism and a return to democratic government. In January of 1990, Bush announced in his State of the Union message that he was going to dramatically cut the number of U.S. troops stationed in Europe. In February, the Bush administration held discussions with the Soviets on the unification of East and West Germany. Before the end of the year, after numerous conferences on the subject, the Soviet Union renounced its occupation rights from World War II, and agreed to the creation of a unified Germany with full membership in NATO. On September 12, 1990, the Treaty on the Final Settlement with respect to Germany was signed in Moscow. In jubilation, the citizens of Berlin got out their sledge hammers, and knocked down the Berlin Wall, bringing to an end more than 40 years of Russian occupation of East Germany.

FYI When the series *Star Trek* hit the airwaves in the late 1960s, people were convinced that Chekov, the Russian crew member on the bridge of the starship *Enterprise,* was pure fantasy on the part of series creator Gene Roddenberry. Yet we now live in a world in which Poland and the Czech Republic, who used to be part of the Warsaw Pact, are part of NATO, and in which Russians are serving with NATO in KFOR, the Kosovo Force. Nothing is stranger for a veteran of the Cold War than to enter a top-secret NATO operations center in Kosovo and see Russian officers with security badges that say "NATO TOP SECRET."

To further deescalate the Cold War, in November the United States and 21 European countries signed a treaty limiting tanks, aircraft, and artillery used by NATO and the Warsaw Pact, which was called the Treaty on Conventional Armed Forces in Europe (CFE). Then, the following year, in July 1991, Bush and Gorbachev signed the Strategic Arms Reduction Treaty, which called for massive cuts in the nuclear arsenals of both the United States and Russia. Then Bush went on to sign an agreement with Boris Yeltsin, president of the new Russian Federation, to eliminate all multiple-warhead missiles by the end of the year 2003. These two agreements, taken together, reduced the number of nuclear warheads in the arsenals of both countries, which numbered more than 21,000, by more than two thirds. With the passage of these agreements between the United States and the USSR, the Cold War was indeed over.

WAR IN THE GULF

The United States had been engaged for many years in a massive military buildup, especially during the Reagan administration. The Bush administration was ready to start thinking about drawing down the military, when a need for this military force suddenly appeared with the Iraqi invasion of Kuwait in August 1990. This created an untenable strategic problem for the United States, which was dependent on oil from the Middle East region. If Iraq, under the leadership of Saddam Hussein, was not checked, then he could threaten Saudi Arabia and other Persian Gulf oil-producing states, ultimately choking off the oil supply.

President Bush immediately condemned the Iraqi invasion, and demanded their immediate and unconditional withdrawal from Kuwait. In the United Nations, the Security Council voted unanimously to condemn the invasion, and also demanded the immediate withdrawal of Iraqi troops from Kuwait. This unanimous action was possible because of the new relationship between the United States and the Soviet Union, who in the past would undoubtedly have opposed the United States in the Security Council. In the weeks following the invasion, the UN Security Council went on to pass 12 more resolutions condemning the Iraqi invasion and imposing wide-ranging economic sanctions on Iraq. The last resolution approved the use of force by UN member states if Iraq did not unconditionally withdraw from Kuwait by January 15, 1991.

Instead of complying with either the U.S. or UN demands, Saddam Hussein instead announced the annexation of the entire sovereign country of Kuwait, making it in effect a province of Iraq. In addition, he rounded up all of the U.S. and British citizens in Kuwait, and announced that they were being held hostage.

President Bush was enraged by Saddam Hussein's obvious disregard of both his ultimatum, and that of the United Nations. Realizing that the United States could not act unilaterally in the region, he put his diplomats to work assembling a military and political coalition, engaging forces from not only the Middle East, but also Asia, Europe, and Africa. President Bush then went onto national television and announced that he was going to deploy U.S. troops to the Middle East.

Even though President Bush had committed troops to the war, he had done so without consulting Congress. Technically, the right to declare war, under the U.S. Constitution, is reserved exclusively to the executive branch. However, since World War II, it had always been the president who had authorized the use of military force in Korea, Vietnam, Panama, and Grenada. Bush did not follow that precedent, however, and he went to Congress for authorization to wage war. On January 12, 1991, three days before the UN deadline for Iraq to leave Kuwait, Congress granted Bush the authority he needed. It was the most sweeping war-making power given a president since World War II.

Saddam Hussein would not withdraw from Kuwait, and immediately after the UN deadline, the coalition forces attacked. The first phase was an air war. For more than a month, the air forces of the United States, Great Britain, France, Italy, Saudi Arabia, and Kuwait pounded vital Iraqi military targets in a campaign called "Desert Storm," which included attacks on communications centers, air-defense artillery, and vital logistic points. With the Iraqi forces in disarray, the coalition then launched their ground campaign, consisting of armored and airborne forces who exercised a "left hook" through the desert, cutting off the remaining Iraqi ground forces, while at the same time, the Marines stormed ashore and liberated the capital of Kuwait. The Iraqi forces were so destroyed by the air campaign, that the ground war lasted less than four days.

FYI Although the administration had a long list of reasons to stop the war short of Baghdad, the real reason can be traced back to the American military experience in Vietnam and Korea, and the psychological effect that it had on senior officers such as Powell and Schwarztkopf, who were Vietnam veterans. In addition, they had seen MacArthur's great victory at Inchon turn into defeat in Korea when he tried to push all the way to the border of China. If they continued the Gulf War, they risked losing. That is not something they could tolerate; they were emotionally incapable of taking that risk.

Saddam Hussein and his military forces were completely defeated, but President Bush, along with Colin Powell, the Chairman of the Joint Chiefs of Staff, and "Stormin" Norman Schwarztkopf, the commander in theater, both advocated stopping the war short of taking Baghdad. The failure of the coalition to achieve complete and total victory would later create problems. Emboldened by the coalition attack, two large minority groups, the Kurds in the North, and the Shiites in the South, had rebelled. When the coalition stopped short of total victory, Saddam Hussein was able to take his remaining military force, and brutally put down these rebellions. In addition, because Saddam was still in power, he was able to frustrate inspectors mandated by the peace treaty and resolutions of the UN Security Council. As a result, Saddam was able to conceal his weapons of mass destruction, and his stockpiles of chemical weapons. Saddam Hussein and Iraq remain a powerful force in the region, and also a powerful ally to radical Islamic terrorists.

Oslo Accords

The Gulf War had an unintended side effect. The coalition had raised relations between the United States and the Arab states to a new high. The United States was able to cash in on this relationship and bring Israel and the Palestine Liberation Organization to the negotiating table. The talks were held first in Madrid, and then continued in Oslo, Norway. In 1993, the agreement was signed at the White House.

Many of the provisions of the Accords were implemented, including the inauguration of the Palestinian National Authority, the handover of land to Palestinian control, and the formation of the Palestinian security forces. However, Palestinian and Israeli negotiators failed to move on from these initial provisions to a permanent status agreement on issues including Jerusalem, borders and refugees.

Frustration at the failure of the peace process to deliver what it promised, and the collapse of last ditch talks chaired by former U.S. President Bill Clinton at Camp David, were partly to blame for the beginning of another Palestinian intifada, or rebellion against Israeli occupation, which began in September 2000.

QUIZ

HOUR'S UP!

1. President Ronald Reagan did all of the following except:

    A. Called Hollywood the Evil Empire

    B. Called the USSR the Evil Empire

    C. Had a plan to defeat the Evil Empire

    D. Wanted to create a weapons system called Star Wars

2. The wall that symbolized the Cold War was the:

    A. Great Wall of China

    B. Berlin Wall

    C. Wall Street

    D. Hadrian's Wall

3. The day that the stock market crashed in 1987 was called:

    A. Black Monday

    B. Ruby Tuesday

    C. Ash Wednesday

    D. Good Friday

4. The first Space Shuttle was called the:

    A. *Constitution*

    B. *Enterprise*

    C. *Discovery*

    D. *Challenger*

5. When George Bush talked about "a thousand points of light," he was talking about:

     A. A trip to the planetarium

     B. His experimentation with drugs

     C. The White House Christmas tree

     D. Volunteering to help others

HOUR 24

The Modern World

CHAPTER SUMMARY

LESSON PLAN:

In this hour, you will learn about the Bull Moose party, the Clinton Years, the second George Bush, September 11, and the War in Afghanistan.

You will also learn ...

- Why one president named George Bush wasn't enough for the American people.
- All about the party for the Bull Moose, and why nobody came.
- That the Dixiecrats were not an all-girl group from south of the Mason-Dixon line.
- How playing the saxophone on the *Arsenio Hall Show* helped one president get elected.

George Bush's run for reelection became a watershed in American politics. At the overwhelmingly successful conclusion of the Gulf War, his reelection had seemed a certainty, yet a short time later, he was defeated by Bill Clinton, a relatively unknown and obscure candidate. Two forces conspired to bring an end to the Republican control of the presidency. One was an incredibly success-ful third-party contender, Ross Perot, whose business-like approach to solving the problems of big government split the vote of the Republican party in much the same way that other third-party candidates, like Teddy Roosevelt, had destroyed their own parties in the past. The second major factor was generational, Bill Clinton's appeal to the baby boomers, who had never before fielded a presi-dential candidate, served to defeat the candidate of the rapidly dying World War II generation.

Clinton entered office immediately after the conclusion of a major war, and ironically he was succeeded in office, after two terms, by the son of the man he had defeated, just as America once more entered a war. Barely was the new president in power, and America was deliberately and brutally attacked by terrorist forces. With the attack on the World Trade Centers and the Pentagon, a new force arose in the world to challenge the American promise of democracy and equality. Like his father, whose response had been definite and decisive, the younger George Bush immediately responded with a show of force in Afghanistan, which had been identified as a training ground and stronghold for terror.

THE 1992 ELECTION

Despite an attempt by conservative journalist Patrick Buchanan to acquire the Republican nomination, President Bush and Vice President Dan Quayle easily won renomination. On the Democratic side, Bill Clinton, governor of Arkansas, defeated a crowded field of candidates to win his party's nomination.

FYI In high school, Bill Clinton was an all-state saxophone player. When running for president in 1992, he donned dark glasses to play "Heartbreak Hotel" on his sax for a national television audience on the *Arsenio Hall Show*. Critic Greil Marcus was the first to name this as the moment that turned Clinton's campaign around, and to make sense of why. According to him, it was the meeting of politics and pop, Bubba and Elvis. And proof that rock and roll can make a president.

The Bush platform was built on the theme traditionally used by incumbents, emphasizing his experience as president and commander in chief. In addition, Bush also drew attention to what he characterized as Clinton's lack of judgment and character. For his part, Bill Clinton organized his campaign around another of the oldest and most powerful themes in electoral politics: change. It was also a battle of generations. George Bush, a product of the World War II generation, faced a young challenger in Bill Clinton who, at age 46, had never served in the military, and had participated in protests against the Vietnam War.

Clinton successfully hammered home his theme of change on the campaign trail, as well as in a round of three televised debates with President Bush and third-party challenger Ross Perot. Bill Clinton won election as the forty-second president of the United States, despite receiving only 43 percent of the popular vote.

PEROT, BULL MOOSE, AND OTHER WILD PARTIES

H. Ross Perot, who ran in the 1992 presidential race against Bush and Clinton, is a prime example of a third-party candidate. In general, third parties organize around a single issue or set of issues, personified in a charismatic leader. They are invariably a disaffected group from one of the two major parties, who split the vote of their mother party. In this election, Perot drew votes away from the Republican Party, ensuring that Clinton would be elected.

An extremely wealthy Texas businessman, Perot got across his message of economic common sense and fiscal responsibility to a wide spectrum of

American people. His campaign organization, "United We Stand," was staffed primarily by volunteers and backed by his personal fortune. Far from resenting his wealth, many admired Perot's business success and the freedom it brought him from soliciting campaign funds from special interests.

Perot received more than 19 million votes, by far the largest number ever tallied by a third-party candidate, and as a percentage of the total, it was second only to Roosevelt's showing in 1912 with the Bull Moose Party. Had he not withdrawn from the race, and then entered again, his total number of votes would probably have been even higher. But in the final analysis, all he succeeded in doing was drawing votes away from the Republicans, and helping to defeat Bush.

The country has produced a number of parties outside the "system." In one state alone during the 1992 presidential election, 58 parties were represented on the ballot, including such obscure organizations as the Apathy, the Looking Back, the New Mexico Prohibition, the Tish Independent Citizens, and the Vermont Taxpayers.

One of the most successful candidates was Theodore Roosevelt, who ran on a third-party ticket after he had already served two terms as president. Declaring himself as fit as a bull moose (hence the party's popular name), his Progressive or Bull Moose Party, a splinter of the Republican Party, won almost a third of the vote in the 1912 election. Roosevelt's effort split the Republican vote, and ensured the election of Democrat Woodrow Wilson.

FYI   For years, those who collect political memorabilia have been debating whether cast-metal moose studs are Roosevelt election buttons, or fraternal pins for the Loyal Order of Moose. People in 1912 wondered the same thing. In fact, the national office of the Moose lodge sued the Progressive Party, saying that Roosevelt supporters were infringing on their lodges' long-standing logo. The Loyal Order of Moose claimed the Progressives had purposely infringed on the lodge's design, hoping to deceive voters into thinking that the tens of thousands of lodge members wearing Loyal Order of the Moose studs were actually Roosevelt supporters.

Another "third party" was the Socialists, which reached its high point in the 1912 election with 6 percent of the popular vote. Perennial candidate Eugene Debs won more than 900,000 votes that year, advocating collective ownership of the transportation and communication industries, shorter working hours and public works projects to spur employment.

Senator Robert LaFollette, who won almost 17 percent of the vote in the 1924 election, was a prime mover in the recreation of the Progressive movement following World War I, backed by remnants of Roosevelt's Bull Moose

Party. Then, the Progressive Party reinvented itself again in 1948 with the nomination of Henry Wallace, a former vice president under Franklin Roosevelt. Unfortunately, his failure to repudiate the U.S. Communist Party, which had endorsed him, undermined his popularity and he wound up with less than 3 percent of the popular vote.

Led by South Carolina governor Strom Thurmond, the Dixiecrats split from the Democrats in 1948 because of their opposition to Truman's civil rights platform. Although they claimed the party stood for "states rights," the party's real goal was continuing racial segregation and the "Jim Crow" laws that sustained it. Similarly, in the 1960s George Wallace, another segregationist Southern governor, built a following through his outrageous attacks against civil rights, liberals and the federal government. His American Independent Party took 13.5 percent of the vote in the 1968 race for president.

THE CLINTON PRESIDENCY

After 12 years of Republican control of the presidency, Clinton came to office amid high expectations for fundamental policy change. Early in his administration he reversed a number of Republican policies. He ended the federal prohibition on the use of fetal tissue for medical research, repealed rules restricting abortion counseling in federally funded health clinics, and used his appointment power to place many women and minorities in prominent government positions.

Although backed by a Congress controlled by the Democratic Party, Clinton found it difficult to change the course of national priorities during his first two years in office. Early in his administration several of his appointees encountered congressional disapproval. His proposal to end the ban on homosexuals in the military met with widespread opposition from Congress, the military, and the public.

FYI Bill Clinton is the only president since World War II not to have served in the military. Eisenhower was a five star general in the Army. Gerald Ford, Lyndon Johnson, and Richard Nixon were lieutenant commanders in the Navy. Harry Truman was a major in the Army. Jimmy Carter was a lieutenant in the Navy and a graduate of Annapolis, and Ronald Reagan was a captain in the Army. George Bush Jr. was a first lieutenant in the Air Force. George Bush Sr. and John F. Kennedy were both lieutenants (junior grade) in the Navy.

Clinton's failure to enact comprehensive health-care reform proved to be a major setback. Widespread public concerns over the proposal's complexity, its reliance on government administration, employer mandates, and levels of services, combined with an effective lobbying campaign by opponents, drained congressional support for this major policy initiative, which had been one of the cornerstones of Clinton's campaign.

Some Clinton White House activities were subjected to criticism, and several alleged scandals became the target of congressional investigations, most notably the "Whitewater affair," an investigation into alleged improprieties by the president and his wife, Hillary Rodham Clinton, in an Arkansas land deal. Other administration actions that became the focus of outside investigations included White House requests for FBI security files, the firing of employees of the White House travel office, and the fund-raising methods used for the 1996 presidential campaign. Yet Clinton's popularity increased as the strength of the economy continued and as the public tired of actions led by the Republican Party, such as congressional investigations, cutbacks in services for the poor, antiimmigrant legislative proposals, and attempts to rescind affirmative-action programs.

In seeking reelection in 1996, Clinton claimed a number of achievements, among them a deficit-reduction plan, a college-loan payback plan, the Family and Medical Leave Act, an anticrime bill, and a welfare reform act that ended federal guarantees and shifted the responsibility for these services to the states. He cut the federal deficit in half, expanded earned-income credits for the working poor, and significantly reduced the number of government workers.

During his first term Clinton succeeded in appointing two members to the U.S. Supreme Court, Ruth Bader Ginsburg and Stephen G. Breyer. These were the first appointments to the high court made by a Democratic president in 25 years.

In the first years of his administration, Clinton's inexperience in foreign affairs was revealed by his inability to establish a consistent U.S. position on issues involving Bosnia, Haiti, the former Soviet Union, Somalia, Cuba, North Korea, and Iraq. Nevertheless, Clinton succeeded in some of his foreign policy efforts. In response to a wave of Cuban refugees seeking entry into the United States in 1994, Clinton reversed the U.S. policy of giving asylum to those seeking to escape Fidel Castro's régime, but worked out an agreement with the Cuban government to allow more refugees into the country. Clinton used the threat of an imminent invasion from the United States to force Haiti's military junta to relinquish power in favor of the democratically elected president, Jean-Bertrand Aristide. A major conflict with North Korea was eased with an agreement offering North Korea assistance with its civilian nuclear program in return for the relinquishment of plutonium-producing nuclear reactors. One of his more controversial foreign policy decisions was to grant U.S. recognition to Vietnam. In 1994, when Iraq appeared to be threatening Kuwait again, Clinton deployed more troops to Kuwait. Two years later he ordered air strikes against Iraq for violating the terms of the peace treaty that had ended the Persian Gulf War.

In the 1996 presidential election, voters chose Clinton by a comfortable margin over Republican nominee Robert Dole, making Clinton the first Democratic president since Franklin Roosevelt to be elected to the office twice, but he was not able to deliver a Democratically controlled Congress. Despite his lack of a majority, he was still able to push through some legislation. In 1997 Congress enacted a major tax cut, the first since 1981, and Clinton negotiated a deficit-reduction package that projected a balanced federal budget by 2002. He also had success with a number of targeted domestic programs on education, health, and the environment, won an increase in the minimum wage, and sponsored a reform bill that established time limits for welfare benefits.

JUST A MINUTE

Clinton could claim credit for a 30-year low in unemployment, and for the fastest real-wage growth in 20 years. The 1998 fiscal year ended with a federal budget surplus of $70 billion, the first surplus in a generation.

Clinton and his foreign policy team, led by Secretary of State Madeleine Albright, achieved considerable diplomatic successes in Northern Ireland and Israel. With Iraq, however, in the wake of ongoing showdowns between Saddam Hussein and UN weapons-inspection teams, the administration realized that diplomatic measures had been exhausted. On December 16, 1998, Clinton, together with British prime minister Tony Blair, authorized renewed air strikes against Iraq.

MONICA AND THE IMPEACHMENT

Independent Counsel Kenneth Starr's investigation of allegations of wrongdoing by Clinton and his wife in the Whitewater affair, begun in 1994, eventually expanded to include charges of perjury, obstruction of justice, and abuse of power.

In the course of his investigations, he uncovered a relationship between the president and a White House intern, Monica Lewinsky. Clinton adamantly denied any sexual involvement with Lewinsky, but this was contradicted by a dress she had saved which contained the president's semen, forcing Clinton to admit to an "inappropriate relationship." Because Clinton had testified under oath both in a civil case and before the grand jury that he had not had such a sexual relationship, he was guilty of perjury.

The House Judiciary Committee began impeachment hearings, which ended in mid-December with the refusal to entertain a Democratic motion for censure and the drafting of four articles of impeachment. On December 16, exactly one day before the full House was scheduled to vote on the articles, Clinton launched renewed air strikes against Iraq, causing his opponents to claim that this was not a valid foreign policy action, but a diversionary tactic to draw attention away from his legal troubles.

On December 19, 1998, the full House approved two of the four articles of impeachment, perjury and obstruction of justice. Clinton thus became the first elected president in U.S. history to be impeached. On January 7, 1999, the Senate trial to remove Clinton from office began. After hearing the evidence, the Senate voted, largely along party lines, and neither article gained a simple majority. The votes were 46–54, and 50–50. Thus, Clinton "beat the rap."

In his final year in office, Clinton was not able to escape the scandal that had led to his impeachment. A committee of the Arkansas Supreme Court recommended that Clinton be disbarred because of his "serious misconduct" in a sexual harassment case brought by a former state employee, Paula Jones.

THE END OF CLINTON'S TERM

The president spent considerable time in his final year in office battling the Republican (GOP) majorities in Congress over a host of issues. He vetoed GOP-passed bills on the repeal of estate taxes and the "marriage penalty," an income tax provision that resulted in unfavorable tax penalties for some married couples. Clinton also battled the GOP over gun control measures, and over a so-called Patient's Bill of Rights, intended to address consumers' grievances regarding health maintenance organizations. One of the president's more controversial moves was to order the release of oil from the nation's strategic oil reserve in an attempt to lower home heating costs. Republicans charged that this was a political ploy designed to aid Vice President Al Gore's chances in the 2000 presidential race.

President Clinton and the GOP-led Congress did come together in bipartisan agreement on the granting of permanent normal trade relations with China, despite a campaign to quell the effort grounded in China's poor record on human rights. Elsewhere, Clinton's efforts to broker a Middle East peace began to crumble as that region became embroiled in renewed violence. Some criticized the president's efforts as having only exacerbated the tensions in the region.

WORLD TRADE CENTER BOMBING

In 1993, terrorists drove a 1,500-pound urea-nitrate bomb, loaded in a Ryder rental van, into the basement parking area of the World Trade Center, set the timer, and left. The explosion rocked the World Trade Center, killed six people, and injured more than a thousand. With this act, a new age in terrorism was introduced. The men that committed this heinous crime were linked to several terrorist groups including the Islamic Jihad, Hamas, and the Sudanese National Islamic Front. A number of the terrorists were subsequently identified, arrested, tried, and convicted.

OKLAHOMA CITY BOMBING

On April 19, 1995, homegrown terrorist Timothy McVeigh parked a Ryder truck outside a government office building in Oklahoma City, loaded with explosives. When it detonated, it killed 168 people, and wounded more than 500. McVeigh was convicted of the bombing, sentenced to death, and executed on June 11, 2001. His accomplice, Terry Nichols, was convicted of manslaughter and conspiracy, and sentenced to life in prison.

KHOBAR TOWERS BOMBING

On the evening of June 25, 1996, terrorists parked a tanker truck in a parking lot adjacent to the Khobar Tower apartment buildings. The sentry on duty realized the threat of a truck bomb and began evacuating the building. Unfortunately, the bomb went off before the building could be completely evacuated, killing 19 servicemen, and wounding hundreds of others. This attack created a swirl of controversy. Two separate Air Force reports found the general in charge had done all he could to keep the event from happening. However, the Defense Departments report found that the general could have done more to protect his troops.

U.S. Embassy Bombings

In 1998, a coordinated attack was made simultaneously by terrorists on the U.S. embassies in Kenya and Tanzania. In Tanzania, a bomb was planted in a refrigeration truck and then parked outside of the embassy. When the bomb exploded, it killed 11 and injured 86. The embassy bombing in Kenya resulted in the deaths of 213 people, 12 of whom were Americans, and more than 5,000 were injured. The United States indicted Osama bin Laden as the mastermind behind the embassy attacks and offered a five million dollar reward for his arrest and conviction.

The U.S. response to the embassy bombings was to attack both Sudan and Afghanistan. The United States attacked an alleged chemical weapons plant in the Sudan, resulting in the death of the night watchmen. This counter-attack came under a great deal of criticism because it was alleged that there was no corroborating evidence to support the attack. The U.S. attack on Afghanistan came in the form of 70 cruise missiles fired at 3 separate terrorist camps. An estimated 24 people were killed, but the attack failed to terminate Osama bin Laden.

Attack on the USS *Cole*

In the year 2000, a group of suicide bombers used a skiff to pull alongside the USS *Cole,* a destroyer, and detonate a bomb. The attack killed 17 sailors and wounded an additional 39. There are eight people being held in connection with the attack. Once again, many believed Saudi Arabian terrorist Osama bin Laden was behind the attack.

The Election Controversy

When Americans went to the polls to vote for president on November 7, 2000, they expected to learn by the end of the night who was going to be elected. However, it wasn't until 36 days later that they would learn George Bush was to be the new president.

Although the vote in a number of states was in dispute, the critical state, with 25 electoral votes, was Florida. As the election results solidified, it soon came down to a simple fact: Florida would decide the election. And because of the extreme closeness of the results in Florida, a recount was automatically triggered under state law. The contested presidential election in Florida put new words and phrases into common usage, most notably *chad.*

STRICTLY DEFINED

> There are multiple types of **chads.** Chad: The tiny square section of a ballot card that is punched out to indicate the voter's preference. Dimpled chad: The chad is dented, but not detached. Pregnant chad: The chad is even more dented, but still attached at all four corners. Hanging chad: a chad attached by one corner. Swinging-door chad: a chad attached by two corners. Tri-chad: a chad attached by three corners.

As Republicans and Democrats alike filed suit at all levels in an attempt to influence the election, the country was subjected to a five-week daily roller-coaster ride through the Florida courts. On December 13, the day after the U.S. Supreme Court ruled against Gore, George W. Bush declared victory. The high court's unprecedented involvement capped the longest election in more than 100 years.

 FYI Twice in the history of the American presidency, a son of a former president has also been elected president. In both cases, they had the same name. John Adams was elected president, and so was his son John Q. Adams. George H. Walker Bush was president, and so is his son George Walker Bush.

Bush clearly benefited in the election from the public's desire for change after eight years of the Clinton–Gore administration. Voter surveys indicated that people perceived Bush as the candidate of change and Gore as the man who represented the status quo.

SEPTEMBER ELEVENTH

On September 11, 2001, terrorists hijacked four commercial jet airliners to be used as ballistic missiles. American Airlines Flight 11 was flown into Tower One of the World Trade Center, and United Airlines Flight 175 was crashed into Tower Two. As the world watched in horror, Tower Two burned, and then collapsed. Shortly afterward, Tower One also fell. This terrorist attack killed thousands of men, women and children from more than 80 nations around the world.

The third plane was American Airlines Flight 77, which was flown by the terrorists into the Pentagon, killing 189 civilians and military personnel. The fourth and last aircraft, United Airlines Flight 93, was believed to be targeted for the Capitol in Washington, D.C. However, on this flight the terrorists got more than they bargained for. The passengers had heard, via cell phone, what had happened to the first three airliners, and they were not going down without a fight. In their attempt to retake the aircraft, the terrorists destroyed the plane. Although everyone on the flight was killed in the attempt, they did save the lives of the innocent victims in the fourth target.

This is a picture of the second attack; World Trade Center One is already burning, as the second aircraft hits World Trade Center Two.

THE WAR ON TERRORISM

That evening, while the rubble of the World Trade Center and the Pentagon was still burning, President Bush spoke to the American people from the Oval Office in a nationally televised address.

QUOTABLE QUOTES

President Bush said, of the terrorist attacks of September 11:

These acts of mass murder were intended to frighten our nation into chaos and retreat. But they have failed, our country is strong. A great people has been moved to defend a great nation. Terrorist attacks can shake the foundations of our biggest buildings, but they cannot touch the foundation of America. These acts shattered steel, but they cannot dent the steel of American resolve. America was targeted for attack because we are the brightest beacon for freedom and opportunity in the world. And no one will keep that light from shining. These terrorist attacks were an act of war against the United States.

The National Security Council identified Osama bin Laden as the leader of al Qaeda, the terrorist group who organized the attacks. He was supported by the government of Afghanistan, known as the Taliban, and his organization was linked to terrorist organizations in 60 other countries, including the Egyptian Islamic Jihad and the Islamic Movement of Uzbekistan. Afghanistan was identified as the country where they were training terrorists in the tactics of terror. As the first campaign in the war on terror, the United States supported the Northern Alliance, a revolutionary army intent on overthrowing the Taliban régime, who subsequently took control of Afghanistan. Osama bin Laden is still a fugitive, although many are convinced that he was killed during the fighting.

Epilogue

From its origins as a set of struggling colonies on the Atlantic coast, the United States has transformed into the first "universal nation," more than 250 million people representing virtually every nationality and ethnic group on the planet. It is also a nation where evolution, whether it be economic, technological, cultural, demographic or social, never stops. The United States is the harbinger of the change that inevitably sweeps through other nations and societies in an increasingly interdependent, interconnected world.

Despite continual change, however, the United States has core values that never waiver. Grounded in the Constitution, the Declaration of Independence, and the Bill of Rights, these values include an undeniable belief in individual freedom, democratic government, social mobility, and equal opportunity for all.

Hour's Up!

1. Saddam Hussein is all of the following except:

    A. Was considered the new Adolf Hitler

    B. Invaded Kuwait, and annexed it to Iraq

    C. Responsible for starting the Gulf War

    D. The first Iraqi leader to come to power in free elections supervised by the United Nations

2. The only president since World War II not to serve in the military was:

    A. Richard Nixon

    B. Ronald Reagan

    C. Bill Clinton

    D. George W. Bush

3. The following have had two members of their biological family with the same last name become president except:

    A. Bush family

    B. Roosevelt family

    C. Adams family

    D. Addams family

4. The United States has had political leaders and parties with all of the following names except:

    A. Webster and the Whigs

    B. Teddy and the Bull Moose's

    C. Strom and the Dixiecrats

    D. Josie and the Pussycats

5. The free trade agreement between the United and Mexico was called:

    A. NATA

    B. NAFTA

    C. BIAFRA

    D. OPEC

APPENDIX A
Test Answers

HOUR 1

1. C. Across a land bridge where the Bering Sea is now located
2. D. Immigration
3. D. Amerigo Vespucci
4. B. Sir Walter Raleigh
5. D. King James I

HOUR 2

1. D. Nobody knows
2. C. The Manhattan Indians
3. A. Lord Baltimore
4. C. U.S. Constitution
5. D. *hood*

HOUR 3

1. C. A learning aid for children
2. D. Electric guitar
3. B. A religious revival
4. D. Emily Post
5. C. Mayflower Compact

HOUR 4

1. D. Sons of Liberty
2. A. Daughters of the American Revolution
3. D. Committee of Correspondence
4. B. Paul Revere
5. C. British regulars made lousy house guests.

Hour 5

1. C. Because they could get ready to fight in a minute
2. C. South Vietnam
3. D. Federalists
4. B. Lexington
5. D. At loggerheads

Hour 6

1. B. To a bar
2. D. Internal Revenue Service
3. D. Lord Leroy Massachusetts
4. D. New England
5. D. Right to life

Hour 7

1. C. Cutting down his father's cherry tree
2. C. King Louis, a French king
3. B. Hamilton favored the farmers and the rural agrarian interests, while Jefferson favored the urban mercantile interests.
4. D. Because the United States didn't have a navy that floated
5. C. Washington

Hour 8

1. C. Is named after Lake Erie
2. B. Cotton gin
3. A. Written by Marilyn Monroe
4. A. Republicans
5. D. George M. Cohan

HOUR 9

1. D. They were intelligent.
2. B. Old Tippecanoe.
3. D. Win the battle of the Alamo.
4. C. Help Wanted. No Irish Need Apply.
5. B. Even though their land was guaranteed by a treaty with the United States, they lost their case in the United States Supreme Court to prevent their removal .

HOUR 10

1. D. A great victory for Texans in their fight for independence from Mexico
2. D. Published right after the end of the Civil War
3. D. Miners, forty-niners, and their daughter, Clementine
4. C. End slavery
5. D. As a slave, Dred Scott did not have the right to travel on the Underground Railroad.

HOUR 11

1. D. The Confederates discovered that the Union army was full of bull.
2. A. Freed the slaves in the North
3. D. A speech given to dedicate the federal cemetery
4. D. Grant and Lee signed a stipulation, in which they agreed to quit fighting.
5. C. Students getting deferments from the draft to attend college

HOUR 12

1. D. Who wasn't in the play
2. C. Inventor of the telephone
3. D. John D. Rockefeller
4. D. Internet
5. D. Promised the former slaves "Forty Acres and a Mule"

HOUR 13

1. D. Trusts were getting too powerful.
2. C. Trust-Buster
3. D. Dr. David Burbank, the sheep-herding dentist
4. C. Defeated Crazy Horse and Sitting Bull at the battle of the Little Big Horn
5. D. The only Roosevelt to be elected president

HOUR 14

1. C. The Boxers were trying to obtain control of the opium trade.
2. D. The Latin word for grain
3. C. Worried about being crucified on a "cross of gold"
4. D. John F. Kennedy
5. A. Christened in a speech by Teddy Roosevelt

HOUR 15

1. B. Square Deal
2. C. Carry a big stick
3. D. Blues
4. D. Veterans' Day
5. B. League of Nations

HOUR 16

1. B. Herbert Hoover
2. C. Prohibition
3. D. New Deal
4. D. Black Friday
5. D. Defendant Scopes was acquitted of all charges

HOUR 17

1. D. The expression Nazis used before they changed to "Haile Hitler"
2. C. Alois Schickelgruber
3. D. First Italian astronaut
4. C. Tojo
5. D. United States of America

HOUR 18

1. D. Cold War
2. D. Communism
3. C. Winston Churchill
4. D. Fade away
5. C. Harry Truman

HOUR 19

1. C. I like Ike.
2. C. A Congressman
3. D. Fair Deal
4. D. Not as annoying as Barney
5. C. Jackie Robinson

HOUR 20

1. C. Separate but equal
2. B. New Frontier
3. C. Unsafe
4. D. To put a man where no man had gone before
5. C. Determined to expel the Communists from his country and turn Vietnam into a democracy

Hour 21

1. D. Martin Luther King
2. D. Limited nuclear weapons
3. B. Gerald Ford
4. D. Donald Duck
5. B. Babies

Hour 22

1. C. Boomers
2. D. Moral Majority
3. D. Gay rights advocate and activist
4. D. Apple
5. D. Drop dead

Hour 23

1. A. Called Hollywood the Evil Empire
2. B. Berlin Wall
3. A. Black Monday
4. B. *Enterprise*
5. D. Volunteering to help others

Hour 24

1. D. The first Iraqi leader to come to power in free elections supervised by the United Nations
2. C. Bill Clinton
3. D. Addams family
4. D. Josie and the Pussycats
5. B. NAFTA

APPENDIX B
More Things to Know

LIST OF U.S. PRESIDENTS AND VICE PRESIDENTS

	Date	President	Vice President
1	1789–1797	George Washington	John Adams
2	1797–1801	John Adams	Thomas Jefferson
3	1801–1809	Thomas Jefferson	Aaron Burr George Clinton
4	1809–1817	James Madison	George Clinton Elbridge Gerry
5	1817–1825	James Monroe	Daniel D. Tompkins
6	1825–1829	John Quincy Adams	John C. Calhoun
7	1829–1837	Andrew Jackson	John C. Calhoun Martin Van Buren
8	1837–1841	Martin Van Buren	Richard M. Johnson
9	1841	William Henry Harrison	John Tyler
10	1841–1845	John Tyler	None
11	1845–1849	James Polk	George M. Dallas
12	1849–1850	Zachary Taylor	Millard Fillmore
13	1850–1853	Millard Fillmore	None
14	1853–1857	Franklin Pierce	William R. King
15	1857–1861	James Buchanan	John C. Breckinridge
16	1861–1865	Abraham Lincoln	Hannibal Hamlin Andrew Johnson
17	1865–1869	Andrew Johnson	None
18	1869–1877	Ulysses S. Grant	Schuyler Colfax Henry Wilson
19	1877–1881	Rutherford B. Hayes	William A. Wheeler

continues

	Date	President	Vice President
20	1881	James A. Garfield	Chester A. Arthur
21	1881–1885	Chester A. Arthur	None
22	1885–1889	Grover Cleveland	Thomas Hendricks
23	1889–1893	Benjamin Harrison	Levi P. Morton
24	1893–1897	Grover Cleveland	Adlai E. Stevenson
25	1897–1901	William McKinley	Garret A. Hobart Theodore Roosevelt
26	1901–1909	Theodore Roosevelt	Charles W. Fairbanks
27	1909–1913	William Howard Taft	James S. Sherman
28	1913–1921	Woodrow Wilson	Thomas R. Marshall
29	1921–1923	Warren G. Harding	Calvin Coolidge
30	1923–1929	Calvin Coolidge	Charles G. Dawes
31	1929–1933	Herbert Hoover	Charles Curtis
32	1933–1945	Franklin D. Roosevelt	John N. Garner Henry A. Wallace Harry S Truman
33	1945–1953	Harry S Truman	Alben W. Barkley
34	1953–1961	Dwight D. Eisenhower	Richard M. Nixon
35	1961–1963	John F. Kennedy	Lyndon B. Johnson
36	1963–1969	Lyndon B. Johnson	Hubert Humphrey
37	1969–1974	Richard M. Nixon	Spiro T. Agnew Gerald Ford
38	1974–1977	Gerald R. Ford	Nelson Rockefeller
39	1977–1981	James Earl Carter	Walter Mondale
40	1981–1989	Ronald W. Reagan	George Bush
41	1989–1993	George H. W. Bush	Dan Quayle
42	1993–2001	William J. Clinton	Al Gore
43	2001–	George W. Bush	Dick Cheney

STATES ADMITTED TO THE UNION

The first 13 states were the original 13 states that united to fight against Great Britain in the Revolutionary War. Even more independent, Vermont (the fourteenth state) was on the verge of war with New York before it, too, joined the rebels to fight for a new nation.

Pennsylvania, Massachusetts, and Virginia were the first of four states that call themselves commonwealths.

South Carolina would later become the first state to secede, provoking the Civil War.

1 Delaware—December 7, 1787

2 Pennsylvania—December 12, 1787

3 New Jersey—December 18, 1787

4 Georgia—January 2, 1788

5 Connecticut—January 9, 1788

6 Massachusetts—February 6, 1788

7 Maryland—April 28, 1788

8 South Carolina—May 23, 1788

9 New Hampshire—June 21, 1788

10 Virginia—June 25, 1788

11 New York—July 26, 1788

12 North Carolina—November 21, 1789

13 Rhode Island—May 29, 1790

Of the last three states admitted in the eighteenth century, Kentucky and Tennessee extended the United States' borders far to the west.

14 Vermont—March 4, 1791

15 Kentucky—June 1, 1792

16 Tennessee—June 1, 1796

During the first half of the nineteenth century, the United States expanded primarily in the Midwest and the South. Ohio, Indiana, and Illinois were ceded to the United States by Great Britain, while Louisiana, Mississippi, and Alabama were obtained from France.

17 Ohio—March 1, 1803

18 Louisiana—April 30, 1812

19 Indiana—December 11, 1816

20 Mississippi—December 10, 1817

21 Illinois—December 3, 1818

22 Alabama—December 14, 1819

Many of the states admitted during the four decades before the Civil War were influenced by the debate over slavery. Missouri, Arkansas, Florida, and Texas entered the Union as slave states, the others as free states. Most were in the Midwest or South. The national boundaries jumped far to the west with the admission of California in 1850 even before hardy settlers were rewarded with the admission of the first Great Plains state, Kansas. (Texas, which lies partly in the Great Plains, was an independent republic for several years. It and California were the first states taken from Mexico, which had won its independence from Spain.)

23 Maine—March 15, 1820

24 Missouri—August 10, 1821

25 Arkansas—June 15, 1836

22 Michigan—January 26, 1837

27 Florida—March 3, 1845

28 Texas—December 29, 1845

29 Iowa—December 28, 1846

30 Wisconsin—May 29, 1848

31 California—September 9, 1850

32 Minnesota—May 11, 1858

33 Oregon—February 14, 1859

34 Kansas—January 29, 1861

West Virginia and Nevada were admitted during the Civil War.

35 West Virginia—June 20, 1863

36 Nevada—October 31, 1864

After the Civil War, the nation again turned its attention westward, annexing most of the Great Plains and Rocky Mountain states. (Utah is often considered a Rocky Mountain state, though it is listed here as a Southwest state.)

Wyoming focused attention on women's rights, while Utah made Americans take a closer look at religion, even as the restless nation's Indian wars were coming to a close.

37 Nebraska—March 1, 1867

38 Colorado—August 1, 1876

34 North Dakota—November 2, 1889

40 South Dakota—November 2, 1889

41 Montana—November 8, 1889

42 Washington—November 11, 1889

43 Idaho—July 3, 1890

44 Wyoming—July 10, 1890

45 Utah—January 4, 1896

Only five states were admitted in the twentieth century, two of them (Alaska and Hawaii) separate from the contiguous 48 states and one (Hawaii) separate from North America. The United States now stretches from sea to sea and beyond.

46 Oklahoma—November 16, 1907

47 New Mexico—January 6, 1912

48 Arizona—February 14, 1912

47 Alaska—January 3, 1959

50 Hawaii—August 21, 1959

U.S. POPULATION

Year	U.S. Population	Year	U.S. Population
2000	275,563,000	1890	62,979,766
1990	248,709,873	1880	50,189,209
1980	226,542,199	1870	38,558,371
1970	203,302,031	1860	31,443,321
1960	179,323,175	1850	23,191,876
1950	151,325,798	1840	17,063,353
1940	132,164,569	1830	12,860,702
1930	123,202,624	1820	9,638,453
1920	106,021,537	1810	7,239,881
1910	92,228,496	1800	5,308,483
1900	76,212,168	1790	3,929,214

Appendix C

American History Chronology

The Colonial Period (1497–1763)

1497	John Cabot lands in North America.
1513	Ponce de Leon claims Florida for Spain.
1524	Verrazano explores North American Coast.
1539–1542	Hernando de Soto explores the Mississippi River Valley.
1540–1542	Coronado explores what will be the Southwestern United States.
1565	Spanish found the city of St. Augustine in Florida.
1579	Sir Francis Drake explores the coast of California.
1607	British establish Jamestown Colony.
1608	French establish colony at Quebec.
1609	United Provinces establish claims in North America.
1612	Tobacco cultivation is introduced in Virginia.
1619	First African slaves are brought to British America.
1619	Virginia begins a representative assembly.
1620	Plymouth Colony is founded.
1636	Rhode Island is founded.

1636	Harvard College is founded.
1650–1696	The Navigation Acts are enacted by Parliament.
1663	Charles II grants charter for Carolina colonies.
1682	Pennsylvania is founded by William Penn.
1689–1713	King William's War (The War of the League of Augsburg).
1692	The Salem Witchcraft Trials.
1696	Parliamentary Act.
1699–1750	Restrictions on colonial manufacturing.
1702–1713	Queen Anne's War (War of the Spanish Succession).
1733	Georgia Colony is founded.
1740–1748	King George's War (War of the Austrian Succession).
1740s	The Great Awakening.
1754–1763	The French and Indian War.
1763	Treaty of Paris ends the French and Indian War.

THE REVOLUTIONARY WAR ERA (1763–1789)

1763	Proclamation of 1763 restricts settlement west of the Appalachians.
1764	The Sugar and Currency Acts are passed.
1765	The Stamp Act is passed.
1767	The Townshend Acts are passed.
1770	The Boston Massacre.
1772	Samuel Adams organizes the Committees of Correspondence.
1772	The Tea Act is passed; the Boston Tea Party.
1774	The Intolerable Acts are passed.
1774	First Continental Congress convenes in Philadelphia.
1775	Battles of Lexington and Concord.
1775	The Second Continental Congress convenes.

1776	American Declaration of Independence.
1776	Thomas Paine's *Common Sense*.
1776	Battles of Long Island and Trenton.
1777	Battle of Saratoga.
1777	Congress adopts the Articles of Confederation.
1777	Vermont ends slavery.
1778	Treaty of Alliance between the United States and France.
1779	Spain declares war on England.
1781	British surrender at Yorktown.
1783	Treaty of Peace is signed.
1785	Land Ordinance of 1785.
1787	Constitutional Convention in Philadelphia.
1787	James Madison develops principles for the U.S. Constitution.
1787	Northwest Ordinance.
1787	Shays's Rebellion.

THE EARLY REPUBLIC (1789–1823)

1789	George Washington is inaugurated first president.
1791	The Bill of Rights is ratified.
1791	First Bank of the United States is established.
1794	Eli Whitney invents the cotton gin.
1794	The Whiskey Rebellion.
1795	Jay Treaty is ratified.
1796	Washington's Farewell Address.
1798	Alien and Sedition Acts.
1803	Louisiana Purchase.
1803	Supreme Court declares parts of the Judiciary Act of 1789 unconstitutional.

1804	New Jersey ends slavery.
1804–1806	Lewis and Clark expedition.
1807	Robert Fulton builds his first steamboat.
1808	African slave trade ends.
1809	Nonintercourse Act.
1812–1814	The War of 1812.
1823	Monroe Doctrine is declared.

THE AGE OF EXPANSION (1820–1865)

1820	The Missouri Compromise.
1825	The Erie Canal is opened.
1830s	The Second Great Awakening.
1830	Baltimore and Ohio Railroad begins operation.
1831	*The Liberator* begins publication.
1831	Nat Turner Rebellion.
1831	Cyrus McCormick invents the reaper.
1831–1838	The Trail of Tears; Southern Indians are removed to Oklahoma.
1836	The Gag Rule.
1837	United States recognizes the Republic of Texas.
1837	Oberlin College enrolls its first women students.
1843	Oregon Trail opens.
1845	Annexation of Texas.
1846	Elias Howe invents the sewing machine.
1846–1848	Mexican-American War.
1848	Gold is discovered at Sutter's Mill in California.
1848	Women's Rights Convention is held in Seneca Falls, New York.
1850	Compromise of 1850.
1853	Commodore Matthew Perry opens Japan to U.S. trade.

| 1854 | The Kansas-Nebraska Act. |
| 1857 | The Dred Scott decision. |

THE CIVIL WAR (1860–1865)

1860	Abraham Lincoln is elected; South Carolina secedes.
1861	Confederates attack Fort Sumter.
1861	First Battle of Bull Run.
1861	Jefferson Davis is elected president of the Confederacy.
1861	George B. McClellan appointed commander of the Union Army.
1861	Trent Affair.
1862	Confederate Congress passes Conscription Act.
1862	Battle of Shiloh.
1862	Robert E. Lee is named commander of the Army of Northern Virginia.
1862	Second Battle of Bull Run.
1862	Battle of Antietam; McClellan is relieved of his command.
1862	Lincoln issues the Emancipation Proclamation.
1862	Homestead Act passed.
1862	Battle of Fredericksburg.
1863	Congress passes the Conscription Act.
1863	Congress passes the National Banking Act.
1863	Draft riots in New York City.
1863	The Emancipation Proclamation.
1863	Battle of Chancellorsville.
1863	Battle of Gettysburg.
1863	Siege of Vicksburg.
1864	Battle of the Wilderness.
1864	Capture of Atlanta.

1864	Sherman's March to the Sea.
1865	Capture of Columbia.
1865	Lee surrenders to Grant at Appomattox Court House.

Reconstruction (1865–1896)

1863	Lincoln announces "10 Percent Plan."
1865	Freedman's Bureau is established.
1865	Lincoln is assassinated.
1865	Johnson's amnesty plan.
1865	13th Amendment is ratified.
1866	Civil Rights Act is passed over Johnson's veto.
1867	Alaska is purchased.
1867	First Reconstruction Act.
1868	Fourth Reconstruction Act.
1868	14th Amendment is ratified.
1868	Ku Klux Klan begins.
1869	Belle Babb Mansfield becomes the first female lawyer in the United States.
1870	15th Amendment is ratified.
1870	Force Act.
1875	Civil Rights Act.
1876	Battle of Little Bighorn.
1877	President Hayes agrees to compromise of 1877.
1881	Tuskeegee Institute is founded.
1887	Pearl Harbor acquired.
1890–1900	Blacks are deprived of the vote in the South.
1895	Booker T. Washington's Atlanta Compromise Speech.
1896	*Plessy* v. *Ferguson*.

THE PROGRESSIVE ERA (1879–1920)

1868	Carnegie Steel Company is formed.
1869	George Westinghouse invents the airbrake.
1870	Standard Oil Company is formed.
1876	Alexander Graham Bell invents the telephone.
1879	Thomas Edison invents the electric light.
1882	Chinese Exclusion Act.
1883	Brooklyn Bridge is completed.
1886	The American Federation of Labor is founded.
1886	Interstate Commerce Act.
1889	Jane Addams founds Hull House.
1890	North American Women's Suffrage Association is founded.
1890	The Sherman Antitrust Act.
1892	The Homestead strike.
1892	General Electric Company is formed.
1894	The Pullman strike.
1895	*U.S. v. E. C. Knight Company.*
1898	Spanish-American War.
1901	U.S. Steel Corporation is formed.
1904	Panama Canal Zone is acquired.
1904	The National Child Labor Committee is formed.
1905	Industrial Workers of the World is formed.
1909	NAACP is founded.
1913	16th Amendment is ratified.
1913	17th Amendment is ratified.
1914	The Federal Trade Commission is established.
1914	The Clayton Antitrust acts are passed.

1914	United States invades Veracruz in Mexico.
1915	The USS *Lusitania* is sunk by a German submarine.
1916	Adamson Act.

WORLD WAR I (1914–1918)

1898	Germany begins its naval buildup.
1902	Britain and Japan conclude a naval alliance.
1905	The First Moroccan Crisis.
1907	Anglo-Russian treaty over Persia.
1907	Triple Entente is completed.
1911	Italy annexes Tripoli.
1912	The First Balkan War.
1913	The Second Balkan War.
1914	The Austrian Archduke Franz Ferdinand is assassinated in Sarajevo.
1914	The Battle of the Marne.
1914	The Ottoman Empire enters the war.
1915	The Armenian Massacre.
1916	The Battle of Verdun.
1917	The February Revolution in Russia.
1917	The United States enters the war on the Allied side.
1918	Germany and the Soviet Union conclude the Treaty of Brest-Litivsk.
1918	President Wilson's Fourteen Points.
1918	Armistice ends the war.
1918	Revolutions in Germany, Austria, and Turkey.
1919	Allied governments intervene in Russia.
1919	The Treaty of Versailles is ratified.

1919	The League of Nations is founded.
1919	The Palmer Raids.
1919	Senate rejects Versailles Treaty.
1919	18th Amendment is ratified, prohibiting alcoholic beverages.
1920	19th Amendment grants women's suffrage.
1920	First commercial radio broadcast.
1921	Margaret Sanger founds the National Birth Control League.
1925	The Scopes "Monkey Trial."
1927	Charles Lindbergh flies solo from New York to Paris.
1929	The Great Depression begins.
1930	The Smoot-Hawley Tariff.
1932	Franklin D. Roosevelt is elected president.
1932	The Reconstruction Finance Corporation is created.
1933	New Deal begins.
1938	End of New Deal Reforms.

THE SECOND WORLD WAR (1931–1945)

1922	The Washington Conference presents a treaty on naval disarmament.
1924	The Dawes Plan ends the crisis in the Ruhr.
1925	The Lacarno Pact.
1928	The Kellogg-Briand Pact.
1929	The Young Plan.
1933	Germany withdraws from the League of Nations.
1935	Hitler denounces the disarmament clauses of the Treaty of Versailles.
1935	The Nuremberg Laws.
1935	Italy invades Ethiopia.

1936	Germany remilitarizes the Rhineland.
1936	The Spanish Civil War begins.
1936	The Rome-Berlin Axis is formed.
1938	The Anschluss: Germany annexes Austria.
1938	The Munich Conference: The Sudetenland is awarded to Germany; Chamberlain announces "Peace in Our Time."
1939	Germany invades Czechoslovakia.
1939	Germany and Italy create the Pact of Steel.
1939	Germany and the Soviet Union form a Nonaggression Pact.
1939	Germany invades Poland.
1940	Germany conquers Denmark and Norway.
1940	Germany conquers the Netherlands, Belgium, and Luxembourg.
1940	Italy enters the war as Germany's ally.
1940	France signs an armistice with Germany.
1940	The Battle of Britain begins.
1940	Italy invades Egypt and Greece.
1941	Germany conquers Yugoslavia and Greece.
1941	Hitler begins Operation Barbarosa and invades the Soviet Union.
1942	British and American forces begin attacking in North Africa.
1943	Roosevelt and Churchill meet at Casablanca.
1943	The Battle of Stalingrad ends with a German defeat.
1943	German and Italian forces in Tunisia surrender.
1943	American and British troops invade Sicily and Italy.
1944	D-Day invasion of Normandy opens up a second front.
1944	The Battle of the Bulge.
1945	The Yalta Conference.
1945	Germany surrenders.
1945	Potsdam Conference.

THE SECOND WORLD WAR: PACIFIC THEATER (1931–1945)

1931	Mukden Incident: Japan invades Manchuria.
1937	Japan attacks China.
1941	Japan attacks Pearl Harbor.
1942	Japan conquers the Philippines.
1942	American forces take Guadalcanal, beginning American island hopping across the Pacific.
1944	American troops under MacArthur land in the Philippines.
1945	Atomic bombs are dropped on the cities of Hiroshima and Nagasaki.
1945	Japan surrenders.

THE COLD WAR (1946–1989)

1947	The Truman Doctrine.
1949	NATO Treaty is signed.
1950	Korean War begins.
1953	Armistice ends fighting in the Korean War.
1954	*Brown v. Board of Education*.
1956	Montgomery bus boycott.
1961	Bay of Pigs invasion.
1962	Cuban Missile Crisis.
1964	Gulf of Tonkin incident.
1964	Civil Rights Act.
1965	President Johnson begins escalation of U.S. role in Vietnamese Civil War.
1965	Medicare Act.
1965	Clean Air Act.
1965–1967	Riots in black ghettos.

1966	National Organization for Women (NOW) is founded.
1968	Martin Luther King Jr. is assassinated.
1969	Astronauts land on the moon.
1972	United States withdraws from Vietnam.
1973	*Roe v. Wade.*
1989	The fall of the Berlin Wall; the Cold War ends.

THE PERSIAN GULF WAR

1990	Iraqi forces invade Kuwait.
1991	UN ground forces liberate Kuwait.
1991	Cease fire signed between the United Nations and Iraq.
1992	United States and Russia sign a treaty officially ending the Cold War.

THE INFORMATION AGE

1993	Bill Clinton is sworn in as the 42nd President of the United States.
1997	Bill Clinton is sworn in as President for a second term.
1998	Terrorist bombs destroy American embassies in Dar Es Salaam, Tanzania and Nairobi, Kenya.
1998	The U.S. House of Representatives approves 2 of 4 Proposed Articles of Impeachment against President Bill Clinton.
1999	NATO begins air strikes against Yugoslavia.
1999	Panama obtains control of the Panama Canal from the United States.
2001	Terrorists Attack the Pentagon and World Trade Center
2002	American ground forces invade Afghanistan.

APPENDIX D

Famous Locations in American History

The following is a list of the National Parks that exist in the United States, where the history of the United States can be found.

ABBREVIATIONS KEY

NB	National Battlefield
NBP	National Battlefield Park
NBS	National Battlefield Site
NHP	National Historical Park
NHS	National Historic Site
NL	National Lakeshore
NM	National Monument
Nmem	National Memorial
NMP	National Military Park
NP	National Park
Npres	National Preserve
NR	National River
NRA	National Recreation Area
NS	National Seashore
NSR	National Scenic River
NST	National Scenic Trail
WSR	Wild and Scenic River

NATIONAL PARKS DATES AND LOCATIONS

1790

- **July 16** District of Columbia authorized, including National Capital Parks, National Mall, White House

1832

- **April 20** Hot Springs Reservation, Arkansas (redesignated Hot Springs NP 1921)

1864

- **June 30** Yosemite State Park, California (incorporated in Yosemite NP 1906)

1866

- **April 7** Ford's Theatre, District of Columbia, acquisition authorized; designated a NHS 1970

1872

- **March 1** Yellowstone NP, Wyoming, Montana, and Idaho

1875

- **March 3** Mackinac NP, Michigan (abolished 1895)

1876

- **August 2** Washington Monument, District of Columbia, accepted; dedicated 1885

1877

- **March 3** Statue of Liberty, New York, accepted; dedicated 1886; designated a NM 1924

1886

- **December 7** National Cemetery of Custer's Battlefield Reservation (redesignated Custer Battlefield NM 1946; redesignated Little Bighorn Battlefield NM 1991)

1889

- **March 2** Casa Grande Ruin Reservation, Arizona (redesignated Casa Grande NM 1918; redesignated Casa Grande Ruins NM 1926)

1890

- **August 19** Chickamauga and Chattanooga NMP, Georgia and Tennessee
- **August 30** Antietam NBS, Maryland (redesignated a NB 1978)
- **September 25** Sequoia NP, California
- **September 27** Rock Creek Park, District of Columbia
- **October 1** General Grant NP, California (incorporated in Kings Canyon NP 1940)
- **October 1** Yosemite NP, California

1894

- **December 27** Shiloh NMP, Tennessee

1895

- **February 11** Gettysburg NMP, Pennsylvania

1899

- **February 21** Vicksburg NMP, Mississippi
- **March 2** Mount Rainier NP, Washington

1902

- **May 22** Crater Lake NP, Oregon
- **July 1** Sulphur Springs Reservation, Oklahoma (redesignated Platt NP 1906; incorporated in Chickasaw NRA 1976)

1903

- **January 9** Wind Cave NP, South Dakota

1904

- **April 27** Sullys Hill NP, North Dakota (transferred to Agriculture Dept. as game preserve 1931)

1906

- **June 8** Antiquities Act
- **June 29** Mesa Verde NP, Colorado
- **September 24** Devils Tower NM, Wyoming
- **December 8** El Morro NM, New Mexico
- **December 8** Montezuma Castle NM, Arizona
- **December 8** Petrified Forest NM, Arizona (redesignated a NP 1962)

1907

- **March 4** Chalmette Monument and Grounds, Louisiana (redesignated Chalmette NHP 1939; incorporated in Jean Lafitte NHP and Preserve 1978)
- **March 11** Chaco Canyon NM, New Mexico (incorporated in Chaco Culture NHP 1980)
- **May 6** Cinder Cone NM, California (incorporated in Lassen Volcanic NP 1916)
- **May 6** Lassen Peak NM, California (incorporated in Lassen Volcanic NP 1916)
- **November 16** Gila Cliff Dwellings NM, New Mexico
- **December 19** Tonto NM, Arizona

1908

- **January 9** Muir Woods NM, California
- **January 11** Grand Canyon NM, Arizona (incorporated in Grand Canyon NP 1919)
- **January 16** Pinnacles NM, California
- **February 7** Jewel Cave NM, South Dakota
- **April 16** Natural Bridges NM, Utah
- **May 11** Lewis and Clark Cavern NM, Montana (abolished 1937)
- **September 15** Tumacacari NM, Arizona (incorporated in Tumacacari NHP 1990)
- **December 7** Wheeler NM, Colorado (abolished 1950)

1909

- **March 2** Mount Olympus NM, Washington (incorporated in Olympic NP 1938)
- **March 20** Navajo NM, Arizona
- **July 12** Oregon Caves NM, Oregon
- **July 31** Mukuntuweap NM, Utah (incorporated in Zion NM 1918)
- **September 21** Shoshone Cavern NM, Wyoming (abolished 1954)
- **November 1** Gran Quivira NM, New Mexico (incorporated in Salinas NM 1980)

1910

- **March 23** Sitka NM, Alaska (redesignated a NHP 1972)
- **May 11** Glacier NP, Montana
- **May 30** Rainbow Bridge NM, Utah
- **June 23** Big Hole Battlefield NM, Montana (redesignated Big Hole NB 1963)

1911

- **February 9** Lincoln Memorial, District of Columbia (dedicated 1922)
- **May 24** Colorado NM, Colorado
- **July 6** Devils Postpile NM, California

1913

- **October 14** Cabrillo NM, California

1914

- **January 31** Papago Saguaro NM, Arizona (abolished 1930)

1915

- **January 26** Rocky Mountain NP, Colorado
- **October 4** Dinosaur NM, Colorado and Utah
- **November 30** Walnut Canyon NM, Arizona

1916

- **February 11** Bandelier NM, New Mexico
- **July 8** Sieur de Monts NM, Maine (redesignated Lafayette NP 1919; redesignated Acadia NP 1929)
- **July 17** Abraham Lincoln NP, Kentucky (redesignated a NHP 1939; redesignated Abraham Lincoln Birthplace NHS 1959)
- **August 1** Hawaii NP, Hawaii (split into Haleakala NP and Hawaii NP 1960; latter redesignated Hawaii Volcanoes NP 1961)
- **August 9** Capulin Mountain NM, New Mexico (redesignated Capulin Volcano NM 1987)
- **August 9** Lassen Volcanic NP, California (incorporated Cinder Cone and Lassen Peak NMs)
- **August 25** National Park Service Act
- **October 25** Old Kasaan NM, Alaska (abolished 1955)

1917

- **February 18** Kennesaw Mountain NBS, Georgia (redesignated a NBP 1935)
- **February 26** Mount McKinley NP, Alaska (incorporated in Denali NP and NPres 1980)
- **March 2** Guilford Courthouse NMP, North Carolina
- **June 29** Verendrye NM, North Dakota (abolished 1956)

1918

- **March 18** Zion NM, Utah (incorporated Mukuntuweap NM; redesignated a NP 1919)
- **September 24** Katmai NM, Alaska (incorporated in Katmai NP and NPres 1980)

1919

- **February 26** Grand Canyon NP, Arizona (incorporated 1908 Grand Canyon NM)
- **December 12** Scotts Bluff NM, Nebraska
- **December 12** Yucca House NM, Colorado

1922

- **January 24** Lehman Caves NM, Nevada (incorporated in Great Basin NP 1986)
- **October 14** Timpanogos Cave, Utah
- **October 21** Fossil Cycad NM, South Dakota (abolished 1956)

1923

- **January 24** Aztec Ruin NM, New Mexico (redesignated Aztec Ruins NM 1928)
- **March 2** Hovenweep NM, Colorado and Utah
- **March 2** Mound City Group NM, Ohio (incorporated in Hopewell Culture NHP 1992)
- **May 31** Pipe Spring NM, Arizona
- **June 8** Bryce Canyon NM, Utah (redesignated Utah NP 1924; redesignated Bryce Canyon NP 1928)
- **October 25** Carlsbad Cave NM, New Mexico (redesignated Carlsbad Caverns NP 1930)

1924

- **April 18** Chiricahua NM, Arizona
- **May 2** Craters of the Moon NM, Idaho
- **October 15** Castle Pinckney NM, South Carolina (abolished 1956)
- **October 15** Fort Marion NM, Florida (redesignated Castillo de San Marcos NM 1942)
- **October 15** Fort Matanzas NM, Florida
- **October 15** Fort Pulaski, Georgia
- **December 9** Wupatki NM, Arizona

1925

- **February 6** Meriwether Lewis NM, Tennessee (incorporated in Natchez Trace Parkway 1961)
- **February 26** Glacier Bay NM, Alaska (incorporated in Glacier Bay NP and NPres 1980)
- **March 3** Fort McHenry NP, Maryland (redesignated Fort McHenry NM and Historic Shrine 1939)
- **March 4** Lee Mansion, Virginia (date restoration authorized; designated Custis-Lee Mansion 1955; redesignated Arlington House, The Robert E. Lee Memorial, 1972)
- **March 23** Mount Rushmore NMem, South Dakota (acquired 1939)
- **September 5** Father Millet Cross NM, New York (abolished 1949)
- **November 21** Lava Beds NM, California

1926

- **May 22** Great Smoky Mountains NP, North Carolina and Tennessee
- **May 22** Shenandoah NP, Virginia
- **May 25** Mammoth Cave NP, Kentucky
- **June 2** Moores Creek NMP, North Carolina (redesignated a NB 1980)
- **July 3** Petersburg NMP, Virginia (redesignated a NB 1962)

1927

- **February 14** Fredericksburg and Spotsylvania County Battlefields Memorial NMP, Virginia
- **March 2** Kill Devil Hill Monument, North Carolina (redesignated Wright Brothers NMem 1953)
- **March 3** Stones River NMP, Tennessee (redesignated a NB 1980)

1928

- **March 26** Fort Donelson NMP, Tennessee (redesignated a NB 1985)
- **May 23** George Rogers Clark Memorial, Indiana (incorporated in George Rogers Clark NHP 1966)
- **May 23** Mount Vernon Memorial Highway (incorporated in George Washington Memorial Parkway 1930)

1929

- **February 21** Brices Cross Roads NBS, Mississippi
- **February 21** Tupelo NBS, Mississippi (redesignated a NB 1961)
- **February 26** Grand Teton NP, Wyoming
- **March 4** Badlands NM, South Dakota (redesignated a NP 1978)
- **March 4** Cowpens NBS, South Carolina (redesignated a NB 1972)
- **April 12** Arches NM, Utah (redesignated a NP 1978)
- **May 11** Holy Cross NM, Colorado (abolished 1950)

1930

- **January 23** George Washington Birthplace NM, Virginia
- **May 26** Sunset Crater NM, Arizona (redesignated Sunset Crater Volcano NM 1990)
- **May 29** Fort Washington Park, Maryland
- **May 29** George Washington Memorial Parkway, Virginia and Maryland (incorporated Mount Vernon Memorial Highway)
- **June 18** Appomattox Court House monument, Virginia (designated Appomattox Court House National Historical Monument 1935; redesignated a NHP 1954)
- **July 3** Colonial NM, Virginia (redesignated a NHP 1936)

1931

- **February 14** Canyon de Chelly NM, Arizona
- **March 3** Isle Royale NP, Michigan
- **March 4** Fort Necessity NBS, Pennsylvania (redesignated a NB 1961)
- **March 4** Kings Mountain NMP, South Carolina

1932

- **March 17** Great Sand Dunes NM, Colorado
- **May 21** Theodore Roosevelt Island, District of Columbia
- **December 22** Grand Canyon NM, Arizona (incorporated in Grand Canyon NP 1975)

1933

- **January 18** White Sands NM, New Mexico
- **February 11** Death Valley NM, California and Nevada (incorporated in Death Valley NP 1994)
- **March 1** Saguaro NM, Arizona (redesignated a NP 1994)
- **March 2** Black Canyon of the Gunnison NM, Colorado (redesignated a NP, 1999)
- **March 2** Morristown NHP, New Jersey
- **June 16** Blue Ridge Parkway, North Carolina and Virginia
- **August 10** Reorganization
- **August 22** Cedar Breaks NM, Utah

1934

- **May 30** Everglades NP, Florida
- **June 14** Ocmulgee NM, Georgia
- **June 19** Natchez Trace Parkway, Mississippi, Alabama, and Tennessee (acquired 1938)
- **June 21** Monocacy NMP, Maryland (reauthorized and redesignated a NB 1976)
- **June 26** Thomas Jefferson Memorial, District of Columbia (dedicated 1943)

1935

- **January 4** Fort Jefferson NM, Florida (redesignated Dry Tortugas NP 1992)
- **June 20** Big Bend NP, Texas
- **August 21** Historic Sites Act
- **August 21** Fort Stanwix NM, New York (acquired 1973)

- **August 27** Ackia Battleground NM, Mississippi (incorporated in Natchez Trace Parkway 1961)
- **August 29** Andrew Johnson NM, Tennessee (redesignated a NHS 1963)
- **December 20** Jefferson National Expansion Memorial, Missouri (Gateway Arch authorized 1954, dedicated 1968)

1936

- **March 2** Richmond NBP, Virginia
- **March 19** Homestead NM of America, Nebraska
- **May 26** Fort Frederica NM, Georgia
- **June 2** Perry's Victory and International Peace Memorial NM, Ohio (redesignated Perry's Victory and International Peace Memorial 1972)
- **June 23** Park, Parkway, and Recreation Area Study Act
- **June 29** Whitman NM, Washington (redesignated Whitman Mission NHS 1963)
- **August 16** Joshua Tree NM, California (incorporated in Joshua Tree NP 1994)
- **October 13** Boulder Dam Recreation Area, Nevada and Arizona (redesignated Lake Mead NRA 1947)
- **November 14** Bull Run Recreational Demonstration Area, Virginia (redesignated Manassas NBP 1940)
- **November 14** Catoctin Recreational Demonstration Area, Maryland (redesignated Catoctin Mountain Park 1954)
- **November 14** Chopawamsic Recreational Demonstration Area, Virginia (redesignated Prince William Forest Park 1948)

1937

- **January 22** Zion NM, Utah (incorporated in Zion NP 1956)
- **April 13** Organ Pipe Cactus NM, Arizona
- **August 2** Capitol Reef NM, Utah (redesignated a NP 1971)
- **August 17** Cape Hatteras NS, North Carolina
- **August 25** Pipestone NM, Minnesota

1938

- **March 17** Salem Maritime NHS, Massachusetts
- **April 26** Channel Islands NM, California (incorporated in Channel Islands NP 1980)

- **June 1** Saratoga NHP, New York
- **June 29** Olympic NP, Washington (incorporated Mount Olympus NM)
- **July 16** Fort Laramie NM, Wyoming (redesignated a NHS 1960)
- **August 3** Hopewell Village NHS, Pennsylvania (redesignated Hopewell Furnace NHS 1985)
- **September 23** Chesapeake and Ohio Canal, Maryland, District of Columbia, and West Virginia (date acquired; designated a NM 1961; incorporated in Chesapeake and Ohio Canal NHP 1971)

1939

- **May 17** Santa Rosa Island NM, Florida (abolished 1946; island included in Gulf Islands NS 1971)
- **May 26** Federal Hall Memorial NHS, New York (redesignated Federal Hall NMem 1955)
- **May 26** Philadelphia Custom House NHS, Pennsylvania (incorporated in Independence NHP 1959)
- **July 1** Mount Rushmore NMem, South Dakota (date acquired)
- **July 25** Tuzigoot NM, Arizona

1940

- **March 4** Kings Canyon NP, California (incorporated General Grant NP)
- **June 11** Cumberland Gap NHP, Kentucky, Virginia, and Tennessee
- **December 18** Vanderbilt Mansion NHS, New York

1941

- **April 5** Fort Raleigh NHS, North Carolina

1943

- **March 15** Jackson Hole NM, Wyoming (incorporated in Grand Teton NP 1950)
- **July 14** George Washington Carver NM, Missouri

1944

- **January 15** Home of Franklin D. Roosevelt NHS, New York
- **June 30** Harpers Ferry NM, West Virginia and Maryland (redesignated a NHP 1963)
- **October 13** Atlanta Campaign NHS, Georgia (abolished 1950)

1945

- **May 22** Millerton Lake Recreation Area, California (abolished 1957)
- **May 22** Shasta Lake Recreation Area, California (transferred to Forest Service 1948)

1946

- **April 18** Lake Texoma Recreation Area, Oklahoma and Texas (transferred to Corps of Engineers 1949)
- **August 12** Castle Clinton NM, New York
- **December 9** Adams Mansion NHS, Massachusetts (redesignated Adams NHS 1952; redesignated Adams NHP 1998)
- **December 18** Coulee Dam NRA, Washington (redesignated Lake Roosevelt NRA 1997)

1947

- **April 25** Theodore Roosevelt National Memorial Park, North Dakota (redesignated a NP 1978)

1948

- **March 11** DeSoto NMem, Florida
- **April 28** Fort Sumter NM, South Carolina
- **June 19** Fort Vancouver NM, Washington (redesignated a NHS 1961)
- **June 22** Hampton NHS, Maryland
- **June 28** Independence NHP, Pennsylvania (incorporated Independence Hall NHS, designated 1943)

1949

- **February 14** San Juan NHS, Puerto Rico
- **June 8** Saint Croix Island NM, Maine (redesignated an International Historic Site 1984)
- **August 17** Suitland Parkway, Maryland and District of Columbia (date acquired; incorporated in National Capital Parks 1975)
- **October 25** Effigy Mounds NM, Iowa

1950

- **August 3** Baltimore-Washington Parkway, Maryland (date acquired; incorporated in National Capital Parks 1975)
- **August 3** Greenbelt Park, Maryland

- **September 14** Grand Teton NP, Wyoming (incorporated 1929 NP and Jackson Hole NM)
- **September 21** Fort Caroline NMem, Florida

1952

- **March 4** Virgin Islands NHS, Virgin Islands (redesignated Christiansted NHS 1961)
- **June 27** Shadow Mountain Recreation Area, Colorado (transferred to Forest Service 1979)
- **July 9** Coronado NMem, Arizona

1954

- **June 28** Fort Union NM, New Mexico

1955

- **July 26** City of Refuge NHP, Hawaii (redesignated Puuhonua o Honaunau NHP 1978)
- **December 6** Edison Home NHS, New Jersey (incorporated in Edison NHS 1962)

1956

- **April 2** Booker T. Washington NM, Virginia
- **July 14** Edison Laboratory NM, New Jersey (incorporated in Edison NHS 1962)
- **July 20** Pea Ridge NMP, Arkansas
- **July 25** Horseshoe Bend NMP, Alabama
- **August 2** Virgin Islands NP, Virgin Islands

1958

- **April 18** Glen Canyon NRA, Utah and Arizona
- **May 29** Fort Clatsop NMem, Oregon
- **August 14** General Grant NMem, New York
- **September 2** Grand Portage NM, Minnesota (designated a NHS 1951)

1959

- **April 14** Minute Man NHS, Massachusetts (redesignated a NHP September 21)
- **September 1** Franklin Delano Roosevelt Memorial, District of Columbia (dedicated 1997)

1960

- **April 22** Wilson's Creek Battlefield NP, Missouri (redesignated Wilson's Creek NB 1970)
- **June 3** Bent's Old Fort NHS, Colorado
- **July 6** Arkansas Post NMem, Arkansas
- **September 13** Haleakala NP, Hawaii (detached from Hawaii NP)
- **December 24** St. Thomas NHS, Virgin Islands (abolished 1975)

1961

- **May 11** Russell Cave NM, Alabama
- **August 7** Cape Cod NS, Massachusetts
- **September 8** Fort Davis NHS, Texas
- **September 13** Fort Smith NHS, Arkansas
- **October 4** Piscataway Park, Maryland
- **December 28** Buck Island Reef NM, Virgin Islands

1962

- **February 19** Lincoln Boyhood NMem, Indiana
- **April 27** Hamilton Grange NMem, New York
- **May 31** Whiskeytown-Shasta-Trinity NRA, California (Whiskeytown Unit)
- **July 25** Sagamore Hill NHS, New York
- **July 25** Theodore Roosevelt Birthplace NHS, New York
- **September 5** Edison NHS, New Jersey (incorporated Edison Home NHS and Edison Laboratory NM)
- **September 5** Frederick Douglass Home, District of Columbia (redesignated Frederick Douglass NHS 1988)
- **September 13** Point Reyes NS, California
- **September 28** Padre Island NS, Texas

1963

- **July 22** Flaming Gorge Recreation Area, Utah and Wyoming (transferred to Forest Service 1968)

1964

- **August 27** Ozark National Scenic Riverways, Missouri
- **August 30** Fort Bowie NHS, Arizona
- **August 31** Allegheny Portage Railroad NHS, Pennsylvania
- **August 31** Fort Larned NHS, Kansas
- **August 31** John Muir NHS, California
- **August 31** Johnstown Flood NMem, Pennsylvania
- **August 31** Saint-Gaudens NHS, New Hampshire
- **September 3** Land and Water Conservation Fund Act of 1965
- **September 3** Wilderness Act
- **September 11** Fire Island NS, New York
- **September 12** Canyonlands NP, Utah
- **December 31** Bighorn Canyon NRA, Wyoming and Montana

1965

- **February 1** Arbuckle NRA, Oklahoma (incorporated in Chickasaw NRA 1976)
- **February 11** Curecanti NRA, Colorado
- **March 15** Sanford NRA, Texas (redesignated Lake Meredith Recreation Area 1972; redesignated Lake Meredith NRA 1990)
- **May 15** Nez Perce NHP, Idaho
- **June 5** Agate Fossil Beds NM, Nebraska
- **June 28** Pecos NM, New Mexico (incorporated in Pecos NHP 1990)
- **July 30** Golden Spike NHS, Utah (designated 1957)
- **August 12** Herbert Hoover NHS, Iowa
- **August 28** Hubbell Trading Post NHS, Arizona
- **August 31** Alibates Flint Quarries and Texas Panhandle Pueblo Culture NM, Texas (redesignated Alibates Flint Quarries NM 1978)
- **September 1** Delaware Water Gap NRA, Pennsylvania and New Jersey
- **September 21** Assateague Island NS, Maryland and Virginia
- **October 22** Roger Williams NMem, Rhode Island
- **November 11** Amistad Recreation Area, Texas (redesignated Amistad NRA 1990)

1966

- **March 10** Cape Lookout NS, North Carolina
- **June 20** Fort Union Trading Post NHS, North Dakota and Montana
- **June 30** Chamizal NMem, Texas
- **July 23** George Rogers Clark NHP, Indiana
- **September 9** San Juan Island NHP, Washington
- **October 15** National Historic Preservation Act
- **October 15** Guadalupe Mountains NP, Texas
- **October 15** Pictured Rocks NL, Michigan
- **October 15** Wolf Trap Farm Park for the Performing Arts, Virginia
- **November 2** Theodore Roosevelt Inaugural NHS, New York
- **November 5** Indiana Dunes NL, Indiana

1967

- **May 26** John Fitzgerald Kennedy NHS, Massachusetts
- **November 27** Eisenhower NHS, Pennsylvania

1968

- **March 12** National Visitor Center, District of Columbia (abolished 1981)
- **April 5** Saugus Iron Works NHS, Massachusetts
- **October 2** National Trails System Act
- **October 2** Wild and Scenic Rivers Act
- **October 2** Appalachian NST, Maine, New Hampshire, Vermont, Massachusetts, Connecticut, New York, New Jersey, Pennsylvania, Maryland, West Virginia, Virginia, Tennessee, North Carolina, Georgia
- **October 2** Lake Chelan NRA, Washington
- **October 2** North Cascades NP, Washington
- **October 2** Redwood NP, California
- **October 2** Ross Lake NRA, Washington
- **October 2** Saint Croix National Scenic Riverways, Minnesota and Wisconsin
- **October 17** Carl Sandburg Home NHS, North Carolina
- **October 18** Biscayne NM, Florida (incorporated in Biscayne NP 1980)

1969

- **January 20** Marble Canyon NM, Arizona (incorporated in Grand Canyon NP 1975)
- **August 20** Florissant Fossil Beds NM, Colorado
- **December 2** Lyndon B. Johnson NHS, Texas (redesignated a NHP 1980)
- **December 2** William Howard Taft NHS, Ohio

1970

- **September 26** Apostle Islands NL, Wisconsin
- **October 16** Andersonville NHS, Georgia
- **October 16** Fort Point NHS, California
- **October 21** Sleeping Bear Dunes NL, Michigan

1971

- **January 8** Chesapeake and Ohio Canal NHP, District of Columbia, Maryland, and West Virginia (incorporated Chesapeake and Ohio Canal NM)
- **January 8** Gulf Islands NS, Florida and Mississippi
- **January 8** Voyageurs NP, Minnesota
- **August 18** Lincoln Home NHS, Illinois

1972

- **March 1** Buffalo NR, Arkansas
- **June 16** John F. Kennedy Center for the Performing Arts, District of Columbia (date acquired; transferred to Kennedy Center Trustees 1994)
- **August 17** Puukohola Heiau NHS, Hawaii
- **August 25** Grant-Kohrs Ranch NHS, Montana
- **August 25** John D. Rockefeller Jr. Memorial Parkway, Wyoming
- **October 9** Longfellow NHS, Massachusetts
- **October 21** Hohokam Pima NM, Arizona
- **October 21** Mar-A-Lago NHS, Florida (designated 1969; abolished 1980)
- **October 21** Thaddeus Kosciuszko NMem, Pennsylvania

- **October 23** Cumberland Island NS, Georgia
- **October 23** Fossil Butte NM, Wyoming
- **October 27** Gateway NRA, New York and New Jersey
- **October 27** Golden Gate NRA, California

1973

- **December 28** Lyndon Baines Johnson Memorial Grove on the Potomac, District of Columbia

1974

- **March 7** Big South Fork NR and Recreation Area, Kentucky and Tennessee
- **August 1** Constitution Gardens, District of Columbia
- **October 1** Boston NHP, Massachusetts
- **October 11** Big Cypress NPres, Florida
- **October 11** Big Thicket NPres, Texas
- **October 26** Clara Barton NHS, Maryland
- **October 26** John Day Fossil Beds NM, Oregon
- **October 26** Knife River Indian Villages NHS, North Dakota
- **October 26** Martin Van Buren NHS, New York
- **October 26** Springfield Armory NHS, Massachusetts
- **October 26** Tuskegee Institute NHS, Alabama
- **December 27** Cuyahoga Valley NRA, Ohio

1975

- **January 3** Canaveral NS, Florida

1976

- **March 17** Chickasaw NRA, Oklahoma (incorporated Platt NP and Arbuckle NRA)
- **June 30** Klondike Gold Rush NHP, Alaska and Washington
- **July 4** Valley Forge NHP, Pennsylvania
- **August 19** Ninety Six NHS, South Carolina
- **October 12** Obed WSR, Tennessee
- **October 18** Congaree Swamp NM, South Carolina

- **October 18** Eugene O'Neill NHS, California
- **October 21** Monocacy NB, Maryland (reauthorization and redesignation of Monocacy NMP)

1977

- **May 26** Eleanor Roosevelt NHS, New York

1978

- **June 5** Lowell NHP, Massachusetts
- **August 15** Chattahoochee NRA, Georgia
- **August 18** War in the Pacific NHP, Guam
- **October 19** Fort Scott NHS, Kansas
- **November 10** Ebey's Landing National Historical Reserve, Washington
- **November 10** Edgar Allan Poe NHS, Pennsylvania
- **November 10** Friendship Hill NHS, Pennsylvania
- **November 10** Jean Lafitte NHP and Preserve, Louisiana (incorporated Chalmette NHP)
- **November 10** Kaloko-Honokohau NHP, Hawaii
- **November 10** Maggie L. Walker NHS, Virginia
- **November 10** Middle Delaware NSR, Pennsylvania and New Jersey
- **November 10** Missouri National Recreational River, Nebraska and South Dakota
- **November 10** New River Gorge NR, West Virginia
- **November 10** Palo Alto Battlefield NHS, Texas
- **November 10** Rio Grande WSR, Texas
- **November 10** Saint Paul's Church NHS, New York (designated 1943)
- **November 10** San Antonio Missions NHP, Texas
- **November 10** Santa Monica Mountains NRA, California
- **November 10** Thomas Stone NHS, Maryland
- **November 10** Upper Delaware Scenic and Recreational River, Pennsylvania and New York
- **December 1** Aniakchak NM, Alaska (incorporated in legislated Aniakchak NM and Aniakchak NPres by ANILCA 1980)

- **December 1** Bering Land Bridge NM, Alaska (redesignated a NPres by ANILCA 1980)
- **December 1** Cape Krusenstern NM, Alaska
- **December 1** Denali NM, Alaska (incorporated with Mount McKinley NP in Denali NP and Denali NPres by ANILCA 1980)
- **December 1** Gates of the Arctic NM, Alaska (incorporated in Gates of the Arctic NP and Gates of the Arctic NPres by ANILCA 1980)
- **December 1** Glacier Bay NM, Alaska (addition to existing NM; total incorporated in Glacier Bay NP and Glacier Bay NPres by ANILCA 1980)
- **December 1** Katmai NM, Alaska (addition to existing NM; total incorporated in Katmai NP and Katmai NPres by ANILCA 1980)
- **December 1** Kenai Fjords NM, Alaska (redesignated a NP by ANILCA 1980)
- **December 1** Kobuk Valley NM, Alaska (redesignated a NP by ANILCA 1980)
- **December 1** Lake Clark NM, Alaska (incorporated in Lake Clark NP and Lake Clark NPres by ANILCA 1980)
- **December 1** Noatak NM, Alaska (incorporated in Noatak NPres by ANILCA 1980)
- **December 1** WrangellBSt. Elias NM, Alaska (incorporated in WrangellBSt. Elias NP and WrangellBSt. Elias NPres by ANILCA 1980)
- **December 1** Yukon-Charley NM, Alaska (redesignated Yukon-Charley Rivers NPres by ANILCA 1980)

1979

- **October 12** Frederick Law Olmsted NHS, Massachusetts

1980

- **March 5** Channel Islands NP, California (incorporated Channel Islands NM)
- **June 28** Biscayne NP, Florida (incorporated Biscayne NM)
- **July 1** Vietnam Veterans Memorial, District of Columbia (dedicated 1982)
- **September 9** USS Arizona Memorial, Hawaii
- **October 10** Boston African American NHS, Massachusetts

- **October 10** Martin Luther King, NHS, Georgia
- **December 2** Alaska National Interests Lands Conservation Act (ANILCA)
- **December 2** Alagnak Wild River, Alaska
- **December 19** Chaco Culture NHP, New Mexico (incorporated Chaco Canyon NM)
- **December 19** Salinas NM, New Mexico (incorporated Gran Quivira NM; redesignated Salinas Pueblo Missions NM 1988)
- **December 22** Kalaupapa NHP, Hawaii
- **December 28** James A. Garfield NHS, Ohio
- **December 28** Women's Rights NHP, New York

1983

- **March 28** Natchez Trace NST, Mississippi, Alabama, and Tennessee
- **March 28** Potomac Heritage NST, Maryland, District of Columbia, Virginia, and Pennsylvania
- **May 23** Harry S Truman NHS, Missouri (designated 1982)

1986

- **October 21** Steamtown NHS, Pennsylvania
- **October 27** Great Basin NP, Nevada (incorporated Lehman Caves NM)
- **October 28** Korean War Veterans Memorial, District of Columbia (dedicated 1995)

1987

- **June 25** Pennsylvania Avenue NHS, District of Columbia (designated 1965)
- **December 23** Jimmy Carter NHS, Georgia
- **December 31** El Malpais NM, New Mexico

1988

- **February 16** Timucuan Ecological and Historic Preserve, Florida
- **June 27** San Francisco Maritime NHP, California (formerly part of Golden Gate NRA)
- **September 8** Charles Pinckney NHS, South Carolina
- **October 7** Natchez NHP, Mississippi

- **October 31** National Park of American Samoa, American Samoa
- **October 31** Poverty Point NM, Louisiana
- **November 18** City of Rocks National Reserve, Idaho
- **November 18** Hagerman Fossil Beds NM, Idaho
- **November 18** Mississippi NR and Recreation Area, Minnesota
- **December 26** Bluestone NSR, West Virginia
- **December 26** Gauley River NRA, West Virginia

1989

- **October 2** Ulysses S. Grant NHS, Missouri

1990

- **June 27** Pecos NHP, New Mexico (incorporated Pecos NM)
- **June 27** Petroglyph NM, New Mexico
- **August 6** Tumacacari NHP, Arizona (incorporated Tumacacari NM)
- **October 31** Weir Farm NHS, Connecticut

1991

- **May 24** Niobrara NSR, Nebraska
- **December 11** Mary McLeod Bethune Council House NHS, District of Columbia (designated 1982)

1992

- **February 24** Salt River Bay NHP and Ecological Preserve, Virgin Islands
- **March 3** Manzanar NHS, California
- **May 27** Hopewell Culture NHP, Ohio (incorporated Mound City Group NM)
- **August 26** Marsh-Billings NHP, Vermont (redesignated Marsh-Billings-Rockefeller NHP 1998)
- **October 16** Dayton Aviation Heritage NHP, Ohio
- **October 21** Little River Canyon NPres, Alabama
- **October 26** *Brown v. Board of Education* NHS, Kansas
- **October 27** Great Egg Harbor Scenic and Recreational River, New Jersey
- **October 27** Keweenaw NHP, Michigan

1994

- **October 31** Death Valley NP, California and Nevada (incorporated Death Valley NM)
- **October 31** Joshua Tree NP, California (incorporated Joshua Tree NM)
- **October 31** Mojave NPres, California
- **October 31** New Orleans Jazz NHP, Louisiana
- **November 2** Cane River Creole NHP, Louisiana

1996

- **November 12** Boston Harbor Islands NRA, Massachusetts
- **November 12** New Bedford Whaling NHP, Massachusetts
- **November 12** Nicodemus NHS, Kansas
- **November 12** Tallgrass Prairie NPres, Kansas
- **November 12** Washita Battlefield NHS, Oklahoma

1997

- **October 9** Oklahoma City NMem, Oklahoma

1998

- **November 6** Little Rock Central High School NHS, Arkansas
- **November 6** Tuskegee Airmen NHS, Alabama

1999

- **November 29** Minuteman Missile NHS, South Dakota

2000

- **October 11** First Ladies NHS, Canton, Ohio
- **October 24** Rosie the Riveter—WWII Home Front NHP, California
- **November 22** Great Sand Dunes NPres, Colorado

2001

- **January 17** Virgin Islands Coral Reef NM, Virgin Islands
- **January 20** Governors Island NM, New York

Index

Treaty on Conventional
 Armed Forces in Europe
 (CFE), 309
tree huggers, 291
Truman, Harry S, 235
 atomic bomb, decision to
  use, 227
 civil rights movement,
  258
 Fair Deal policies,
  247-249
 Korean War, 240-243
 middle name, explanation
  of, 249
 reelection of, 249
Tyler, John, 115

U

Uncle Tom's Cabin, 134
Underground Railroad, 130
unions (labor), formation of,
 186-187
United Empire Loyalists, 70
United Nations, establish-
 ment of, 234-235
University of Pennsylvania,
 founding of, 36
Unsafe at Any Speed: The
 Designed-In Dangers of the
 American Automobile, 269
USS Cole, terrorist attack on,
 323

V

Vallee, Rudy, 209
Van Buren, Martin, presidential election of, 115

Vanderbilt, Cornelius, 162
Verrazano, Giovanni da, 10
Verrazano Bridge, 10
Vespucci, Amerigo, 9
Veterans' Day, creation of,
 200
vice presidents, early system
 of, 109
Vietnam War, 269-272
Villa, Pancho, 180
Virginia Slave Codes, 25
Voting Rights Act of 1965,
 281

W

Wall Street, construction of,
 32
Wallace, George, 271, 318
Wallace, Henry, 318
Wallace, Lew, 172
Walsh, Thomas J., 204
Wampanoag Indians, 18
War of 1812, 96-98
"War on Drugs" campaign,
 Bush, George, 307-308
Warren, Earl, 261
Washington, Booker T., 171
Washington, George, 76-77
 American Revolution
  Battle of Long Island,
   65
  crossing of the
   Delaware, 65
  Valley Forge, 66
 commander-in-chief, nam-
  ing of, 62
 foreign policies, 90
 French and Indian War,
  46

myths, 88
 presidential election of,
  87-89
 retirement of, 92
 slavery, view of, 104
Water Quality Improvement
 Act, 291
Watergate scandal, 277-278
Weaver, James B., 183
Webster, Daniel, 115
Weems, Parson, 88
Welles, Gideon, 143
westward expansion, United
 States, 118-120
Wheelock, Eleazar, 38
Whig Party, 108
 establishment of, 115
Whitney, Eli, 105
Wigglesworth, Michael, 37
Wilderness, Battle of the
 (Civil War), 149
Wilkie, Wendell, 221
Williams, Roger, 19
Wilson, Woodrow
 education of, 194
 League of Nations, pro-
  posal of, 200-201
 presidential election of,
  194
 World War I, 198
Winthrop, John, 19-20
witch hunts, 34
witchcraft trials, 34
Wobblies, founding of, 187
women's liberation move-
 ment, 282-284
women's rights movement,
 122
 19th Amendment to the
  Constitution, 203
Women's Rights National
 Historical Park, 123

X–Y–Z